Understanding the Many Faces of Human Security

Studies in International Minority and Group Rights

VOLUME 13

The titles published in this series are listed at *brill.com/imgr*

Understanding the Many Faces of Human Security

Perspectives of Northern Indigenous Peoples

Edited by

Kamrul Hossain
Anna Petrétei

BRILL
NIJHOFF

LEIDEN | BOSTON

Library of Congress Cataloging-in-Publication Data

Names: Hossain, Kamrul, editor. |Petrétei, Anna, 1987- editor.
Title: Understanding the many faces of human security : perspectives of northern indigenous peoples / edited by Dr. Kamrul Hossain, Ms. Anna Petrétei.
Description: Leiden ; Boston : Brill Nijhoff, 2016. | Series: Studies in international minority and group rights ; volume 13 | Includes bibliographical references.
Identifiers: LCCN 2016023667 (print) | LCCN 2016024082 (ebook) | ISBN 9789004314382 (hardback : alk. paper) | ISBN 9789004314399 (E-book)
Subjects: LCSH: Indigenous peoples--Legal status, laws, etc.--Arctic regions. | Indigenous peoples--Arctic regions--Economic conditions. | Basic needs--Law and legislation--Arctic regions.
Classification: LCC K3247 .U53 2016 (print) | LCC K3247 (ebook) | DDC 342.08/7209113--dc23
LC record available at https://lccn.loc.gov/2016023667

Want or need Open Access? Brill Open offers you the choice to make your research freely accessible online in exchange for a publication charge. Review your various options on brill.com/brill-open.

Typeface for the Latin, Greek, and Cyrillic scripts: "Brill". See and download: brill.com/brill-typeface.

ISSN 2210-2132
ISBN 978-90-04-31438-2 (hardback)
ISBN 978-90-04-31439-9 (e-book)

This book is printed on acid-free paper and produced in a sustainable manner.

Contents

Foreword

Understanding the Many Faces of Human Security: Perspectives of Northern Indigenous Peoples is a compilation of important articles written by well-known authors of indigenous studies. In recent years, studies on the rights of indigenous peoples have gained momentum. The indigenous movements for an increased voice in the decision-making processes concerning matters that affect indigenous peoples have achieved wide recognition. The 2007 United Nations Declaration on the Rights of the Indigenous Peoples, which was adopted with broad support, is a landmark achievement that furthered indigenous peoples' rights. Relevant policy processes that address indigenous peoples' rights in most cases affirm the normative importance of indigenous rights endorsed in the Declaration. Today, the Free, Prior, and Informed Consent (FPIP) principle, especially regarding the right of indigenous peoples, has become an established norm. The treaty-monitoring bodies within the mainstream human rights instruments, such as the two Covenants—the International Covenant on Civil and Political Rights (ICCPR) and the International Covenant on Economic, Social and Cultural Rights (ICESCR), the International Convention on Elimination of All Forms of Racial Discrimination, the Convention on the Elimination of All Forms of Discrimination against Women—repeatedly emphasize the importance of the rights of indigenous peoples.

This book addresses the challenges of the realization of the rights of indigenous peoples from a "security" point of view. By the term "security," the book generally refers to the human dimension of security. Although several chapters refer to the Copenhagen School that promoted the theory of "securitization," which identified five security objects (military, political, economic, environmental, and societal), the book generally presents all aspects of security other than the military aspect as far as they are relevant to promote the rights of indigenous peoples.

Also important is that the focus of the book is "the North"—mainly the Arctic and sub-Arctic region. The ongoing and rapid transformation, new industrial developments, as well as other economic practices taking place in the region naturally have repercussions that adversely affect the rights of the groups of indigenous peoples who are scattered across this region. The chapters of the book provide new knowledge based on recent developments. Consequently, socio-economic, environmental, cultural, and health-related concerns of the Ainu, Inuit, Nenets, Sámi, and Mongolian indigenous peoples that present several security challenges connected to their rights, have been successfully captured in the book. It also addresses the importance of developing policy measures to better implement the rights of these peoples making "security" as a referent object. I believe this new dimension is important to understand the current challenges to indigenous rights; and this dimension, in my view, will be of interest to academic and non-academic readers who take indigenous rights seriously.

Timo Koivurova
Research Professor, Director
Arctic Centre, University of Lapland

Preface

In March 2014, we organized a seminar entitled "Cultural Resilience and Human Rights—Perspectives of Northern Indigenous Peoples" as a joint project between the Arctic Centre of the University of Lapland and the College of Liberal Arts of the Muroran Institute of Technology of Japan. In the seminar, we brought scholars, indigenous peoples' representatives, and non-academic policy makers and stakeholders together to share their knowledge and views on the concerns of indigenous peoples located in the Arctic and sub-Arctic region. The seminar focused on inter-disciplinary aspects of the challenges facing indigenous peoples living in the Northern Hemisphere. The outcome of the seminar motivated us to prepare a funding application to the Academy of Finland for a research project entitled "Human Security as a Promotional Tool for Societal Security in the Arctic: Addressing Multiple Vulnerabilities in the Population with Specific Reference to the Barents Region" (HuSArctic). By the end of 2014, our application had been approved, and we continued working on this volume. As one of the first steps of the research project, we organized a kick-off meeting in April 2015, at which we continued our research on this interesting topic, and finalized the chapters published in this volume. Most of the authors of this book are team members of the HuSArctic research project.

We thank all contributing authors of this volume, the reviewers of the chapters, and the interns at the Northern Institute for Environmental and Minority Law of the Arctic Centre of the University of Lapland, in particular Camille Burlet and Filip Holienčin, who assisted in the technical editing processes. Our special thanks go to Prof. Hiroshi Maruyama, who helped us receive generous grants from the Muroran Institute of Technology that allowed us to cover the travel costs of the scholars who attended the March 2014 seminar. We are also grateful to the Arctic Centre for offering us venues and administrative support, and its personnel, in particular Ms. Raija Kivilahti, for her practical support. Finally, we are grateful to the Academy of Finland for supporting our research through funding for the HuSArctic project.

Dr. Kamrul Hossain
Ms. Anna Petrétei

List of Figures and Tables

Figures

Tables

List of Abbreviations

AB	Appellate Body
ACIA	Arctic Climate Impact Assessment
AEC	Arctic Economic Council
AHDR	Arctic Human Development Report
ANCSA	Alaska Native Claims Settlement Act
APNN	Greenland Department of Fisheries, Hunting and Agriculture
BEAC	Barents Euro-Arctic Council
CEACR	Committee of Experts on the Application of Conventions and Recommendations
CHS	Commission on Human Security
CPA	Ainu Culture Promotion Act
DSB	Dispute Settlement Body
DV	domestic violence
EFSA	European Food Safety Authority
EIA	environmental impact assessment
EU	European Union
FPIC	free, prior, and informed consent
GATT	General Agreement on Tariffs and Trade
HDR	Human Development Report
HRC	Human Rights Committee
IBA	Impact and Benefit Agreements
ICC	Inuit Circumpolar Council
ICCPR	International Covenant on Civil and Political Rights
ICERD	International Convention on the Elimination of All Forms of Racial Discrimination
ICESCR	International Covenant of Economic, Social and Cultural Rights
ICRW	International Convention for the Regulation of Whaling
IPCC	Intergovernmental Panel on Climate Change
IFAW	International Fund for Animal Welfare
ILO	International Labour Organization
IPCC	Intergovernmental Panel on Climate Change
ITK	Inuit Tapiriit Kanatami
IWGIA	International Work Group for Indigenous Affairs
KHMAO	Khanty-Mansiysky Autonomous Okrug
MMPA	US Marine Mammal Protection Act
MEP	Member of Parliament
NAO	Nenets Autonomous Okrug

NATO	North Atlantic Treaty Organisation
NLCA	Nunavut Land Claims Agreement
NPO	Non-Profit Organization
POP	persistent organic pollutants
RAIPON	Russian Association of the Indigenous People of the North
RCMP	Royal Canadian Mounted Police
SAR	Search and Rescue Agreement
ST	securitization theory
Tukes	Turvallisuus- ja kemikaalivirasto (The Finnish Safety and Chemicals Agency)
UN	United Nations
UNDP	United Nations Development Programme
UNDRIP	United Nations Declaration on the Rights of Indigenous Peoples
UNESCO	United Nations Educational, Scientific and Cultural Organization
WTO	World Trade Organization
YNAO	Yamalo-Nenets Autonomous Okrug

Notes on Contributors

Shahnaj Begum

Shahnaj Begum is working as a researcher (Doctoral candidate) at the Unit for Gender Studies in the Faculty of Education of the University of Lapland. Her research focuses on Northern elderly well-being (including Sámi elderly) and gender issues in the context of Arctic change. She has published recently a number of articles in regarded journals, such as in the Yearbook of Polar Law (Brill Academic Publishers), in the Polar Record (Cambridge University Press) etc. She is also working as project coordinator of the project "The Arctic Change and Elderly Exclusion: A gender-based perspective", funded by Nordic Council of Ministers. Begum has also extensive experiences in working with the elderly people at the old home service institutions in Helsinki. She has also received a number of prestigious research grants awarded by various Finnish foundations, such as Finnish Cultural Foundation.

Heather Exner-Pirot

Heather Exner-Pirot is the Managing Editor of the Arctic Yearbook, a regular contributor to Radio Canada's Eye on the Arctic, an Editorial Board member of the Canadian Journal of Foreign Policy, a Research Fellow at the EU Arctic Forum, and a Board Member of the Saskatchewan First Nations Economic Development Network. She received her PhD in Political Science at the University of Calgary in 2011. She is currently a Strategist for Outreach and Indigenous Engagement at the University of Saskatchewan. She has formerly held positions with the International Centre for Northern Governance and Development and the University of the Arctic.

Wilfrid Greaves

Wilfrid Greaves holds a PhD in Political Science from the University of Toronto. His research has examined security and environmental change in the circumpolar Arctic, Canadian foreign policy, natural resource extraction and climate change, and human security and complex peace operations. He is Lecturer at the Trudeau Centre for Peace, Conflict and Justice at the University of Toronto.

Filip Holienčin

Filip Holienčin is working as a researcher at the Northern Institute for Environmental and Minority Law (NIEM) in the Arctic Centre, University of

Lapland, Finland. He earned his law degree with a master thesis on The Elements of Natural Law in Roman Law from Masaryk University, Czech Republic, where he is currently studying a bachelor programme of Scandinavian Studies in Swedish language. As an exchange student, he also studied 2 semesters at the University of Iceland in Reykjavík, specializing on Environmental Law. His research interests are indigenous peoples', environmental and security related issues in the Arctic with a main emphasis on Nordic countries. He is currently working on a project "Demilitarisation in an increasingly militarized world" examining Svalbard and Åland.

Kamrul Hossain

Dr. Kamrul Hossain is an Associate Professor and Director of the Northern Institute for Environmental and Minority Law (NIEM) at the Arctic Centre in the University of Lapland. He is also an Adjunct Professor of International Law and served as an acting Professor of Public International Law at the Faculty of Law of the University of Lapland. At present he leads the research project – HuSArctic, funded by the Academy of Finland. He has actively been involved, and acted as key person, in a number of significant research projects funded within the framework of, for example, the European Union, Nordic Council of Ministers, Academy of Finland etc. Dr. Hossain has extensively published scholarly articles in high quality international journals. He served as the Special Editor for Volume 3 of the Yearbook of Polar Law published in 2011. He regularly teaches at the University of Lapland, and periodically at other foreign universities. He completed visiting fellowships at a number of foreign universities including the University of Toronto in Canada, Scott Polar Research Institute of the University of Cambridge in the U.K., and Muroran Institute of Technology in Japan. He has received a number of prestigious awards including SYLFF Fellowship at the University of Helsinki. In 2012, he was awarded a Faculty Research Fellowship by the Canadian Department of Foreign Affairs and International Trade (DFAIT).

Hiroshi Maruyama

Hiroshi Maruyama is Guest Professor at the Hugo Valentin Centre Uppsala University and Professor Emeritus at the Muroran Institute of Technology in Japan. In January 2016, he was awarded Honorary Doctorate by Uppsala University. He has devoted himself to research for and with minorities who struggle against the authorities in search of local autonomy and social justice over environmental issues and the revitalization of their distinct languages and cultures. He has published monographs and articles on environmental issues and indigenous policies, including Japan's policies towards the Ainu language and culture with special reference to North Fennoscandian Sámi policies (2015, Acta Borealia). He is pioneering the following fields: environmental issues in rural areas of Japan in the light of decision making processes, Japan's policies towards the Ainu in the international context, comparative studies between Sámi and Ainu for their indigenous rights.

Masumi Matsumoto

Masumi Matsumoto is professor at Muroran Institute of Technology in Hokkaido, Japan and guest professor of Institute of Technology of Inner Mongolia, China. She was associate professor (1998–2005) and professor at Keiwa College, Japan (2005–2014). She received her PhD from Niigata University, Japan. She has written a number of papers and books on national integration of China in Chinese, English and Japanese. She is known as a specialist of Islam in China, including its modern history and gender issues. Major publications: "Islamic Education in China: Triple Discrimination and the Challenge of Hui Women's Madrasas", in Sakurai and Adelkhah eds, The Moral Economy of Madrasa: Islam and Education Today, (London: Routledge, 2011), "Rationalizing Patriotism among Muslim Chinese", in Dodoigion, Kosugi, Komatsu (eds) Intellectuals in the Modern Islamic World (London: Routledge, 2006), "Protestant Missions to Muslims in China" Annals of Japan Association for Middle East Studies, 21(1): 141–171 (2005), "Islamic Reform in Muslim Periodicals in China" Etudes Orientales 21/22: 88–104 (2005), Study of China's Policy toward Ethnic Minorities (Tokyo: Taga Shuppan, 1999, in Japanese) (Chinese version, Zhongguo Minzu Zhengce de Yanjiu, Beijing: Minzu Chubanshe, 2003).

Päivi Naskali

Päivi Naskali is working as a Professor of Gender Studies at the University of Lapland and as a Dean of the Faculty of Education. She has supervised a large number of Master's degrees and many doctoral theses concerning gender issues in Lapland. She is a head of the Finnish University Network of Gender Studies, has worked actively in the National Doctoral School in Gender Studies and edited the Journal of Women's Studies. Her research interests include gender and ageing in the times of neoliberalism, educational gender politics and feminist pedagogy and philosophy. She has worked as an expert in the Arctic Council project Gender Equality in the Arctic (2014) and in the Rector's Forum of The University of Arctic (2014). She has, e.g., been organizing the Arctic Council Conference on Gender Equality and Women in the Arctic, Taking Wing, in 2002. She has involved in the research projects Enterprising Self and Tasuko (Equality and gender knowledge in teacher education), and been a member of different research and development projects that have analysed gender segregation in the labour market in Finnish Lapland. She has lately been leading a research project The Arctic Change and Elderly Exclusion: A Gender-based Perspective.

Anna Petrétei

Anna Petrétei is working as a researcher at the Northern Institute for Environmental and Minority Law (NIEM), and is a PhD candidate at the University of Lapland, Faculty of Law. She graduated as a lawyer at the University of Pécs, Hungary. She wrote her master's thesis on the rights of the Sámi minority, about which she also published articles in Hungary. She is carrying out research on the rights of indigenous peoples. She is currently involved in a project focusing on human security in the Arctic region (Human Security as a promotional tool for societal security in the Arctic: Addressing Multiple Vulnerability to its Population with Specific Reference to the Barents Region), where she examines different aspects of societal and indigenous security. She has published several articles on indigenous rights related to mining activities. Besides studying Sámi rights and traditional livelihoods, she continues her research by expanding her approach to other indigenous peoples. Her research interests are minority law, indigenous rights, traditional livelihoods and mining law from the viewpoint of indigenous peoples.

Øyvind Ravna

Øyvind Ravna is professor in jurisprudence (Dr. Juris) at the Faculty of Law, University of Tromsø – The Arctic University of Norway, where he teaches Sámi Law, property law and human rights. He holds a doctoral degree in law on legal clarification of reindeer husbandry rights from University of Tromsø (2008) and a master in property law and land consolidation from the Norwegian University of Life Sciences (1987). His field of research is indigenous law, especially protection and recognition of culture, land rights and livelihood, including the adaption and impact of the 2005 Finnmark Act. He has been the head of the research group on Sámi and indigenous law at the University of Tromsø 2008 – 2012 and is currently the head of the Arctic Thematic Networks subgroup on Indigenous Peoples' Law. He has served as a land consolidation judge and head of the land consolidation court in Finnmark County and been engaged in research and investigation for the Sámi Right Committee, the Finnmark Commission, and the Reindeer pasture rights committee for Finnmark. Ravna is editor–in–chief of *Arctic Review on Law and Politics*. He has edited four academic anthologies in the period of 2007 to 2012 and the author of *Finnmarksloven – og retten til jorden i Finnmark* (*The Finnmark Act – and the right to the land of Finnmark*), published by Gyldendal Academic in 2013.

J. Miguel Roncero Martin

Born in Toledo, Spain, in 1986. Studied Political Sciences at the Complutense University of Madrid and International Relations at Webster University (Vienna campus), with stays in Bergen, Norway, and Geneva, Switzerland. PhD candidate in Political Science at the University of Vienna, Austria. His research focuses on security and cooperation in the Arctic, humanitarian issues, responsibility to protect (R2P), energy security and corruption. Project manager and international development practitioner working within the United Nations system.

Nikolas Sellheim

Nikolas Sellheim holds a PhD in law from the University of Lapland. His research examines the interconnection between the EU seal products trade ban and living conditions in seal hunting communities. He works as Editor for Polar Record, the journal of the Scott Polar Research Institute, University of Cambridge, UK. He holds degrees in Polar Law, Circumpolar Studies and Scandinavian Studies. His ongoing and previous research on Arctic law and governance has by and large linked empirical with legal elements, a path he continues in his future research. Nikolas previously worked as Book Reviews Editor for Polar Record, in the International Secretariat of the University of the Arctic (UArctic), as research assistant for the Arctic Council's CAFF Working Group and on several projects relating to the EU and the Arctic.

Vigya Sharma

Vigya Sharma is a Research Fellow with the Energy and Poverty Research Group, at the University of Queensland (UQ), Australia. She is also an Honorary Fellow with the Centre for Social Responsibility in Mining (CSRM), Sustainable Minerals Institute at UQ where she was a Postdoctoral Fellow until May 2015.

Her final project at CSRM examined the nexus of climate change-influenced natural disasters, mining and traditional livelihoods in Mongolia. The project brought together more than 120 representatives from the mining industry, local, regional and central government agencies, local herding groups and the civil society to partake in multiple capacity buildings workshops across Mongolia.

Vigya has a PhD in sustainability and international development from the University of Adelaide, Australia. Her broad interests are in the areas of sustainability, poverty and livelihoods, climate change adaptation, natural disasters, mining, and energy for development.

Michael Sheehan

Michael Sheehan is Professor of International Relations, and Director of the Callaghan Centre for the Study of Conflict, at Swansea University. He was formerly Director of the Scottish Centre for International Security at Aberdeen University. He is published widely on the theory and application of the concept of security and is the author of 11 books on security, including, Arms Control: Theory and Practice (1988), The Balance of Power: History and Theory, (1996), National and International Security, (2000), International Security: An Analytical Survey, (2005) and Securing Outer Space, (2009), co-edited with Natalie Bormann. He is currently researching the relationship between current approaches to security and the experience and understanding of security by European indigenous people's.

Elena Tonkova

Elena Tonkova is an associate professor at the Syktyvkar State University, Russia. She was awarded PhD in Philosophy of Culture from the Lomonosov Moscow State University. Dr. Tonkova has worked as dean of the Faculty of Humanities and as director of the Social Technologies Institute at the Syktyvkar State University. In 2010 she was a Fulbright scholar at the Kennan Institute of the Woodrow Wilson International Center for Scholars where she conducted substantial research on the topic of multiculturalism. Her research interests lie in the area of social justice and cultural diversity, which cover both theoretical perspectives (mainly focusing political philosophy) and their practical applications through the prism of series of case studies, conducted in cooperation with international academic teams. Dr. Tonkova's research has already resulted in the publication of several articles and the development of academic courses for students at various levels.

Svetlana Vinogradova

Svetlana Vinogradova graduated from the Leningrad State University (1989), three-year PhD educational courses on the Institute of Economic Problems of the Kola Scientific Center, Russian Academy of Sciences (2005, specialty – regional economy); defended PhD thesis on "Indigenous peoples in context of the regional policy for labour market development (case of the Murmansk Region)", Apatity, RSC RAS, 2006.

Since 1996, working in the Center of the Humanities of the Kola Science Centre RAS; present position – Leading Researcher. Fields of scientific interests – sustainable development, social aspects of the Northern and Arctic policy, indigenous peoples. More than 10 years has been studying the problems of the indigenous population of the Kola Peninsula – Saami, including international projects and research supported by industrial companies to assess the social impacts; acted as an expert for the government of the federal and regional levels on indigenous issues.

Introduction: Indigenous Peoples of the North and Human Security

Kamrul Hossain, J. Miguel Roncero Martin, Anna Petrétei and Filip Holienčin

Indigenous peoples have inhabited the Arctic and sub-Arctic for millennia. They are the foundations of human presence in the High North, a presence that, according to the recent discovery in Siberia of a "butchered wooly mammoth," can be traced back forty-five thousand years.[1] Today, the region is home to a significant number of indigenous peoples, herein referred to as indigenous peoples of the North, who together total some four hundred thousand individuals. They include, among others, Inuit in North America, Greenland, and Russia; Sámi in the Nordic countries and on the Kola Peninsula in Russia; diverse groups of small indigenous peoples in the Russian North; and the Ainu in Japan. The indigenous peoples of the North conquered a land that others saw as inhospitable and uninhabitable; they made it their home, and thrived.

Despite ethnic and cultural differences, indigenous peoples from all over the globe present unique lifestyles developed around the common denominator of the ice and the sea as well as common elements. One of these elements is that they maintain, and intend to promote, nature-based sustainable livelihoods to maintain their identity as a distinct people within a given geographic region. The indigenous peoples of the North are no exception in this regard. However, today, the traditional worldviews of many of these groups are being challenged, while the world they have known for generations is literally and figuratively melting away. Since the region as a whole experiences numerous pressures from various sources, these groups of indigenous peoples often face new challenges linked to rapid modernization and development, resource-driven industrialization, demographic pressure, and cultural changes driven by external cultures. Considerable attention has been paid to the consequences of climate change as the region is warming at a rate twice as fast[2] as the global average

1 Scientific American, "Mammoth Find Moves Humans in Arctic Back 10,000 Years," (2016). Available online at: http://www.scientificamerican.com/podcast/episode/mammoth-find-moves-humans-in-arctic-back-10-000-years/ (Accessed 15 January 2016).

2 National Oceanic and Atmospheric Administration – United States Department of Commerce (NOAA), "Arctic Report Card: Update for 2014 – Tracking recent environmental changes," (2014). Available online at: http://www.arctic.noaa.gov/reportcard/ (Accessed 10 August 2015).

 | DOI 10.1163/9789004314399_002

resulting in overwhelming repercussions for the region's ecosystems,[3] such as measurable changes in the ice thickness and observable changes in animal migration patterns. These changes affect human and animal populations, which rely on predictable ecosystems for survival. In addition, other human-induced actions, such as extractive industrial developments, the construction of dams, ports, and pipelines in some locations, the overall process of globalization driven by economic development, and the emergence of a market economy, result in harmful effects on the environment, lives, and traditional ways of living of indigenous peoples, who generally live in harmony with nature and whose traditional and collective identity is based on a deep spiritual relationship with the surrounding nature and the natural environment. Although these groups of peoples are often characterized by their ability to be resilient, adaptive, ingenious, and flexible in their ways of living, the increasingly accessible economic potential endangering the region's environmental integrity together with changing climate patterns put these groups under diverse security threats connected to the groups' cultural identity and political integrity.

Today, the Arctic is still a scarcely populated region whose inhabitants are concentrated in small population pockets; infrastructure of all types is still very limited, and if it exists, sometimes, it serves national or state interests instead of those of the indigenous peoples of the North. However, the potential natural resources have made the region very attractive to large extractive industries. Although some argue that large-scale industrial activities, as well as other economic activities in the region, such as tourism, may enable these populations to strengthen their purchasing power, thus enhancing their economic capability and fostering socioeconomic development, a study suggested that these activities bring little economic benefit to the permanent communities in the vicinity.[4] In fact, industry-driven economic development may have "extremely negative consequences for indigenous societies" in the Arctic.[5] The dynamics

3 McKarthy, J.J. et al., ed., *Climate Change 2001: Impacts, Adaptation and Vulnerability, Contribution of Working Group II to the Third Assessment Report of the Intergovernmental Panel on Climate Change* (Cambridge University Press: Cambridge, 2001).

4 Greaves, Wilfrid (2010), "Insecurity of non-dominance: Re-theorizing human security and environmental change in developed states," Chapter 5 *in Critical environmental security: Rethinking the links between natural resources and political violence*, ed. Matthew A. Schnurr and Larry A. Swatuk (Centre for Foreign Policy Studies Dalhousie University). Available online at: http://www.dal.ca/content/dam/dalhousie/pdf/cfps/pubs/critical-environmental-security/chapter5.pdf (Accessed 10 August 2015).

5 Fjellheim, R.S. and Henriksen, J.B., "Oil and Gas Exploitation on Arctic Indigenous Peoples' Territories" in *Gáldu Čála – Journal of Indigenous Peoples Rights* No. 4/2006. Available online at: http://caid.ca/Arctic2006.pdf (Accessed 10 January 2015).

of change for traditional Arctic economies brought by extractive industry-driven development may have extremely negative effects, as pointed out by several studies. For example, a commercial market-based economy is less effective for Arctic inhabitants in remote areas and thus weakens their economic self-sufficiency; however, once introduced within the context of a traditional Arctic economy, this socioeconomic modernization substantially displaces traditional economic systems. Additionally, younger generations used to the comforts of a market-based economy may be uninterested in learning traditional lifestyles. As a result, the combined effect of environmental degradation and economic stagnation may cause high unemployment rates hand-in-hand with weakened economic self-sufficiency, among other problems.[6] This modernization also opens up economic opportunities to individuals elsewhere, which results in a population movement to the High North, changing population patterns and potentially jeopardizing indigenous rights and cultures, as the indigenous peoples become smaller minorities within their homelands. Climate change is another factor that alters landscape realities and biodiversity by, for example, triggering the northward movement of species or contaminants detrimental to human health; because the Arctic populations are exposed to a new and different lifestyle resulting from globalization and climate change, adapting to new realities often causes other social problems, such as high rates of alcoholism, suicidal tendencies, and others.[7] All these factors, alone or in combination, result in critical threats to the indigenous peoples of the North. In addition to these studies, and although perhaps just symbolically, environmental non-governmental organizations (NGOs) such as Greenpeace[8] and publications such as National Geographic[9] have collected testimonies of representatives and individuals of Arctic indigenous peoples opposing the development of hydrocarbons in the region. The voices express legitimate opinions, fears, and self-perceived threats to security that must be considered and addressed.

The security challenges vary depending on the prevailing context of each area in the region, each indigenous group, and even each specific community.

---

6 Arctic Climate Impact Assessment (ACIA). (New York: Cambridge University Press, 2005), 657.

7 Arctic Human Development Report (AHDR). (Akureyri: Stefansson Arctic Institute, 2004).

8 Greenpeace, "Arctic Indigenous People Say No to Arctic Oil Drilling", Available online at http://www.greenpeace.org/international/en/multimedia/slideshows/Arctic-Indigenous-Peoples-conference-/ (Accessed on 10 January 2016).

9 Folger, Tim, "Melting Away," in *National Geographic* (National Geographic Society, November 2015).

However, the indigenous groups in the region generally face multiple vulnerabilities that represent aspects of human security threats in a range of issues: from societal and cultural to economic, environmental, and legal. In recent years, the momentum of these particular aspects has increased due to the ongoing transformation of the region. The Arctic is a region where traditional perspectives need to be rethought. Cartography, for example, is one, as the most common map projections fail to truly capture the essence of a region where cardinal points seem somehow out of place. This, of course, can also be applied to other fields of study; here is where the concept of human security comes in, challenging traditional assumptions at the ontological, epistemological, and methodological levels. Ontologically, the concept of human security belongs to the broadened understanding of security itself, of what can be securitized, and who the securitizing actors are; epistemologically, it allows for the inclusion of many issues that have been dismissed as suitable or appropriate for security studies and provides a new approach in which the well-being of individuals and communities is key to achieving an authentic security; methodologically, human security is an effective tool for analyzing security threats as perceived by the affected actors and for giving voice to these actors—in our case, the indigenous peoples of the North. In this perspective, human security is also a tool for promoting the empowerment of indigenous peoples of the North, and within them, the more vulnerable or ignored groups such as women and the elderly.

The concept of human security was initially developed by the United Nations (UN) in its 1994 Human Development Report, with the aim of broadening the understanding and scope of security.[10] The human security approach, as an analytical tool, offers an inclusive framework for an expanded understanding of security that identifies vulnerabilities, self-perceived threats, and ignored risks that affect the collective security of the indigenous peoples of the North. As a concept, human security presents a broad meaning; it can include virtually everything that challenges human well-being, from natural catastrophes to human-induced actions that cause adverse consequences to the general well-being of individuals and the community.[11] The concept is most fiercely contested on the point that if everything is addressed by human security, then nothing can really be prioritized, and therefore, tackling security problems

10 United Nations Development Programme (UNDP), "Human Development Report: New Dimensions of Human Security," (1994). Available online at: http://hdr.undp.org/sites/default/files/reports/255/hdr_1994_en_complete_nostats.pdf (Accessed 11 January 2016).

11 Hossain, Kamrul, "Securing the Rights: A Human Security Perspective in the Context of Arctic Indigenous Peoples," in *The Yearbook of Polar Law* (Brill, 2013), 494. Available online at: http://ssrn.com/abstract=2505482 (Accessed 10 August 2015).

under the umbrella of human security may become a challenge. However, we endeavor to consider the prevailing challenges facing the specific region of the Northern Hemisphere and, in particular, its indigenous peoples in response to the rapid transformation of the region. We do not stick to one definition of human security, we present the vulnerabilities that indigenous peoples of the North face from various perspectives on each group in each sub-region of the North. The term "vulnerability" refers to "the conditions determined by physical, social, economic and environmental factors or processes, which increase the susceptibility of a community to the impact of hazards."[12] The existing vulnerabilities have a direct impact on how the indigenous peoples of the North can tackle the challenges they face and accentuate their fears and desires.

Consequently, each chapter discusses one or more of these phenomena, which result mainly from the risks of environmental change and the rapid yet industry-dependent economic transformation that eventually culminates in greater economic disparity and other forms of inequality as well as socio-cultural threats to the community's traditional relation to its environment and, ultimately, existence. Traditionally, these vulnerabilities have not been linked to threats to security but to social or economic challenges. Therefore, the vulnerabilities have received limited attention at the policy level. Yet the threats exist and are perceived as such by the indigenous peoples of the North. Mitigating the threats and empowering indigenous peoples to address their concerns through implementing legal and policy tools, enhancing the role of indigenous institutions, and adopting local, regional, and sub-regional policy measures, such as strengthen their traditional occupations, languages, and linguistic identity as well as the identity based on cultural practices, are crucial for indigenous peoples to be empowered and resilient on their own terms in relation to the rapidly changing world and the stressors that follow the transformations. Today, the developments within the human rights framework, the introduction of new instruments and programs to strengthen and monitor indigenous peoples' rights, the broadening of what is understood as threats to security, and developments concerning increasing awareness of a political agenda to promote influence on their own issues that focus on the maintenance of culture and language issues have influenced greater participation in the international scene and promoted their political identity on the global scene, which particularly empower indigenous peoples.

Therefore, we address a number of issues that different groups of indigenous peoples face. However, although these groups are different from each

12 United Nations – Secretariat of the International Strategy for Disaster Reduction, "Terminology: Basic terms of disaster risk reduction," (2004). Available online at: http://www.unisdr.org/2004/wcdr-dialogue/terminology.htm (Accessed 10 August 2015).

other, the issues the peoples face present commonalities linked to a changing natural and social environment. The range of issues includes general and specific perspectives of indigenous (human) security in thirteen chapters. Although threats on a general level are presented from various aspects and points of view, such as indigenous security understanding, governance, sustainability, livelihood practices, mining and other economic uses, as well as nature-based resources and land use management, the specific aspects of the threats include issues related to gender and the elderly, two groups that present specific vulnerabilities and that are often forgotten when human and other aspects of security are addressed. In our analyses, we also present approaches that can contribute to improving the socioeconomic, sociocultural, environmental, and structural conditions of the region, so that the legitimate concerns and interests of the indigenous peoples of the North can be addressed, and the challenges they face and threats they perceive can be mitigated. The approaches we offer also attempt to promote a greater inclusion of indigenous voices through strengthening the role of existing indigenous institutions and by creating new institutions at the local and regional levels.

The issues presented in this work are linked to the Japanese Ainu, the Canadian Inuit, the Russian Nenets, the Sámi peoples in four countries (Finland, Norway, Russia, and Sweden), and Mongolian indigenous herders. Here we can already see one of the most important characteristics of the Arctic and the indigenous peoples of the North: an interstate and transboundary reality. Despite common 'circumpolar' approaches and efforts, these groups live in separate states and are subject to different legal frameworks that limit and shape the group's actions and, to some extent, their voices.

Our first chapter thus focuses on the constraints and shortcomings that state-based national and international legal systems impose on the indigenous peoples of the North. Kamrul Hossain illustrates the governance approaches—both legal and institutional—in order to demonstrate how indigenous security is structured, in particular concerning the Arctic. Hossain shows that the existing indigenous governance framework includes a variety of international instruments, such as the UN Declaration on the Rights of Indigenous Peoples, the International Labour Organization (ILO) Convention 169, the International Covenant on Civil and Political Rights, and the Convention on Biodiversity and its protocols. According to Hossain, although references to indigenous issues can be found either directly or indirectly in these documents, they have significant shortcomings in terms of mitigating particular challenges that the indigenous peoples of the Arctic face. These shortcomings are addressed in numerous policy papers and the academic literature. Consequently, Hossain concludes that a better governance regime should include relevant legal and policy options, developed by state, regional, international, as well as indigenous, institutions, in a more holistic manner in order to promote the governance of indigenous security.

The first focus on a particular indigenous group brings us to North America (Alaska and northern Canada), Greenland, and Russia, the wider home of the Inuit. Drawing upon the Copenhagen school securitization theory, Wilfrid Greaves examines the perception of "in/security" from the perspective of the Inuit in the Arctic region of northern Canada. By assessing various data, comprising surveys, public documents, articles, academic sources, speeches, and interviews, Greaves examines how the Inuit and their political leaders and organizations have understood the meaning of security over the past two decades. The data suggest that the Inuit perceive the concept of Arctic security mainly within three categories: the natural environment, indigenous identity and culture, and Inuit political autonomy. The Inuit perceive Arctic security as strongly connected to the changing climate, whereas Canada still asserts its policy, which remains fundamentally colonial and focuses on extracting Arctic resources instead of mitigating the impact of climate change on the (cultural) survival and well-being of the Inuit. Nikolas Sellheim illustrates the European discourse on the Inuit seal hunt, which presents threats to Inuit sustainability. According to Sellheim, although the current seal hunting policy effectively barred from the European domestic market all products stemming from commercial seal hunts with the exemption of those conducted by Inuit and other indigenous communities, the blanket characteristic of this "indigenous exemption" and the distinctiveness of Inuit regions with their complex economic systems and increased exposure to detrimental impacts of climate change, have imposed adverse effects on Inuit livelihoods. Thus, Sellheim argues, this exemption, based on a stereotypical perception of indigenous communities using narratives that do not correlate with the realities of Arctic life, has resulted in an unfortunate distinction between "good" indigenous hunts and "bad" commercial hunts. In contrast, Heather Exner-Pirot shows various interpretations of economic security at a general level, particularly focusing on the balance between development and sustainability in the context of the North American Arctic. According to Exner Pirot, the transition from a subsistence economy to a wage economy had a severe impact on the population, and a return to a traditional lifestyle is no longer possible or desirable. The case studies suggest, for example, that the established practice of Impact and Benefit Agreements in Canada aimed to ensure benefits for local communities in exchange for cooperation, or the support of Greenlandic Inuit governments to exploit, although as sustainably as possible, the island's hydrocarbon and mineral resources have made the return to a subsistence economy unlikely.

According to Exner-Pirot, and due to this new reality, economic security is just as important to human well-being as environmental security, meaning that the failure to address threats to economic security will have a negative impact on the well-being of individuals and communities.

From the Inuit, we move to two less well-known indigenous groups who live in the Arctic and sub-Arctic region: the Ainu, who are present on Hokkaido and the Sakhalin and Kuril islands, and the Nenets in Northern Russia. Addressing issues that affect these less well-known groups is vital, first, to give voice to groups and communities largely ignored and, second, to enable comparative analyses and the potential application of transboundary solutions. Thus, Hiroshi Maruyama presents the security threats to the Ainu that arise out of the construction of dams on the Saru River system located in Biratori on Hokkaido in Japan. Maruyama highlights the opinion of the Sapporo District Court on illegal actions of the Japanese government concerning the construction of the Nibutani Dam and expropriation of Ainu lands. By showing the adverse consequences of the construction of the dam for the Ainu, Hiroshi Maruyama argues that the Japanese government is still not in compliance with the court's ruling and thus is violating the rights of the Ainu as an indigenous people. On the same issue, Masumi Matsumoto focuses on the situation of Ainu women, which, according to Matsumoto, is probably the most ignored Ainu issue in general. Although Matsumoto shows the adverse consequences of long-term discrimination, she also describes the fascinating story of an elder Ainu woman who represents an inspiring example of the promotion of non-discrimination and empowerment. Elena Tonkova addresses security pertaining to the livelihood of the Nenets of the Russian North. Tonkova argues that although the Nenets enjoyed relative freedom and continued to develop reindeer husbandry with only minimal influence from imperial Russia, intensive state interventions of sedentarization and collectivization during the Soviet era, together with industrial development, had an immensely adverse impact on the Nenets' social structures and livelihoods. The subsequent collapse of the Soviet Union made the Nenets' effort to continue with their traditional livelihoods even harder and exposed their fragile economic and social structures to the new unregulated Russian capitalism. As a result, despite the Nenets' historically developed strategy of adapting to new situations, challenges emerging from industrial activity that has caused serious environmental damage, such as drilled mud spills, air pollution, acid rain, the release of chemicals including heavy metals, together with a decrease in biodiversity as well as climate change impacts such as ice-on-snow effects, early snow melting, and changes in wind and migration routes, all represent serious threats to the Nenets' livelihood practices. However, Tonkova concludes that the preservation of the traditional lifestyle and more effective support and aid from the state for promoting their well-being are important. Tonkova also emphasizes the importance of various inclusive policies to increase the political representation of the Nenets to support their cultural needs.

The Sámi are perhaps, together with the Inuit, one of the best-known indigenous groups in the Arctic and sub-Arctic region. However, the Sámi also face challenges to their security derived from existing vulnerabilities, and thus, Sámi issues all across the Nordic and northwestern Russian region are covered in five chapters. Michael Sheehan opens this section by covering general Sámi security and taking into consideration societal, economic, and environmental perspectives by using the broader approach to security referred to in the Copenhagen school. According to Sheehan, societal security represents the core of Sámi security issues, since many other security issues derive from it. In this regard, he shows the interactions of several objects of security threats, for example, socio-environmental, economic, and cultural threats that affect the identity of the Sámi. Based on a literature review and data gathered from interviews, Sheehan concludes that a more holistic approach to security to better address Sámi security is needed since they face highly interrelated security challenges.

The transforming economy based on the rapid development of extractive industries in the North also has an impact on Sámi communities. Balancing economic development with the maintenance of traditional lifestyles is not an easy task, as conflicting views emerge from the different groups involved, both indigenous and non-indigenous. Three authors explore the delicate balance between indigenous rights and the global desire to develop the vast natural resources in the region. Anna Petrétei starts this analysis by investigating emerging mining activities taking place across the Sámi homelands in Russia and the Nordic countries, and the effects on Sámi culture and livelihood. Petrétei argues that traditional livelihood needs typically compete with other interests of society (such as the promise of greater income), which create tension. Although the growing need for natural resources has led to mining operations, among others, in Sámi homelands, which has had a positive effect on local economies, the actions also have negative impacts not only on the environment but also on the livelihoods that the Sámi maintain. Petrétei adopts a rights based approach to analyze Sámi security in response to activities concerning natural resource extraction and other major development projects in or near Sámi territories. The analysis continues with Øyvind Ravna, who examines legal questions pertaining to the Sámi's right to lands and connected livelihood and natural resources practices in light of ILO Convention 169, which addresses the rights of indigenous and tribal peoples. Ravna specifically focuses on the Sámi who inhabit Finnmark County of Norway regarding the commitment undertaken by Norway under that convention. Ravna highlights specific legislation (the Finnmark Act) that Norway has adopted pursuant to its obligations under Articles 14 and 15 of the ILO Convention 169. Although, according to Ravna, the act ensures the Sámi's rights to land and natural resources by transferring the previous state land to a regional ownership body and by prescribing the legal identification of and clarification process for land, Ravna maintains that the government should take on a more proactive role to effectively realize the Sámi's right to lands and natural resources in Finnmark County.

The Sámi groups are not identical and do not face the same challenges. Due to the Sámi's transboundary situation, some enjoy a more responsible legal and political framework than others. In this light, Svetlana Vinogradova investigates security challenges to the Russian Sámi in their current legal and political condition. Vinogradova not only presents the security threats to this group of people located on the Kola Peninsula of Russia but also analyzes the applicable legal instruments that promote their security concerns. Vinogradova argues that the colonization of the Barents Sea coast has adversely affected the Sámi's traditional culture and economy; during the Soviet transformations in the last century, these destructive pressures further intensified causing drastic impacts on the social structures and well-being of Russian Sámi resulting in massive unemployment and poverty. In addition to these challenges, the recently added industrial expansion, such as mining, has put extra pressure on the communities. For example, the system of local settlements lacks direct consultation mechanisms between local communities and the mining companies. According to Vinogradova, although the Russian Sámi are protected by an extensive legal framework consisting of federal and regional laws, Sámi political activity remains limited. Their integration in common regional political processes is quite low, and the processes are promoted slowly.

Vulnerable groups within Sámi communities, such as the elderly and the vulnerabilities they experience, are also addressed. The changes experienced in the Arctic as well as the new security challenges could arguably have a greater social and emotional impact on the elderly, a group that does not necessarily have the skills or the desire to adapt to the changing modern world. Shahnaj Begum and Päivi Naskali present experiences pertaining to the human security threat to elderly Sámi living in Finnish and Swedish Lapland. Begum and Naskali gather various data from numerous interviews, studies, field studies, and literature reviews. While assessing how elderly Sámi are affected by ongoing transformations in this region from the viewpoint of economic, food, health, environmental, personal, and community security, Begum and Naskali offer recommendations for promoting the well-being of elderly Sámi.

The last chapter brings us to Mongolia and the human security concerns of Mongolian indigenous herders. In this chapter, Vigya Sharma identifies opportunities for innovations to mitigate human security threats. Sharma adopts a comparative approach between the indigenous peoples of the Arctic and those of Mongolia in presenting the threats related to the herding business. According to Sharma, there are many similarities between these two regions. Since approximately 40 percent of all Mongolians are currently involved in herding for their primary livelihood, herding-based lifestyles provide much more than just livelihoods: a traditional lifestyle to which many indigenous peoples of the North can relate. Therefore, Sharma emphasizes the endorsement of approaches that are grounded in the local context while addressing threats to human security, instead of leaning solely on, for example, mining as the most profitable source of revenue. This comparative study between Mongolia and the Arctic shows the high relevance and applicability of the study of threats and vulnerabilities faced by the indigenous peoples of the North. The Arctic, as a landscape of fast-paced environmental and socioeconomic change, can serve to illustrate alternative approaches to address these vulnerabilities in other regions.

The thirteen chapters presented in this volume offer a comprehensive overview of a number of common and specific vulnerabilities and threats to security faced by indigenous peoples of the North. The "human security" approach followed in this volume provides a broadened and inclusive understanding of security, addressing areas often neglected in traditional approaches, such as economic, food, health, environmental, personal, community, and political security. During an era when traditional military-driven security and rampant *Realpolitik* resulting from the promise of vast natural resources seem to be the norm driving the development and implementation of policies, human security is an effective tool to give voice to the indigenous peoples of the North, to identify and address their vulnerabilities, and to promote policies that are aligned and responsive to the indigenous views and problems, foster indigenous governance, and enable the implementation of sustainable policies for socioeconomic development as well as the preservation of traditional lifestyles. The traditional knowledge of the indigenous peoples of the North can and must be acknowledged and included within development policies. The peoples' vulnerabilities must be addressed, and their legitimate perceptions should be acknowledged. Their long presence, based on adaptability, resilience, respect for their environment, and sustainability, ought to be a major driving force for sustainability in the Arctic. This is a lesson taught by history, as evidenced by the long-gone Viking settlements in Greenland.[13]

Put bluntly, without the indigenous peoples of the North, there is no Arctic.

13 Diamond, J., *Colapse* (London: Penguin books, 2011) 248–276.

CHAPTER 1

Indigenous Security Governance in the North: Structure and Promotional Tools

*Kamrul Hossain**

Abstract

This chapter addresses important questions related to the governance of indigenous security in response to various challenges prevailing in the North. While the region generally has fairly good regional governance framework, indigenous peoples' concerns still call for significant advancement in terms of tackling socio-cultural and environmental problems. The existing indigenous governance framework includes a variety of international instruments, such as the UN Declaration on the Rights of Indigenous Peoples, ILO Convention 169, International Covenant on Civil and Political Rights, Convention on Biodiversity and its protocols etc. References to indigenous issues can be found either directly or indirectly in these documents. However, they also have significant shortcomings in terms of mitigating particular challenges. These shortcomings are addressed in numerous policy papers and academic literatures. Regional institutions and concerned states have endorsed policies and strategies to mitigate indigenous security challenges. Against this background, this chapter aims to draw the existing structure of the indigenous security framework; thereafter, it intends to identify various options that can be materialized to promote the governance of indigenous security in the particular context of the North.

1 Introduction

In this article, the North refers to the circumpolar Arctic region and, to a certain extent, the sub-circumpolar Arctic region.[1] The entire region is home to a significant number of diverse groups of indigenous peoples. These groups of peoples traditionally rely on nature-based livelihood practices, which enable

* Kamrul Hossain, Associate Professor and Director of the Northern Institute for Environmental and Minority Law (NIEM) at the Arctic Centre in the University of Lapland.

1 There is no precise definition of the Arctic region. The article addresses, among others, the Barents region because of the institutional framework of the region.

 | DOI 10.1163/9789004314399_003

cultural survival, economic sustenance, and spiritual well-being. Today, the region has experienced rapid transformation owing to a variety of reasons. One of the major causes of this transformation is climate change, which drastically affects both the Arctic and sub-Arctic regions.[2] Consequently, these groups of indigenous peoples face numerous challenges that threaten their physical survival and cultural identity. Generally, indigenous peoples and their rights are directly or indirectly addressed in relevant human rights instruments by which they enjoy some form of protection in terms of maintaining their culture, cultural rights, and identity. However, the implementation of the collective component of the rights of indigenous peoples is difficult. Except for International Labour Organization (ILO) Convention 169,[3] there are no other legally binding international instruments that comprehensively focus on indigenous peoples' rights. The mainstream human rights instruments—the International Covenant on Civil and Political Rights (ICCPR)[4] and the International Covenant on Economic, Social and Cultural Rights (ICESCR)[5] have not referred to the term "indigenous peoples." Moreover, the International Convention on the Elimination of All Forms of Racial Discrimination (ICERD)[6] also does not have any similar reference. However, reference to indigenous peoples has appeared in the subsequent treaty interpretation conducted by Treaty monitoring bodies within the auspices of the abovementioned instruments.[7] Yet, it is important to note that these abovementioned instruments embodied rights that belong to individuals only. Therefore, while individual members of the indigenous community—as with other individuals in the states that have ratified the

2 Gruber, Stefan, "The Impact of Climate Change on Cultural Heritage Sites: Environmental Law and Adaptation," *Carbon and Climate Law Review* (2011): 209–219, http://ssrn.com/abstract=1285741.

3 Convention Concerning Indigenous and Tribal Peoples in Independent Countries (1989) (No. 169), 72 ILO Official Bull. 59; 28 ILM 1382 (1989), http://www.ilo.org/dyn/normlex/en/f?p=NORMLEXPUB:12100:0::NO::P12100_ILO_CODE:C169.

4 International Covenant on Civil and Political Rights, opened for signing December 16, 1966, 999 U.N.T.S. 171 (entered into force March 23, 1976), http://www.ohchr.org/en/professionalinterest/pages/ccpr.aspx.

5 International Covenant on Economic, Social and Cultural Rights, opened for signing December 16, 1966, 993 U.N.T.S. 3 (entered into force January 3, 1976), http://www.ohchr.org/EN/ProfessionalInterest/Pages/CESCR.aspx.

6 International Convention on the Elimination of All Forms of Racial Discrimination, opened for signature December 21, 1965, 660 U.N.T.S. 195 (entered into force January 4, 1969), http://www.ohchr.org/EN/ProfessionalInterest/Pages/CERD.aspx.

7 See, for example, Committee on the Elimination of Racial Discrimination, General Recommendation XXIII: Indigenous Peoples, U.N. Doc. CERD/C/51.Misc.13/Rev.4 (Aug. 18, 1997).

treaties—are protected, it is not certain how community rights or group rights as a whole can be protected. The United Nations Declaration on the Rights of Indigenous Peoples (UNDRIP) adopted in 2007 is the only instrument that sets out comprehensive rights of indigenous peoples. Nevertheless, the Declaration, because of its nature as a non-legally binding instrument, does not create any binding obligation upon the states.

Indigenous groups often advocate for collective enjoyment of the rights attached to them. Lack of adequate protection of indigenous rights broadens the threats to their overall survival from diverse angles, which can be explained from the security viewpoint, given that the human rights framework has limitations. The term "security" here refers to human dimensions of security, which is today broadly understood as human security. According to my understanding, the human security concept is one of the most appropriate tools available to comprehend indigenous peoples' present day struggle. However, as there are apparent regional differences in the understanding of the concept of human security, in this chapter, I intend to explore the applicability of the concept in the context of the Arctic and its indigenous communities. The peoples in the Arctic suffer from a range of human security challenges mainly due to a rapid transformation of the region, the major driver of which is climate change. While addressing these concerns, I refer to the normative developments that occurred relatively recently in connection with the human rights regime, which today includes a set of group rights known as third-generation human rights.[8] Such rights broadly comprise, among others, the rights to environment and development, the realization of which is dependent—in the case of indigenous peoples—on the enjoyment of a set of rights, including the right to self-determination.[9] However, the legal framework for the attainment of these rights is unclear. Therefore, in this chapter, I argue that a governance framework within the scope of human security would help realize the entitlements of these groups of indigenous peoples.

The remainder of this chapter is structured in the following manner: First, I address the concept of human security and its applicability to the region's

8 Marks, Stephen, "The Human Right to Development: Between Rhetoric and Reality," *Harvard Human Rights Journal* 17 (2004): 137–168, 138. See also Maggio, Greg and Owen J. Lynch, "Human Rights, Environment, and Economic Development: Existing and Emerging Standards in International Law and Global Society" (Center for International Environmental Law, 1997). Accessed November 2, 2014, http://www.ciel.org/Publications/olp3i.html.

9 The understanding of self-determination increasingly invokes self-government in internal matters without necessarily arguing for a secession from the existing state. See for example Cassese, Antonio, *Self-Determination of Peoples: A Legal Reappraisal*. (Cambridge: Cambridge University Press, 1995), 53.

indigenous peoples. This is intended to promote an understanding of the challenges facing the region's indigenous peoples. Second, I assert the aspects of existing institutional structures available to address these challenges. In this endeavor, I analyze how the relevant provisions of these instruments capture the security threats where the referent objects are the indigenous peoples. Finally, I show the shortcomings of the existing structure in addressing the security threats that the groups of indigenous peoples of the North encounter. In conclusion, I provide some remarks to promote indigenous human security in the context of the North.

2 A Brief Overview of the Concept of Human Security

The concept of human security is a policy tool, the foundation of which is underlined in the United Nations (UN) Human Development Report (HDR) adopted in 1994.[10] The primary idea underlying the concept is to address security at a sub-national level, extending to individuals or communities beyond state-centric security, which is sovereignty oriented. However, the concept as a whole complements the traditional notion of state-centric security in the sense that a state is not secure unless its subjects are secure. The author of the HDR, Dr. Mahbubul Hoq, defined the concept in the following manner:

> Human security is not a concern with weapons. It is a concern with human dignity. In the last analysis it is a child who did not die, a disease that did not spread, and an ethnic tension that did not explode, a dissident who was not silenced, a human spirit that was not crushed.[11]

According to the HDR, the concept of human security is understood as a means of safeguarding two aspects, namely the "freedom from fear" and the "freedom from want," the absence of which constitutes multiple security threats, where individuals remain at the centre. While "freedom from fear" is about ensuring security from physical violence, the "freedom from want" is about ensuring that the economic, social, and cultural demands of individuals and community

10 See *United Nations Human Development Report* (UNHDR) *1994*. Published for the United Nations Development Programme. (New York and Oxford: Oxford University Press, 1994), http://hdr.undp.org/en/content/human-development-report-1994.

11 Ibid., 22.

are met.[12] The former addresses concerns associated with violent conflict, such as conflicts led by poverty, inequality, etc.; the latter addresses, amongst the other issues, diseases or health-related aspects, hunger, natural disaster, environmental catastrophes, etc. It is said that these elements are crucial as they are inseparable in the understanding of the root cause of all insecurity. It is also said that these elements kill far more people than war, genocide, and terrorism combined. They represent seven categories of threats, as identified in the HDR.[13] Consequently, the human dimension of understanding security is crucial to protect human communities from apparently non-violent but serious threats, which represent the root cause of both national and international security threats. Therefore, the concept as a whole is about the promotion of human wellbeing, focusing on individual or community security at sub-state as well as regional and international levels.[14] A broad range of issues are included to promote the understanding of security: from response to physical threat to political stability, from management of natural disaster to environmental protection, and from poverty reduction to economic development. Considering the presence of this broad range of aspects, it is unlikely that there can be any single definition of human security to be constitutive of a norm.[15] However, there are both narrow and broad conceptions in the understanding of the concept.[16] The narrow approach is based on natural rights and the rule of law that are attached to basic human rights, whereas the broad view includes a larger agenda of economic globalization, environment, and sustainability in connection to the assurance of welfare at the individual and community levels. As a "foundational concept," human security brings values and ethical norms

12 The concept as a whole is argued to include seven categories of security: economic, health, food, personal, political, community, and environment. See ibid.

13 Ibid., 24–25.

14 Ruiz De Garbay, Daniel, "Securing Humans in a Dangerous World," *Human Security Journal* 3 (2007): 1–23. See also Cilliers, Jakkie, Human Security in Africa A conceptual framework for review (African Human Security Initiative, 2004), 10. Accessed November 18, 2012, http://dspace.cigilibrary.org/jspui/bitstream/123456789/31497/1/AHSIMONO1.pdf?1. A state can for example, be as thoroughly disrupted by internal challenges as they can be by external forces. Human security is therefore a relationship of in/securities emanating from the level of the individual or non/sub-state level. The manifestation of in/securities depend on the context.

15 Owen, Taylor, "Human Security – Conflict, Critique and Consensus: Colloquium Remarks and a Proposal for a Threshold-Based Definition," *Security Dialogue* 34 (2004): 373–387, 384.

16 Oberleitner, Gerd, "Human Security and Human Rights," *Occasional Paper Series 8*, European Training and Research Centre for Human Rights and Diplomacy, 2002.

to security debates when such a broad formulation is constructed.[17] While some argue that a narrowed down approach is more easily operationalized, as a policy tool, human security is not confined to any limited scope that restricts security threats only to physical violence.[18] Even though a broad formulation of the concept causes ambiguity in the context of a coherent, uniform, and common understanding,[19] the utility of human security lies in addressing policy problems[20] by considering the prevailing context with regard to particular geographical regions. It is concerned with the threats actually affecting people, regardless of its arbitrary broad or narrow formulations.[21] The idea is to integrate both negative (protection) and positive (empowerment) aspects of security in the promotion of human wellbeing in a particular society, while taking into consideration specific regional characteristics.

3 Human Security and Its Arctic Relevance

To the extent human security threats address the policy problems prevailing in a particular region, it is influenced by the characteristics of the regional structure. As security threats vary significantly across countries and communities, human security questions of the global South are not akin to those prevailing in the Northern region, such as in the Arctic. The causes and expressions of human security depend on a complex interaction of international, regional, and local factors. As a broad, dynamic, and flexible framework, human security captures such variation in specific contexts, builds processes that are based on people's own perceptions of fear and vulnerability, identifies the concrete

17 See generally Shahrbanou, Tadjbakhsh and Anuradha M. Chenoy, *Human Security: Concepts and Implications*. London & New York: Routledge, 2007.

18 Taylor Owen 2004, *supra* note 15, 384.

19 Fukuda-Parr Sakiko and Carol Messineo, "Human Security: A critical review of the literature." CRPD *Working Paper* No. 11. (Centre for Research on Peace and Development, 2012). Accessed February 26, 2014, http://soc.kuleuven.be/web/files/12/80/wp11.pdf. See also Yuen Foong, Khong "Human Security: A Shotgun Approach to Alleviating Human Misery?" *Global Governance* 7 (2001): 231–236, 233. It is often criticized that making everything a security concern for an individual effectually brings no benefits for anyone, and in so doing, no priority can be given to addressing policy problems.

20 Taylor Owen 2004, *supra* note 15, 377. Such problems have been successfully addressed, for example, in the International Convention to Ban Landmines, the International Criminal Court, small arms, and child soldiers, which are often attributed to the human security agenda.

21 Ibid., 382.

needs for people under stress, enables solutions based on local realities, helps identify priority security needs at the local level, and examines the impact of global developments on different communities.[22] By providing holistic and contextual account of peoples' concrete needs and the factors endangering their security, the concept, when applied, is capable of analysing overall social impact.[23] Such an understanding of human security needs prevails in the Arctic, particularly in the context of its indigenous peoples facing numerous human security challenges.

4 Arctic Indigenous Peoples and Human Security Challenges

The Arctic presents unique environmental conditions that are generally regarded as pristine, and its ecosystem is sensitive to any external interference. However, the region is undergoing an increasing number of changes. Climate change and related consequences are argued to be the major factors responsible for the environmental changes occurring in the Arctic.[24] For example, temperature rise is expected to contribute to rapid melting of Arctic sea ice, which will lead to numerous human activities including shipping, fishing, and extraction of mineral resources. The Arctic is generally regarded as a resource-rich region, both in terms of living natural resources and the huge potential of inland and offshore resources.[25] Consequently, a move to the increasingly accessible Arctic is not a far cry. The seasonally opened water around the Arctic seas has already shown an increase in the volume of vessels sailing through the Arctic sea routes.[26] With this development, it is obvious that there will be new sources of pollution that will affect the region. With regard to mineral

---

22 See "Human Security in Theory and Practice", Human Security Unit, Office for the Coordination of Humanitarian Affairs, United Nations, 9–11. Accessed February 26, 2014, http://hdr.undp.org/en/media/HS_Handbook_2009.pdf.

23 See ibid.

24 Gruber, Stefan, "The Impact of Climate Change on Cultural Heritage Sites: Environmental Law and Adaptation," *Carbon and Climate Law Review* (2011), 209–219, http://ssrn.com/abstract=1285741.

25 Agarwal, Sunil Kumar, "The Arctic Climate Impacts and International Law: Issues and Challenges" (May 20, 2011), National Maritime Foundation, http://ssrn.com/abstract=1866114 or http://dx.doi.org/10.2139/ssrn.1866114.

26 Donald R. Rothwell, "Arctic Ocean Choke Points and the Law of the Sea," ANU College of Law Research Paper No. 10–81, 2010. Canadian Council of International Law Annual Meeting, Ottawa, October 28–30, 2010, 3–4, http://ssrn.com/abstract=1697882 or http://dx.doi.org/10.2139/ssrn.1697882.

resources, the offshore Arctic in particular is regarded as the next reservoir of the world's untapped hydrocarbon resources.[27] While it may be observed that increasing demands of oil and gas in the world market would create competition over these resources, the likelihood of any tension of interstate conflict affecting regional security appears to be non-existent, at least in the near future, considering the present settings of Arctic geopolitics.[28] However, the range of activities will result in various tensions in terms of environmental sustainability and benefit sharing amongst various interests groups at local and regional levels, thereby presenting human security threats from multidimensional aspects. Because the changes occurring in the region create increasingly vulnerable social, economic, and environmental conditions, those that define human security for the local and indigenous communities[29] are at the centre of these tensions.[30] For example, oil and gas development, which has already been implicated in increased climate change, is expected to intensify in the future, which would then contribute to local and indigenous peoples' capacity to adapt by providing access to resources—and the resources themselves—at risk.[31] The consequences of climate change drastically alter ecosystems, such that both human and non-humans must either significantly adapt or be wiped

27 The United States Geological Survey estimates that reserves are plentiful. US Geological Survey (USGS), "Circum-Arctic Resource Appraisal: Estimates of Undiscovered Oil and Gas North of the Arctic Circle", U.S. Geological Survey Fact Sheet 2008–3049, 2008, http://pubs.usgs.gov/fs/2008/3049/.

28 This is mainly due to the fact that the resources located in the Arctic are, in most cases, within the sovereign jurisdiction of each of the Arctic states. Moreover, thus far, the circumpolar states have shown strong commitment to play along the rules of international law. It is argued that the Arctic has been, and will be, a peaceful region even in the foreseeable future from the interstate conflict viewpoint, unless something dramatic happens. See, for example, Berkman, Paul Arthur and Alexander N. Vylegzhanin, "Building Common Interests in the Arctic Ocean," in *Environmental Security in the Arctic Ocean*, ed. Paul Arthur Berkman and Alexander N. Vylegzhanin, 371–404, NATO Science for Peace and Security Series C. Environmental Security, 2013.

29 Lukovich, Jennifer Verlaine and Gordon A. McBean, "Addressing Human Security in the Arctic in the Context of Climate Change through Science and Technology," *Mitigation and Adaptation Strategies for Global Change* 14 (2009): 697–710, 699.

30 See Arctic Climate Impact Assessment (ACIA). (New York: Cambridge University Press, 2005), 95. According to the ACIA report, the indigenous peoples' future is at stake; therefore, it is important to ensure their ability for them to make choices and changes for their very survival.

31 IPCC, *Climate Change 2007 – The physical science basis.* (Cambridge: Cambridge University Press, 2008).

out.[32] Some communities benefit from diverse human activities occurring in the Arctic, but the others suffer from the devastations caused by these activities. For example, fishing communities or reindeer-herding communities suffer from loss of their traditional livelihood activities.[33] In sum, it may be argued that there will be both negative and positive developments; however, it is uncertain how these developments would embrace the human security challenges of these communities, as their lives and livelihood practices are regarded vulnerable to threats, such as those from health security, food security, community security, etc.

The Arctic contains diverse groups of indigenous peoples; their numbers vary depending on how they are counted. However, approximately 400,000 indigenous persons divided into close to 40 different groups inhabit the region. They include the Inuit from North America to the Sámi in the Nordic countries, to small indigenous peoples of the Russian North. They account for 10 percent of the entire population of the region.[34] This number is significant, and given that these peoples in many parts of the Arctic continue traditional activities as part of their livelihood— and other practices that they inherited from their ancestors— there are substantial impacts from the transformation of the region. In the most remote areas of the North, many are still engaged in traditional hunting and fishing practices. In other areas, they practice traditional activities, such as reindeer and caribou herding. Although recent developments suggest that many indigenous communities, particularly amongst the ones living in the Nordic countries, are increasingly engaged in small-scale tourism activities, for example, building summer cottages, it appears that traditional livelihood practices—even despite modern means and technology—still offer important roles for these peoples in order for them to maintain their unique identity among the rest of the inhabitants. Thus, even though security threats non-discriminately affect all the inhabitants of the region, the community identity of indigenous peoples is of significance, thereby making them more vulnerable than others.

While this vulnerability aspect is connected to security, it is not clear how the challenges facing communities can be addressed from the viewpoint of security. Tylor Owen argues for a threshold-based approach, which is

32 Hoogensen, Gunhild, "Human Security in the Arctic–Yes, it is relevant!" *Journal of Human Security* 5 (2009): 1–10, 4.

33 Ibid.

34 For more information see also Arcic Centre, "Arctic Indigenous Peoples," http://www.arcticcentre.org/EN/SCIENCE-COMMUNICATIONS/Arctic-region/Arctic-Indigenous-Peoples.

conceptualized as limited to the severity of risks.[35] However, the problem is that the list of all relevant risks to people is vast and measuring severity is context-dependent. Narrowing the focus on this list of risks depends on the surrounding characteristics of a particular region. In the Arctic, for its indigenous peoples, the list is exhaustive; narrowing down of the risks, to whatever category they may belong to, is not my objective here in the chapter. Moreover, I do not intend to prioritize issues such as subsistence livelihood practices, competition over land use and resources, and food and health concerns over other issues, like suicide and mental health, domestic violence, substance abuse and drug addiction, and lack of adequate housing, etc. I only address some of the challenges, which can either they can be viewed from the vulnerability viewpoint or from a narrowed-down threshold-based approach which would require effective instructional tools for better implementation.[36] In this analysis, security is understood as the ability of the Arctic indigenous peoples not only to identify the risks and threats to their wellbeing and values, but also to determine the ways to end, mitigate, and/or adapt to the risks identified.[37]

These groups of indigenous peoples face a number of security threats, namely threat to environmental security, economic security, community security, food security, health security, etc. These aspects of security challenges are interconnected and tied to each other. One security threat influences the others. They also lead to a number of other societal problems that are contributory to human security threats, such as unemployment, family violence, alcoholism, etc. For example, threat to environmental security threatens the security of the maintenance of indigenous culture, which is related to community security. Environmental pollution contaminates the traditional food supply chain that affects food security, which then further contributes to a threat to health security. Simultaneously, one aspect of security undermines another component of security. For example, economic security undermines environmental security.

As a resource rich region, the Arctic attracts international investments both for inland and offshore resources. In recent years, mining activities in many parts of the Arctic, including in the region of Lapland and the Northern part of

35 Liotta, P.H. and Owen, Taylor, "Why Human Security?" *The Whitehead Journal of Diplomacy and International Relations* (2006), 51.

36 See Section 5 of this chapter.

37 This sort of analysis is found in the work of Gunhild Hoogensen and positive and negative security. See Hoogensen 2009, *supra* note 32, 3.

Russia, have increased significantly.[38] Many of these areas are regarded as the homeland for indigenous peoples. Clearly, these developments thus contribute to tension over the economic and environmental interests of these groups of peoples. As far as environment is concerned, changes occurring in the Arctic have a significant impact on the continuing practice of traditional culture. Take an example of reindeer herding in Fennoscandia. Reindeer-herding practices are common means of subsistence for many Sámi in the region.[39] In Norway and Sweden, it is only the Sámi who can practice reindeer herding, whereas in Finland there are no such restrictions.[40] Yet, in Finland it is significantly only the Sámi who practice herding activities. Even though new methods are used today as part of herding practices—such as the use of snowmobiles and, to a certain extent, helicopters—as well as in the processing of the end products,[41] the practice itself is regarded as a Sámi emblem in the region in terms of understanding their culture and cultural identity.[42] The impact of climate change on reindeer herding are noticeable in many ways. Recent research reveals that due to climate change, reindeer herding is becoming less and less resilient than it was before.[43] Although changes have always occurred in the natural environment, the current changes are more drastic.[44] In addition, the amount

38 Wilson, Alana, F. McMahon and Miguel Cervantes, *Annual Survey of Mining Companies*. Vancouver: Fraser Institute, 2013, https://www.fraserinstitute.org/uploadedFiles/fraser-ca/Content/research-news/research/publications/mining-survey-2012-2013.pdf. Accessed April 16, 2015.

39 *Arctic Human Development Report – Regional Processes and Global Linkages* (AHDR), TemaNord2014: 567. (Copenhagen, Nordic Council of Ministers, 2014), 136.

40 Timo Koivurova, Vladimir Masloboev, Kamrul Hossain, Vigdis Nygaard, Anna Petrétei, Svetlana Vinogradova: *Legal Protection of Sami Traditional Livelihoods from the Adverse Impacts of Mining: A Comparison of the Level of Protection Enjoyed by Sami in Their Four Home States*. In: Arctic Review on Law and Politics, Vol. 6, No. 1, 2015, pp. 11–51.

41 Reindeer meats are processed in industries, exported in other regions, and traditional practices are replaced by more commercial practices.

42 Irja Seurujärvi-Kari *et. al.*, *The Sámi The Indigenous People of Northernmost Europe*. (Brussels: European Bureau for Lesser Used Languages, 1997), 21.

43 See findings of the project "Reindeer Herding, Traditional Knowledge and Adaptation to Climate Change and Loss of Grazing Land", ed. Ole Henrik Magga *et al.*, a project led by Norway and Association of World Reindeer Herders (WRH) in Arctic Council, Sustainable Development Working Group (SDWG), http://reindeerherding.org/wp-content/uploads/2013/06/EALAT-Final-Report.pdf.

44 Furberg, Maria, Birgitta Evengard and Maria Nilsson, "Facing the Limit of Resilience: Perceptions of Climate Change among Reindeer Herding Sami in Sweden," *Global Health Action* (4) 2011, 8417–8427, doi: 10.3402/gha.v4i0.8417.

of grazing land for reindeer has gradually shrunk because of new forms of land use behavior, including mining.

Similarly, the effects of climate change impact other traditional practices, such as traditional fishing activities amongst the Sámi. For many coastal Sámi, fishing is becoming increasingly difficult, as commercial fisheries extend to the North because of the wider access resulting from more open water throughout the coastal region. Even inland fisheries, such as salmon fishing, have become threatened as outside interests grow. For example, the Deatnu River Valley, which is located between Norway and Finland and is the home of Sámi people on both sides of the border, is increasingly attracting tourists for salmon fishing.[45] According to statistics, the average total haul made by tourists between 1972 and 2011 constitutes 25% of the total; on the other hand, the haul made by tourists from Finland has in recent years constituted 30% of the total haul.[46] As such, the increase appears to be a threat in the maintenance of traditional fishing as representative of not only the Sámi culture and cultural identity but also subsistence practices. Similar threats are also apparent in other parts of the Arctic. In the North American Arctic, where one of the core cultural practices of the Inuit communities is to live in harmony with nature and to depend on hunting, fishing, and trapping for traditional livelihood practices, many are finding the changes extremely difficult to the extent that the maintenance of traditional cultural practices are concerned. Even though culturally theses peoples are capable of adapting to changes, the rapid fluctuations in environmental changes cause them to become increasingly disconnected from the lands and areas that they use for livelihood practices. Today, they are unable to predict natural processes as they used to earlier.[47] Moreover, harsh climatic conditions as well as the thinning and breaking sea ice makes hunting and fishing practices extremely life threatening, let alone the threat to food security.

As mentioned earlier in this article, food is part of the community culture in a particular society, particularly for indigenous peoples, as they maintain various rituals related to food habits that are common among the indigenous

45 According to statistics, the average haul made by tourists between 1972 and 2011 constitutes 25% of the total haul; in recent years, the haul made by tourists from Finland amounted to up to 30% of the total haul. See "Catch-statistics Norwegian and Finnish catch of salmon", Deatnu River fishing administration website, http://tanafisk.no/en/statistikk/fangststatistikk.

46 See "Catch-statistics Norwegian and Finnish catch of salmon", Deatnu River fishing administration website, http://tanafisk.no/en/statistikk/fangststatistikk.

47 Downing, Ashleigh and Alain Cuerrier, "A synthesis of the impact of climate change on the First Nations and Inuit of Canada," *Indian Journal of Traditional Knowledge* 10 (2011): 57–70, 57.

peoples of the Arctic. Whaling is an example for many communities both amongst the Inuit of North America and Greenland as well as some Sámi in Northern Norway.[48] Food does not only serve as a physical commodity, it also serves as a cultural property for these communities, which is connected to their cultural identity; thus, an adverse effect on food impacts their community wellbeing. While food security is understood as "all people at all-time have physical, social and economic access to safe, sufficient and nutritious food that meets their dietary needs and … for an active and healthy life,"[49] it has to be noted that for the Arctic indigenous communities, traditional food plays the most important role in providing all their dietary needs for healthy life. Traditional food includes a variety of berries, mushrooms, and animal food products. In addition to increasing obstacles to accessing traditional food resources, contamination through pollution, mainly of marine sources, affects the safety of these traditional food chains. For example, fishery resources have been found to be contaminated in many Arctic areas.[50] On land infrastructural development, expansion of new industrial activities and other human activities, such as shipping and offshore resource developments, also pollute the food supply chain. Although alternative food supply was provided from the flow of globalization from the south, which is mostly referred to as "Western food," southern foods do not meet the required dietary needs for the communities inhabiting the North. Research suggests that imported food contributes to various health-related risks for the local and indigenous communities of the North. Diseases such as campylobacteriosis, risk of cancer, obesity, diabetes, and cardiovascular diseases are apparently on the rise.[51] Consequently, there appears to be a dual phenomenon in the context of food security—on the one hand, traditional foods gradually become unavailable, and where they are available, they are not safe anymore because of contamination; on the other hand, Western

48 For more information see also "Sami Culture The Coastal Sami of Norway," http://www.utexas.edu/courses/sami/dieda/hist/nor-sami.htm.

49 "The state of food insecurity in the world 2001". Rome: Food and Agriculture Organization, 2001. Accessed March 9, 2015, http://www.fao.org/docrep/003/y1500e/y1500e00.htm.

50 Letcher, Robert J. *et al.*, "Exposure and effects assessment of persistent organohalogen contaminants in Arctic wildlife and fish," *Science of the Total Environment* 408 (2010): 2995–3045.

51 See for example Hedlund, Christina, Yulia Blomstedt and Barbara Schumann, "Association between climatic factors and infectious diseases in the Arctic and subarctic region – A systematic review," *Global Health Action*, 7 (2014): 24161–24176; Jorgenson, M., Y. Kue, "Cardiovascular Diseases, Diabetes, and Obesity," in *Health Transitions in Arctic Populations*, ed. Young, T. Kue and Peter Bjerregaard, 291–307. (Toronto, Buffalo and London: University of Toronto Press, 2008), 291.

food does not fulfill the dietary needs of indigenous peoples, thereby resulting in health-related risks that affect health security. Moreover, the remoteness of the region is also a factor that offers threats to health security since access to health care facilities is not well developed in the North. Indigenous communities in the North are structurally sparsely populated communities that suffer from these various threats.

One of the other aspects of relevance from the viewpoint of Arctic indigenous communities is that the region, particularly the remote areas, suffers from poverty. Even though almost all the other areas of the circumpolar region, except for the Russian North, are more or less covered by their states' social security network providing minimum means of financial support for economic survival, it is nevertheless not sufficient in many cases unless the creation of new jobs is secured. Additionally, lack of responsive tools to enhance resilience and adaptability also threaten many aspects of the human security of these groups of peoples, which necessitates an effective governance mechanism for addressing these challenges.

5 Indigenous Security Governance

Very generally, governance is interpreted as an institutional mode of societal coordination by which states or actors produces rules, regulations, policies, strategies, action plans, etc. It has two components: structure and process.[52] Structure implies actor-institution constellations, whereas process implies interactions amongst institutions and actors to produce the rules, regulations, policies, strategies, etc. The process varies depending on the particular environmental consideration. Consequently, the governance of indigenous security must involve an interaction between structure and process, where tradition or culture coincides.[53] A project such as this requires integrating flexible policy tools within the governance framework. Implementation of human security is exercised through various existing mechanisms, both norm-oriented and policy oriented. The norm-oriented form can be found within a human rights framework, while the policy-oriented form can be found in various policy

52 Hunt, Janet and Diane Smith, "Strengthening Indigenous Community Governance: A step towards advancing Reconciliation in Australia." Paper presented at Peace, Justice and Reconciliation in the Asia-Pacific Region Conference, April 1–3, 2005, Queensland University. Accessed February 14, 2015, http://caepr.anu.edu.au/sites/default/files/Publications/topical/Hunt_Smith_Governance.pdf.

53 Ibid.

documents developed through local, national, and regional institutions. The concept as a whole must not necessarily be integrated; a fragmented approach is undertaken in understanding particular security threats, given that the characteristics of each of the Arctic regions vary because of geographical locations, socio-cultural practices, and environmental and climatic conditions. However, it is important to identify the most urgent issues relevant for a particular region and in the context of particular communities. Thus, the governance approach of human security integrates this prioritization.

The Norm-Oriented Approach

The human rights framework primarily addresses almost all aspects of the components that the concept of human security encompasses. Some of these aspects are objective, while some others are subjective. They are often categorized as first, second, and third generations of human rights. While the first and second generations represent civil and political rights, and economic, social and cultural rights, respectively, third-generation human rights represent the group component of human rights leading to, for example, the right to environment and right to development.[54] While the former discusses the concrete rights guaranteed by internationally agreed treaties and treaty mechanisms, the latter is more linked to offering normative guidance. While the ultimate objective of the third-generation human rights is to promote human wellbeing, the human security tool is used to identify the collectivity of these rights.

The mainstream structure of human rights comprises three documents: the Universal Declaration of Human Rights adopted in 1948 and the two Covenants adopted in 1966—the ICCPR and ICESCR—referred to in the introduction. These three documents are occasionally referred to as the international bill of rights.[55] However, the bill of rights only addresses rights belonging to individuals and does not mention the term "indigenous peoples," even though the common article 1 of both Covenants highlights peoples' right to self-determination. Yet, one article of the ICCPR, namely article 27, mentions culture and cultural components of rights of the "minority", which can be interpreted as including indigenous peoples. This article protects the rights of individuals belonging to a minority to enjoy his or her culture "in community" with other members of the group. The fact is that indigenous peoples form a minority in most

54 Hannan, Muhammed Abdul, "Third Generation Human Rights and the Good Governance," OIDA *International Journal of Sustainable Development* 2 (2010), 41–50, http://ssrn.com/abstract=1717075.

55 Perry, Michael J., "The Morality of Human Rights: A Nonreligious Ground?" *Emory Law Journal* 54 (2005): 97–150, 101, http://ssrn.com/abstract=685550.

countries; hence, the article applies to them. The members of indigenous groups, as with other citizens of the country concerned, are protected by the bill of rights as far as they are affected individually, regardless of their group component of rights that is linked to the enjoyment of the right to self-determination.[56] While interpreting indigenous right to self-determination, it is mostly argued from the viewpoint of the cultural component of indigenous peoples, as far as culture is largely connected to lands and land-based activities.[57] As discussed previously, culture offers community security with regard to the unique identity of indigenous peoples, and the maintenance of which is associated with, among others, environmental sustainability. For example, in *Länsman et al. v. Finland*, the Human Rights Committee (HRC) clearly indicated that culture cannot be determined in "abstracto"; it may have components that require adaptation to the changes occurring in response to commercial activities occurring on the lands of the Sámi people, thereby having significant impacts on the practice of culture due to adverse effects on the disturbed environment.[58] Despite this clear articulation by the HRC, it must be mentioned that by virtue of the Optional Protocol to the ICCPR, a group as a whole cannot bring a communication; rather, only an individual or, in the opinion of the HRC, a group of individuals who are equally affected[59] can submit a complaint against any violation of the rights guaranteed under article 27 of the Covenant. Consequently, there have been serious debates in legal literature on whether this minority protection article has strong influence in promoting rights associated with indigenous peoples. Even though various interpretations promoted by the HRC suggest an interconnection between articles 27 and 1, particularly paragraph 2 of the Covenant, with regard to self-determination of indigenous peoples in the context of resource management, the procedural mechanisms

56 Scheinin, Martin, "Indigenous Peoples' Land Rights under the International Covenant on Civil and Political Rights," Norwegian Centre for Human Rights, 2004, http://www.galdu.org/govat/doc/ind_peoples_land_rights.pdf.

57 See Human Rights Committee (HRC) interpretations in e.g., Länsman *et al.* v. Finland, Communication No 511/1992, U.N. Doc. CCPR/C/52/D/511/1992 (1994). Accessed February 2015, http://www1.umn.edu/humanrts/undocs/html/vws511.htm

58 See Länsman *et al.* v. Finland, Communication No. 511/1992, U.N. Doc. CCPR/C/52/D/511/1992 (1994), para 9.3., http://www1.umn.edu/humanrts/undocs/html/vws511.htm.

59 For more information see also United Nations Human Rights, "Human Rights Treaty Bodies – Individual Communications", Office of the High Commissioner for Human Rights, http://www.ohchr.org/EN/HRBodies/TBPetitions/Pages/IndividualCommunications.aspx.

appear to be ambiguous in terms of how indigenous peoples can effectively enjoy the right and thereby secure themselves from various aspects of threats.

The normative development concerning the specific rights of indigenous peoples began developing in the late 1970s. The first international treaty addressing the concerns of indigenous peoples is the ILO Convention No. 169 adopted in 1989. The particularly important aspects of the Convention are the commitments for non-discrimination, recognition of the culture and cultural identity of indigenous peoples, their participatory rights, right to be consulted in matters that affect them, and a right to decide the matters that are of priority for them.[60] However, while all these elements offer significant aspects of human security components, the most important is the promotion of their identity as distinctive community. Even though the term "peoples" has been frequently used, clearly, a right to "self-determination" has not been mentioned in the Convention. Nevertheless, the recognition of their culture, which is in most cases related to their land and land-based resources, make sense of the rights to enjoy a secure environment and sustainable economic development. Despite this structural development, one should bear in mind that there are fundamental gaps in addressing specific elements of rights pertaining to guaranteeing human security of indigenous peoples. First, the nature of Convention No. 169 is general, and thus, applicable to all the indigenous peoples of the world with no room to focus on specific regional aspects prevailing in the North. Even though it serves as an important document to promote the realization of the basic rights of the indigenous peoples, it does not have a strong component of a right to self-determination—an inherent right giving greater room for promoting indigenous security. While participation and consultation have been invoked, there was nothing about "free consent," implying a right to veto in matters that affect indigenous peoples in response to the activities occurring on their lands. Second, the Convention lacks universal recognition with regard to the norms endorsed in it, because of the small number of ratifications.[61] Third, amongst the Arctic states, it applies only to Norway and Denmark, where the latter does not have indigenous peoples in its main land territory. While it is applicable for Greenlandic peoples, Greenland, the majority of whose population is indigenous peoples, enjoys a relatively larger form

60 Articles 2, 3, 6, 7 of the ILO Convention, *supra* note 3.

61 For information on the ratifications, see also International Labour Organization (ILO), "NORMLEX Ratification by Conventions", Ratifications of 169 Indigenous and Tribal Peoples Convention, 1989 (No. 169), http://www.ilo.org/dyn/normlex/en/f?p=NORMLEXPUB:11300:0::NO:11300:P11300_INSTRUMENT_ID:312314:NO.

of autonomy by its home rule government, thereby making the relevance of the Convention less important for it.

However, the most rewarding achievement for indigenous peoples is the endorsement of the UN Declaration on the Rights of Indigenous Peoples (UNDRIP) in 2007. The Declaration contains comprehensive rights applicable to indigenous peoples, including the right to self-determination. While, self-determination has been clearly explained with further clarity that the right extends to include self-government, the concept has nevertheless endorsed a procedural element in it to implement the right—free, prior, and informed consent.[62] In at least four places in the Declaration, the phrase "free, prior, and informed" consent is endorsed.[63] The Declaration does have significant impacts in the realization of indigenous rights, unlike a treaty intended to be binding, although its character is only of a non-legally binding document. Yet, it is used as a guiding document to raise concrete concerns on the rights of indigenous peoples. This guiding structure has both legal and policy implications.

Since the Declaration has received tremendous recognition amongst the international community,[64] some of its provisions are argued to be creating customary norms, which in international law do have binding legal character. For example, free, prior, and informed consent endorsed in the Declaration, is argued to be an existing and widely recognized concept of public international law.[65] One example is the case of *Saramaka People v. Suriname*, where the Inter-American Court of Human Rights clearly referred to the UN Declaration, in particular its article 32. Referring to Suriname's endorsement of the Declaration, the court articulated the importance of achieving free, prior, and informed consent of the indigenous peoples concerned.[66] Similarly, such an approach was undertaken by the HRC in 2009 in *Ángela Poma Poma v. Peru*

62 See article 4 of the UNDRIP, which states: "Indigenous peoples, in exercising their right to self-determination, have the right to autonomy or self-government in matters relating to their internal and local affairs, as well as ways and means for financing their autonomous functions." United Nations Declaration on the Rights of Indigenous Peoples (UNDRIP) (2007), A/61/L.67/Annex, art. 4.

63 Articles 10, 11, 19, 28, 29 of the UNDRIP.

64 The UNDRIP was adopted by 144 countries, with 11 abstentions and 4 countries voting against it.

65 See for example Göcke, Katja, "The Case of Ángela Poma Poma v. Peru before the Human Rights Committee," in *Max Planck Yearbook of United Nations Law* 14 (2010), ed. Armin von Bogdandy and Rüdiger Wolfrum, 337–370. (Leiden, Martinus Nijhoff 2010), 367.

66 Case of the Saramaka People v. Suriname, Judgment of November 28, 2007, Inter-American Court of Human Rights, para. 131, http://www.corteidh.or.cr/docs/casos/articulos/seriec_172_ing.pdf.

case.[67] The HRC explicitly set the requirement of obtaining free, prior, and informed consent from members of the potentially affected indigenous community. At a general level, the other legally binding instruments referred to elsewhere in this chapter have also shared similar legal importance of the Declaration.[68] In addition, the Convention on Biological Diversity of 1992 and its Nagoya Protocol adopted in 2010 have endorsed provisions concerning indigenous peoples' right to hold the ownership of traditional knowledge, which today is threatened by external use, thus leaving them with no remedy because of lack of effective enforcement mechanisms.[69] Despite this legal importance, the challenge remains with respect to translating the normative elements into a reality in which security concerns can be ameliorated, if not completely eliminated.

The Policy-Oriented Approach

One way of giving real meaning to the comprehensive provisions of the UN Declaration is to absorb them into policy strategies within international, regional, and national frameworks. As international and regional actors, indigenous peoples themselves are engaged in various international and regional fora. At the international level they participate, for example, in the International Work Group for Indigenous Affairs (IWGIA) and the UN Expert Mechanism on the Rights of Indigenous Peoples. In the context of the Arctic, they also participate in a number of relevant regional bodies including the Arctic Council, Barents Euro-Arctic Council (BEAC) etc. In addition, they are also organized at both

67 Ángela Poma Poma v. Peru, Human Rights Committee, Communication No. 1457/2006, U.N. Doc. CCPR/C95/D1457/2006 of 27 March 2009.

68 For example, the Committee on the Elimination of Racial Discrimination (CERD) recommended in its 2008 Concluding Observations on the United States "that the declaration be used as a guide to interpret the State party's obligations under the Convention relating to indigenous peoples". It also recommended that the Declaration be applicable as a legally binding instrument to all United Nations Member States, even the ones that had voted against it. See Committee on the Elimination of Racial Discrimination, Concluding Observations on the United States of America, U.N. Doc. CERD/C/USA/Co/6 of 5 March 2008, para. 29; a similar approach is also undertaken by the Committee on the Rights of the Child, see Committee on the Rights of the Child, General Comment No. 11: Indigenous Children and Their Rights under the Convention, U.N. Doc. CRC/C/GC/11 of January 12, 2009, para 82.

69 "Convention on Biological Diversity. Text of the CBD," http://www.cbd.int/convention/text/default.shtml; "The Nagoya Protocol on Assess to Genetic Resources and the Fair Equitable Sharing of Benefits Arising from their Utilization to the Convention on Biodiversity: text and annex." Montreal: Secretariat on the Convention on Biological Diversity, 2011, http://www.cbd.int/abs/doc/protocol/nagoya-protocol-en.pdf.

national and transnational levels by means of forming indigenous organizations, such as the Inuit Circumpolar Council (ICC) or at the national level, for example, through the Sámi Parliaments in three Nordic countries. Such institutions produce policy documents in which both the overarching spirit of the Declaration as well as particular regional concerns can be reflected with a view to promoting greater rights of the indigenous peoples, which would then essentially promote indigenous security.

Regionally, thus far, the Arctic has achieved significant improvement in recognizing the concerns of indigenous peoples. Institutional development in this region with a focus on indigenous peoples is most advanced compared to other regions of the world. They enjoy the status of "permanent participants" within the structure of the Arctic Council, which some authors refer to as unique in the development of international norm building.[70] It is the structure of the Arctic Council—an inter-governmental body comprising eight Arctic states. The organizational structure includes six Arctic's indigenous peoples' organizations as "permanent participants." In addition, a number of other non-Arctic states and inter-, and non-governmental organizations participate as "observers" in the Council. Decision-making at the Arctic Council is done with the strong involvement of these permanent participants. It is said that a decision is not likely where permanent participants collectively reject it and, in this sense, they enjoy some form of *de facto* veto right.[71] Moreover, the unique status of permanent participants is occasionally argued to enjoy higher status than some of the state actors, such as observer states, which is noteworthy in the development of international law.[72] The Arctic Council adopts policy documents wherein at almost all levels indigenous issues are highlighted, thereby providing for greater concerns that are relevant for the indigenous security of the circumpolar north. Today, it is also said that the Arctic Council is gradually becoming a venue for treaty negotiation at the regional level. Two recently adopted treaties under the auspices of the AC support this development.[73] What

70 Koivurova, Timo and Leena Heinämäki, "The participation of indigenous peoples in international norm making in the Arctic," *Polar Record* 42 (2006): 101–109, doi:10.1017/S0032247406005080.

71 Ibid.

72 For more information on the role of indigenous peoples as permanent participants in the Arctic Council, see also Koivurova, Timo, "The Status and Role of Indigenous Peoples in Arctic International Governance," in *The Yearbook of Polar Law* 3 (2011), ed. Gudmundur Alfredsson and Timo Koivurova, 169–192. (Leiden, Martinus Nijhoff, 2011), http://ssrn.com/abstract=2429175.

73 "Agreement on Cooperation on Aeronautical and Maritime Search and Rescue in the Arctic." Final for signature April 21, 2011, http://www.arctic-council.org/index.php/en/

is important here is that these treaties also have strong components to protect the concerns of these groups of indigenous peoples. Take the 2011 Search and Rescue agreement as an example. The indigenous peoples of the Arctic, particularly the ones inhabiting the coastal areas, travel far north for hunting and fishing. Tough and unpredictable weather conditions, as well as unanticipated thinning sea-ice, cause life-threatening situations for both indigenous and non-indigenous populations travelling far north for various reasons. The idea of the SAR agreement is to promote cooperation among the Arctic states to ensure both physical security as well as use of indigenous knowledge for the purpose of rescue operations. As a living organization, thus far, the Arctic Council has endorsed a number of assessment reports through its various working groups,[74] the main purpose of which is to promote sustainable Arctic environment. As said earlier, environmental sustainability is part and parcel of maintaining indigenous identity in the Arctic.

In addition to the Arctic Council, at the regional level BEAC performs an important role. Composed of European Arctic nations, the BEAC's members are: Denmark, Finland, Iceland, Norway, Sweden, Russia and the European Commission. Amongst its structure, it includes the Working Group of Indigenous Peoples whose goals are to promote education, language, health, cultural exercise, usage of indigenous knowledge and competence, institution buildings and socio-cultural and economic wellbeing.[75] Hence the policy documents and strategies are assumed to address aforementioned issues to promote indigenous security. Among the other prevailing structures in the region, the Inuit Circumpolar Council (ICC) plays an important role in the promotion of Inuit security, in particular. In addition to stimulating dialogue, the ICC has produced a number of widely cited documents for the for the promotion Inuit security, such as the Circumpolar Inuit Declaration on Resource Development Principles in Inuit Nunaat[76] and the Circumpolar Inuit Declaration on

document-archive/category/20-main-documents-from-nuuk, choose Arctic Search and Rescue Agreement; "Agreement on Cooperation on Oil Pollution, Preparedness and Response in the Arctic." April 2013, http://www.arctic-council.org/index.php/en/document-archive/category/425-main-documents-from-kiruna-ministerial-meeting.

74 Examples include Arctic Biodiversity Assessment, Arctic Species Trend Index, Arctic Marine Biodiversity Monitoring Plan, International Arctic Vegetation Database, Arctic Flora and Fauna Status and Trends, etc.

75 See Barents Euro-Arctic Council (BEAC), "Working Group of Indigenous Peoples," http://www.beac.st/in-English/Barents-Euro-Arctic-Council/Working-Groups/Working-Group-of-Indigenous-Peoples.

76 See Inuit Circumpolar Council Canada, "Circumpolar Inuit Declaration on Resource Development Principles in Inuit Nunaat," http://www.inuitcircumpolar.com/resource-development-principles-in-inuit-nunaat.html.

Sovereignty in the Arctic.[77] Both these documents address various aspects of human security, including environment, community, and economic sustainability both from the top-down and bottom-up approaches. The ICC played a key role in the petition submitted by Inuit leader Sheila Watt-Cloutier against the United States government for its failure to take meaningful action to curtail its greenhouse gas emissions, which have caused devastating climate change impacts both globally and regionally, in particular in the Arctic.[78] These impacts have proven particularly damaging for the Inuit and other indigenous peoples. The other example is the response of the Inuit to EU legislation that put a ban on the import of seal products into the internal market. As the legislation calls for huge impacts on the traditional economy of the Inuit, they have filed a lawsuit in the European General Court to overturn EU legislation seeking annulment of Regulation (EC) No. 1007/2009 of the European Parliament and Council of September 16, 2009 on trade in seal products. In the lawsuits, despite the fact that the WTO eventually rendered its decision in 2014 in favor of the EU, it is important to note that the Inuit were represented by their organizations, including the Inuit Tapiriit Kanatami and Inuit Circumpolar Council.[79]

In the three Nordic countries, Sámi Parliaments act jointly to promote Sámi rights. They agreed to adopt a regional legal document, the Nordic Sámi Convention, to address specific issues facing the transnationally located Sámi. With a twofold purpose—the promotion of Sámi rights and elimination of problems caused by territorial divides—the Convention aims at developing the Sámi people's language, culture, livelihoods, and way of life. Therefore, it is regarding ensuring a strengthened role of the transnational Sámi with the least possible interference from national borders. Even though the Convention has not yet been materialized into a final legal document, based on the Draft of the document, it may be argued that the Convention will certainly help strengthen the security of the Sámi once it is adopted.

77 See Inuit Circumpolar Council Canada, "Circumpolar Inuit Declaration on Sovereignty in the Arctic." Adopted by the Inuit Circumpolar Council April 2009, http://www.inuit circumpolar.com/sovereignty-in-the-arctic.html.

78 See Petition to the Inter American Commission on Human Rights Seeking Relief from Violations Resulting from Global Warming Caused by Acts and Omissions of the United States, Submitted by Sheila Watt-Cloutier, with the support of the Inuit Circumpolar Conference, on behalf of all Inuit of the Arctic regions of the United States and Canada. December 7, 2005, http://www.inuitcircumpolar.com/uploads/3/0/5/4/30542564/final petitionicc.pdf.

79 Fur Institute of Canada, "The overview of the case as of April 2013," http://www.seal harvest.ca/site/pdfs/Overview%20of%20Legal%20Case.pdf. Accessed April 16, 2015.

6 Conclusion

Human rights tools are formally structured and developed by means of international treaties and national constitutions. The tools create a legal framework, and it has naturally legally binding force. States are the duty bearers in the protection and promotion of the human rights of its subjects. While international law also provides rights for states, such as protecting its sovereignty, as duty-bearers they commit to protect the basic fundamental rights of their subjects. Thus, the subjects are also right holders both under international as well as domestic law. In the Arctic, with regard to the rights of the indigenous peoples, on one hand, the debate is usually based on the tension regarding the right to resource development, and on the other hand, on the right to be protected from environmental degradation. Often, the human rights tool reveals its limitation as the identification of the risks or threats as well as their mitigation or implementation within the framework are the sole responsibility of the states. However, as a flexible policy tool, human security addresses urgent needs and prioritizes the issue areas to be safeguarded for the greater wellbeing of communities with their own involvement. Nevertheless, the best realization of human security is achieved through the framework of established legal structures offered by the human rights framework. However, addressing priority-based, region-specific, and selected problems requires complementary structure alongside the human rights framework. This is particularly important for Arctic indigenous peoples as they are vulnerable to rapid environmental changes facing the region and affecting their human security challenges. The governance of human security of Arctic indigenous peoples is considered within the structure of both legal norms and policy tools. Legal norms are mainly offered with respect to the human rights structure and policy tools are developed through prevailing regional institutional cohesion, for example, the actions of the Arctic Council. A combination of these two does not only protect the indigenous peoples from threats but also offers them tools for empowerment to be self-sustaining. As indicated above, the governance approach includes promotion of both negative and positive aspects of security, which in addition to offering protection, enhances strategies to develop capacity and confidence by means of the actor-institutions constellation. Thus, apart from using available normative tools, developing relevant strategy and effective policy structures reflexive to regional changes by using existing regional bodies will arguably contribute to better governance of human security applicable to the indigenous peoples in the Arctic.

CHAPTER 2

Environment, Identity, Autonomy: Inuit Perspectives on Arctic Security

*Wilfrid Greaves**

Abstract

This chapter examines what security means from the perspective of Inuit in the Arctic region of northern Canada. It undertakes a discursive analysis of the security claims articulated by organizations and leaders representing Inuit in Canada, whose traditional territories comprise the majority of the Canadian North. The first section lays out an interpretivist approach to studying in/security building on securitization theory (ST). This approach views security as socially constructed and constituted through the shared understanding of particular sets of social actors, including Indigenous peoples. The second section details Inuit understandings of security in the Canadian Arctic region. The data suggest that Inuit primarily identify referent objects of security within three categories: the natural environment, Indigenous identity and culture, and the maintenance of Inuit political autonomy in the context of the Canadian settler state. The concluding section argues that Indigenous identity is a key analytical variable for explaining the exclusion of Inuit views within Canadian Arctic security discourse, and proposes an explanatory framework for the structural exclusion of the understandings of in/security articulated by non-dominant groups from state security discourse. This framework offers an empirical approach to securitization in settler-colonial contexts and suggests possible directions for further research.

Constructing (Indigenous) In/Security

Security is now widely recognized as an essentially contested concept that has no inherent or natural meaning but is contextual, ambiguous, and inherently political.[1] Indeed, the term 'security' may be more fruitfully replaced with

* Wilfrid Greaves, PhD, Lecturer, Trudeau Centre for Peace, Conflict and Justice University of Toronto.

1 Buzan, Barry and Lene Hansen, *The Evolution of International Security Studies*. Cambridge: Cambridge University Press, 2009; Smith, Steve, "The Contested Concept of Security," in *Critical Security Studies and World Politics*, ed. Ken Booth, 27–62. Boulder: Lynne Rienner, 2005; Wolfers, Arnold, "'National Security' as an Ambiguous Symbol," *Political Science Quarterly* 67 (1952).

 | DOI 10.1163/9789004314399_004

'in/security', since the latter captures how security scholarship focuses on the existence of threats, rather than their absence, and how every articulation identifying conditions of security simultaneously depicts a situation considered insecure. Security and insecurity are two sides of the same conceptual coin, thus: in/security. One prominent framework for engaging in/security as socially constructed is securitization theory, a "radically constructivist" approach developed by the members of the Copenhagen School to explain the changing nature of security threats in the post-Cold War period.[2] Securitization explains how, rather than providing an objective analysis of in/security in a given context, security discourses transform political issues *into* security issues through the (re)production of particular phenomena as threatening.

Securitization refers to the process through which a given phenomenon is constructed as a threat through the shared agreement of particular social actors. This process occurs when an actor articulates, depicts, or otherwise makes a security claim, called a *securitizing move*. Securitizing moves employ the grammar and vocabulary of in/security – security, insecurity, threat, danger, survival, etc. – to identify a *referent object* whose survival or wellbeing is endangered by a specified threat. However, it is only when a securitizing move is accepted by an *authoritative audience* with the power to respond to the threat that it transforms into a complete or successful securitization.[3] Drawing on the linguistic theory of John Austin, Buzan, Wæver and de Wilde describe three "facilitating conditions" that structure the likely success of a securitizing move: use of the grammar of security, the social capital and authority of the securitizing actor, and the features of the object held to be threatening.[4] These conditions shape whether securitizing moves are likely to be accepted, whether certain actors will be heard, and whether certain phenomena can be credibly securitized. As such, security is "a self-referential practice, because it is in this practice that the issue becomes a security issue – not necessarily because a real existential threat exists but because the issue is presented as such a threat".[5] Securitizing moves are situated within specific political contexts and are usually constrained by prior security discourses, though they can either reinforce or challenge existing meanings of in/security. By making a securitizing move, an actor seeks to elevate that threat-referent relationship to the highest level

2 Buzan, Barry, Ole Wæver, and Jaap de Wilde, *Security: A New Framework for Analysis*. Boulder: Lynne Rienner, 1998, 35; Wæver, Ole, "Securitization and Desecuritization," in *On Security*, ed. Ronnie D. Lipschutz, 46–86. New York: Columbia University Press, 1995.

3 Balzacq, Thierry, ed. *Securitization Theory: How Security Problems Emerge and Dissolve*. New York: Routledge, 2011; Buzan, Wæver, and de Wilde 1998, *supra* note 2.

4 Buzan, Wæver and de Wilde 1998, *supra* note 2, 33.

5 Buzan, Wæver, and de Wilde 1998, *supra* note 2, 24.

of political priority, thus mobilizing political and material resources to defend the specified referent object.

The social constructedness of in/security is illustrated by the fact that, particularly since the end of the Cold War, there has been a proliferation of securitizing moves associated with radically distinct political issues. Security is ubiquitously employed as a suffix to characterize conditions of crisis, risk, or instability associated with terms such as: national, international, global, human, environmental, ecological, physical, political, societal, cultural, identity, border, health, and energy. Some of these constitute what Buzan, Wæver, and de Wilde describe as sectors of security, namely categories for classifying different types of security issues affecting sovereign states. But others are different; rather than categories of security issues, they function as shorthand for commonly cited threat-referent relationships, most notably the case of 'national security' denoting the military defence of the sovereign state. By contrast, terms such as human security contain alternative normative claims about human beings as the appropriate object of security analysis, and imply a commitment to broadening security studies away from a strict focus upon sovereign states. Though diverse and often contradictory, such in/security claims share an understanding that, in the contemporary global context, security language can be employed to mobilize political attention and resources across disparate policy realms. They also signify that in/security is no longer confined to defence of the sovereign state against military threats to its territory and core national interests.[6] Security means more than national security, even if what it means in a given context or through a particular usage is sometimes unclear. By offering an explanatory framework for how in/security is constructed, securitization theory demonstrates how defining in/security is a political act that is *always* susceptible to contestation.

One of the key variables in securitization processes is identity, though there is no consensus on what role it plays or the extent of its significance in the construction of security issues. Initially, the Copenhagen School focused primarily on identity as a referent object to be secured through state action. Identity was central to their conception of societal security, wherein "the referent object is large-scale collective identities that can function independent of the state".[7] Subsequent analysts have theorized different relationships between identity and in/security, such as: how identity is (re)produced through

6 Walt, Stephen M., "The Renaissance of Security Studies," *International Studies Quarterly* 35 (1991).

7 Buzan, Wæver, and de Wilde 1998, *supra* note 2, 22; Wæver, Ole *et al.*, *Identity, Migration and the New Security Order in Europe*. London: Pinter, 1993.

practices or discourses of in/security;[8] how identity constrains what issues can be considered threatening;[9] and the specific threats facing marginalized or non-dominant identity groups within a given political community.[10] Most securitization scholars, including the Copenhagen School, also recognize security as a "structured field" characterized by unequal "social power" which shapes the capacity of actors to successfully securitize 'their' issues.[11] Tacitly or explicitly, this position necessarily recognizes the importance of who makes a securitizing move, with the identities of the securitizing actor acting "as a catalyst or gatekeeper in accepting a particular idea as a threat".[12] Since it contributes to the likelihood of securitizing moves succeeding, identity is key to understanding the facilitating conditions that structure the outcomes of securitization processes.

In the context of the circumpolar Arctic, one relevant set of identities for securitization analysis is that of Indigenous peoples. Though historically marginalized within their respective states, Indigenous peoples have emerged as key actors in circumpolar politics.[13] Nearly half a million Indigenous people reside across the Arctic region, though their political, economic, and social circumstances vary considerably across countries. Most enjoy some degree of self-government, but all are represented in regional politics through the six Permanent Participants of the Arctic Council, which Indigenous peoples were integral in helping establish.[14] With the exception of Russia, Arctic Indigenous peoples also enjoy benefits as citizens of wealthy states in the Global North,

8 Campbell, David, *Writing Security: United States Foreign Policy and the Politics of Identity.* Minneapolis: University of Minnesota Press, 1998; McSweeney, Bill, *Identity, Interests, and Security: A Sociology of International Relations.* Cambridge: Cambridge University Press, 1999.

9 Hayes, Jarrod, "Securitization, Social Identity, and Democratic Security: Nixon, India, and the Ties That Bind," *International Organization* 66 (2012).

10 Hoogensen, Gunhild and Svein Vigeland Rottem, "Gender Identity and the Subject of Security," *Security Dialogue* 25 (2004).

11 Buzan, Wæver, and de Wilde 1998, *supra* 2, 3; Balzacq, Thierry, "The Three Faces of Securitization: Political Agency, Audience and Context," *European Journal of International Relations* 11 (2005): 190–191.

12 Sjöstedt, Roxanna, "Ideas, Identities and Internalizations: Explaining Securitizing Moves," *Cooperation and Conflict* 48 (2013): 153.

13 Koivurova, Timo and Leena Heinämäki, "The Participation of Indigenous Peoples in International Norm-Making in the Arctic," *Polar Record* 42 (2006); Tennberg, Monica, "Indigenous Peoples as International Political Actors: A Summary," *Polar Record* 46 (2010); Young, Oran, "Governing the Arctic: from Cold War Theater to Mosaic of Cooperation," *Global Governance* 11 (2005).

14 English, John, *Ice and Water: Politics, Peoples, and the Arctic Council.* Toronto: Penguin, 2013.

including: strong legal frameworks respecting certain Indigenous rights; certain social benefits including public welfare, employment insurance, health services, and support for Indigenous language and education; and, in some cases, recognized rights to land use, title, and collective ownership.

Compared to the challenges facing Indigenous populations in much of the world, Arctic Indigenous peoples enjoy relatively good qualities of life, relatively high degrees of political autonomy, and relatively benign contemporary relationships with the settler-colonial governments under whose sovereign authority they live. Without minimizing the significant challenges confronting Indigenous peoples across the circumpolar region[15] the political inclusion of Indigenous peoples is one of the central features of political order in the post-Cold War Arctic, characterized by the high degree of political agency they now exercise. Inherent in this agency is the fact that Indigenous peoples have distinct sets of political interests, including understandings of in/security concerning what types of issues are threatening to them, in what ways, and what responses are appropriate. But despite their relatively advantageous social and political positions compared to other Indigenous populations, Arctic Indigenous peoples experience significant restraints on their capacity to successfully transform their security concerns into complete securitizations. As illustrated by the case of Inuit in Canada, Arctic Indigenous peoples appear to have their securitizing moves consistently rejected by the governments of their respective states, resulting in the general exclusion of Indigenous security concerns from state policy and official security discourse.

Inuit Securitizing Moves

Though not the only Indigenous people in the Canadian Arctic, Inuit are the most numerous and politically empowered, and are central to the region's social fabric and political institutions. Approximately 55,000 Inuit live in 53 small communities, forming a plurality of the permanent population of Northern Canada. Four Inuit regions – Nunavut, the Inuvialuit Settlement Region (Northwest Territories), Nunavik (northern Quebec), and Nunatsiavut (northern Labrador) – comprise over 20% of Canada's total area and are collectively known as *Inuit Nunangat*, which itself forms only part of the wider Inuit homeland of *Inuit Nunaat*, which includes territories in Alaska, Greenland,

15 Poppel, Birger, ed., *SLiCA: Arctic Living Conditions – Living Conditions and Quality of Life Among Inuit, Saami and Indigenous Peoples of Chukotka and the Kola Peninsula.* Copenhagen: Nordic Council of Ministers, 2015.

and Russia. One of the last Indigenous peoples in the Americas to experience extensive contact with European settlers and their descendants, Inuit are one of three constitutionally recognized groups of Aboriginal people in Canada. Inuit are also sophisticated political actors, with pan-Canadian representation through Inuit Tapiriit Kanatami (ITK), the national Inuit organization; membership in the Inuit Circumpolar Council (ICC), one of the Permanent Participants of the Arctic Council; a range of local and regional organizations and governments; and the Government of Nunavut, where Inuit make up approximately 85% of the territorial population.[16]

A variety of data support the claim that Inuit understand and articulate a distinct, and oppositional, conception of Arctic security to that of the Canadian state. These are drawn from different sources, including: textual analysis of publicly available documents; surveys; published articles, speeches, and policies; parliamentary testimony; and interviews with Inuit leaders. Though not exhaustive, this section provides a representative compilation and analysis of Inuit securitizing moves related to the Canadian Arctic. Overall, Inuit articulate an understanding of Arctic security that identifies a variety of referent objects pertaining to the natural environment, including plants and wildlife; Inuit identity and culture; and Inuit political autonomy within the context of the Canadian settler state. These objects are often not viewed separately, but seen as inter-related and mutually reinforcing, and consistent with a broad conception of human security.[17] For instance, Mary Simon, former president of both ICC and ITK and a former federal Ambassador for Circumpolar Affairs, notes that Inuit "subscribe to the concept that security should be understood in a broad sense. Just as health is more than the absence of disease, so, too, security is more than the absence of military conflict".[18] Rosemarie Kuptana, also former president of ITK and a pioneering contributor to the Arctic Council, concurs: "Security is more than about arms build-up. Security is about ensuring that Inuit are equal members of the human family and have the economic base to ensure a reasonable life-style as defined by contemporary Canada…Security

16 Shadian, Jessica, "From States to Polities: Reconceptualizing Sovereignty through Inuit Governance," *European Journal of International Relations* 16, (2010); Simon, Mary, "Canadian Inuit: Where We Have Been and Where We Are Going," *International Journal* 66, (2011); Smith, Heather A. and Gary Wilson, "Inuit Transnational Activism: Cooperation and Resistance in the Face of Global Climate Change," in *Indigenous Diplomacies*, ed. J. Marshall Beier, 171–186. New York: Palgrave MacMillan, 2009.

17 UNDP, Human Development Report 1994: New Dimensions of Human Security. New York: United Nations Development Program, 1994.

18 Simon 2011, *supra* note 15, 891.

to Inuit was, and is, having food, clothing and shelter".[19] Udloriak Hanson, a former official with ITK, answers her own question: "What does security mean to Inuit? Security doesn't come from the comfort that some find in icebreakers, sonar detectors and Arctic military capabilities. Security from our societal perspective comes from access to the basic essentials of life – food, shelter and water".[20] Many Inuit representatives acknowledge the validity, even necessity, of military activity as a component of Arctic security, but they are unanimous that it is insufficient for a complete understanding of what Inuit require to be secure. In contrast, Nancy Karetak-Liddell, former federal Member of Parliament for Nunavut, describes security for Inuit as "feeling safe on our lands, in our communities, having the ability to freely move around, the ability to practice our own way".[21]

Broad evidence of Inuit conceptions of Arctic security can also be drawn from the 2011 *Arctic Security Public Opinion Survey*. When unprompted as to the meaning of security, a plurality of 27% of Northerners (including Indigenous and non-Indigenous respondents) indicated the most pressing Arctic security issue to be "protecting Canada's borders from international threats." When the word 'security' was omitted, however, and respondents were asked to simply list the most pressing Arctic issues, 33% of Northerners listed the environment first, followed by housing and community infrastructure (9%), and the economy, jobs and employment (7%),[22] meaning that by a ratio of more than 3:1 Northerners consider the environment to be the most important Arctic issue. Moreover, when prompted with a list of various dimensions of security, fully 91% of Northerners considered environmental security to be important to their definition of Arctic security, with 90% also identifying as important social security including basic access to health care, education, housing and community infrastructure. 66% felt cultural and language security was important, though this increased to 74% in Nunavut where Inuit form a majority.[23] Northerners were also more likely than Southerners (78%–71%) to agree that "strengthening Canada's climate

19 Kuptana, Rosemarie, "The Inuit Sea," in *Nilliajut: Inuit Perspectives on Security, Patriotism, and Sovereignty*, ed. Scot Nickels, 10–13. (Ottawa: Inuit Tapiriit Kanatami, 2013), 11–12.

20 Hanson, Udloriak, "Foreword," in *Nilliajut: Inuit Perspectives on Security, Patriotism, and Sovereignty*, ed. Scot Nickels. Ottawa: Inuit Tapiriit Kanatami, 2013, 2.

21 *Nilliajut: Inuit Voices on Arctic Security*. Directed by Jordan Konek, Curtis Konek and Ian Mauro. Ottawa: Inuit Qaujisarvingat, 2013. Accessed April 7, 2015. http://www.inuitknowledge.ca/content/nilliajut-inuit-perspectives-arctic-security-1.

22 EKOS, *Rethinking the Top of the World. Arctic Security Public Opinion Survey*. Toronto: Walter and Duncan Gordon Foundation and the Munk School of Global Affairs, 2011, 13.

23 EKOS 2011, *supra* note 21, 14–15.

change policies is a critical step in ensuring the security of Arctic residents," and less likely (52%–60%) to agree that "Canada should strengthen its military presence in the North in order to protect against international threats".[24] The survey's authors conclude that Northern respondents "see environmental security and social security as key elements to protecting the Canadian Arctic. National security, while still seen as important, does not seem to be a leading priority".[25] While there are important similarities between Northern and Southern Canadians, the survey suggests the environment is prioritized more highly by Northerners, who are also less inclined to see national security or sovereignty as important Arctic issues. Finally, Northerners are less supportive of the view that increased military activities will contribute to Arctic security, while considering their own habitation to be an important contributing factor to asserting Canada's Arctic interests. These findings are similar to those for Indigenous peoples across the circumpolar region: "On average three out of four [Arctic] indigenous people perceive climate change to be a problem in their communities, and more than 50 per cent mention local contaminated sites, pollution of local lakes and streams and pollution from industrial development as problems in the region".[26] Overall, insofar as Northern Canadians think in terms of 'Arctic security' it seems clear they do so with respect to the environmental, social, and cultural challenges affecting their communities and ways of life.

Environment

Foremost in Inuit articulations of security are the impacts of the changing Arctic environment. Other dimensions of security, such as culture and identity, are often linked to the environment and seen through the prism of human-caused environmental change. In addition to "environmental damage from past and present military and industrial activities",[27] much of which originates from past activities of the Soviet/Russian military, the Arctic is undergoing climate change more acutely than anywhere else in the world, and Indigenous peoples are experiencing an ecological transformation that implicates every aspect of individual and community life. Ecological changes such as erratic weather, increased lake temperatures, thawing permafrost, stress on plant and animal populations, melting glaciers, rising sea levels, and disappearing sea ice are

24 EKOS 2011, *supra* note 21, 23.

25 EKOS 2011, *supra* note 21, 13.

26 Poppel 2015, *supra* note 14, 56.

27 AHDR, *Arctic Human Development Report*. Akureyri: Steffanson Arctic Institute, 2004, 210.

occurring across the region.[28] Particularly in the Western Arctic, "communities reported concern that the coasts and riverbanks in this region have been falling into the water at an alarming rate. Homes and buildings…have already been relocated as a result, and the communities are concerned about the possibility of the need for complete community relocation in the future".[29] Arctic communities universally require outside support to adapt to their changing ecological context, but some will simply be unable to survive in their present form, requiring relocation and reconstruction for their residents to continue living in the North.[30]

Climate change also exacerbates longstanding environmental issues such as pollution, particularly the human and animal health impacts of persistent organic pollutants (POPs) in the Arctic ecosystem. It was concern over POPs in the 1980s that catalyzed wider scientific and political interest in the Arctic region, with Inuit in Canada identified as having the highest concentrations of heavy metal contamination of any population on the planet.[31] These chemical compounds, mainly produced by heavy industries located far to the south, biomagnify along the food chain and concentrate in the fatty tissue of marine animals eventually consumed by Northerners, "threaten[ing] not only the well-being of wildlife, but the health of northern residents heavily dependent on country foods".[32] The effects of POPs, including higher rates of cancer and neurological damage in children, are aggravated by climate change because warmer weather increases their relative toxicity and speeds their degradation

28 ACIA, Impacts of a Warming Climate: Arctic Climate Impact Assessment. Cambridge: Cambridge University Press, 2004; IPCC, *Climate Change 2007: Synthesis Report.* Intergovernmental Panel on Climate Change Fourth Assessment Report. Cambridge: Cambridge University Press, 2007; IPCC, "Summary for Policymakers," in *Climate Change 2013: The Physical Science Basis. Contributions of Working Group I to the Fifth Assessment Report of the Intergovernmental Panel on Climate Change.* Cambridge: Cambridge University Press, 2013.

29 Nickels, Scot *et al.*, *Unikkaaqatigiit: Putting the Human Face on Climate Change – Perspectives from Inuit in Canada*. Ottawa: Joint Publication of Inuit Tapiriit Kanatami, Nasivvik Centre for Inuit Health and Changing Environments at Université Laval and the Ajunngi niq Centre at the National Aboriginal Health Organization, 2005, 83.

30 ACIA, *supra* note 27, 80–81.

31 Downie, David Leonard and Terry Fenge, eds., *Northern Lights Against POPs: Combatting Toxic Threats in the Arctic*. Montreal-Kingston: McGill-Queen's University Press, 2003.

32 VanderZwaag, David, Rob Huebert and Stacey Ferrarra, "The Arctic Environmental Protection Strategy, Arctic Council and Multilateral Environmental Initiatives: Tinkering While the Arctic Marine Environment Totters," *Denver Journal of International Law and Policy* 30 (2003): 132.

into the local ecology.[33] Environmental changes thus pose both immediate and long-term challenges to human wellbeing in the Arctic, and have necessitated a range of adaptation responses by local communities and other organizations because of the emergent hazards to Indigenous ways of life.[34]

Numerous data suggest that Inuit in Canada have principally operationalized Arctic security in terms of the direct and indirect effects of climate change. For instance, of the securitizing moves made between 2001 and 2011 in all of the publicly accessible online documents from the three Permanent Participants of the Arctic Council representing Canadian Indigenous peoples, 20 out of 25 were made by organizations representing Inuit, and all of these used securitizing language to describe the direct and indirect effects of climate change.[35] The referent objects invoked include: the environment overall; food security, especially the welfare of caribou herds; culture, language, or traditional ways of life; Indigenous health; and Indigenous rights. In fact, there were no securitizing moves captured in this study that did not identify environmental change as the source of threat. While the total number of securitizing moves is not large, use of security language by Inuit was effectively reserved for climate change, and the multiple ways in which it is affecting the material and cultural wellbeing of Inuit and other Arctic Indigenous peoples.

Examples of discourse employed by Inuit leaders also illustrate this point. Terry Audla, current president of ITK, situates climate change as "a formidable threat that confronts all of humanity, but with particularly dire challenges to Inuit," before specifying the environmental hazards affecting the security of his people:

> In the Arctic, our physical security has already been challenged by such things as changes to wildlife patterns, unreliable wind and temperature patterns and associated thawing and freezing cycles, rising sea levels, and shifting building foundations due to permafrost variation. Nature is never stable, and life close to nature always brings its own insecurities, as well as benefits. Climate at a rate and of an intensity that appears unprecedented, and well outside Inuit cultural memory, creates insecurities of an entirely new nature, generating concerns about the sustainability of

33 Noyes, P.D. *et al.*, "The Toxicology of Climate Change: Environmental Contaminants in a Warming World," *Environment International* 35 (2009).

34 Nickels *et al.*, 2005, *supra* note 28, 95.

35 Greaves, Wilfrid, "Turtle Island Blues: Climate Change and Failed Indigenous Securitization in the Canadian Arctic," *Working Papers on Arctic Security No.* 2, 1–27. Toronto: Munk-Gordon Arctic Security Program, 2012.

> large aspects of our inherited and acquired patterns of life...[sic] our very sense of who and what we are as Inuit.[36]

In the words of Sheila Watt-Cloutier, another former president of ICC, "climate change is threatening the lives, health, culture and livelihoods of the Inuit".[37] The scale of environmental change in the Arctic is such that it is now the lens through which Inuit evaluate other important regional issues. For instance, The *Circumpolar Inuit Declaration on Resource Development Principles* reserves the right of Inuit to benefit from the development of natural resources in their territories, but stipulates that "Inuit and others – through their institutions and international instruments – have a shared responsibility to evaluate the risks and benefits of their actions through the prism of global environmental security... To minimize the risk to global environmental security, the pace of resource development in the Arctic must be carefully considered".[38] Inuit leaders acknowledge the potential benefits of resource development, but clearly identify the objects of value that will be threatened by unrestricted extraction or the local damage that would be caused by an industrial accident. As one Inuit elder put it: "The circumpolar North is increasingly opening up very quickly now, and coming with that is offshore oil and gas development. To me, the greatest risk to our security is these companies that operate offshore could do major damage to our marine biology".[39] Overall, the local and global dimensions of environmental change and degradation are central to how Inuit leaders and organizations articulate the security interests of their people.

Identity

Inuit also identify their identity and cultural practices as referent objects to be protected, but link these to environmental change because of the connection between Inuit identity and their natural environment. For many Indigenous peoples around the world, identity and cultural practices are predicated upon a close relationship between indigeneity and the natural environments of their ancestral territories: "cultural survival, identity and the very existence

36 Audla, Terry, "Inuit and Arctic Security," in *Nilliajut: Inuit Perspectives on Security, Patriotism, and Sovereignty*, edited by Scot Nickels. Ottawa: Inuit Tapiriit Kanatami, 2013, 8.

37 Watt-Cloutier, Sheila. *Petition to the Inter-American Commission on Human Rights Seeking Relief From Violations Resulting From Global Warming Caused by Acts and Omissions of the United States*. 2005, 7. Accessed April 18, 2014. http://www.inuitcircumpolar.com/inuit-petition-inter-american-commission-on-human-rights-to-oppose-climate-change-caused-by-the-united-states-of-america.html.

38 ICC, *A Circumpolar Inuit Declaration on Resource Development Principles in Inuit Nunaat*. Nuuk: Inuit Circumpolar Council, 2011, 5.1, 5.5.

39 *Nilliajut* 2013, *supra* note 20.

of Indigenous societies depend to a considerable degree on the maintenance of environmental quality. The degradation of the environment is therefore inseparable from a loss of culture and hence identity".[40] Environmental changes that alter traditional patterns of subsistence and undermine multi-generational knowledge of weather and climate patterns, animal movements, and methods of hunting, gathering, and survival have far-reaching implications for Indigenous identities. For Inuit, this relationship is exemplified by environmental issues such as the reduced quality and availability of traditional country foods, including game, fish, and berries. "To hunt, catch, and share these foods is the essence of Inuit culture. Thus, a decline in [country foods]… threatens not only the dietary requirements of the Inuit, but also their very way of life".[41] In response, research on food security in the Canadian North has increasingly called for policymakers to recognize the cultural importance of traditional foods for Indigenous peoples, and the integral link between food security and climate change.[42]

Certain practices central to Inuit identity are also threatened by non-environmental factors. Most notably, the hunting of marine mammals, particularly seals, has been the subject of significant popular attention and criticism, as well as external political opposition. Environmental groups' longstanding opposition to the seal hunt has been characterized as a dispute between animal rights and Indigenous peoples' human rights,[43] and has framed ongoing disputes between Inuit and conservation and animal rights groups, and between Canada and the European Union (EU). In 2009, the EU implemented a ban on imported seal products that reflected popular concerns over the manner in which seals were hunted and perceptions that seal populations are endangered. Although the ban provides an exemption for seal products hunted by Inuit or other Indigenous communities, Canada expressed its opposition diplomatically and by filing a complaint with the World Trade Organization (WTO). The WTO ultimately upheld the validity of the seal ban on moral grounds, though it also noted the ban's inconsistent and arbitrary nature and the preferential

40 Cocklin, Chris, "Water and 'Cultural Security'," in *Human Security and the Environment: International Comparisons*, ed. Edward A. Page and Michael Redclift. Northampton: Edward Elgar, 2002, 159.

41 ACIA, *supra* note 27, 94.

42 Lambden, Jill, Olivier Receveur and Harriet V. Kuhnlein, "Traditional Food Attributes Must be Included in Studies of Food Security in the Canadian Arctic," *International Journal of Circumpolar Health* 66 (2007); Power, Elaine M, "Conceptualizing Food Security for Aboriginal People in Canada," *Canadian Journal of Public Health* 99 (2008).

43 Wenzel, George, *Animal Rights, Human Rights: Ecology, Economy and Ideology in the Canadian Arctic*. Toronto: University of Toronto Press, 1991.

treatment afforded Greenlandic, as opposed to Canadian, seal products. Observers note the ban's effect on reducing the commercial seal product market within the EU negatively affects Inuit's ability to gain supplemental income from seal hunting, resulting in reduced financial capacity to sustain their hunting activities. According to Nunavut Premier Peter Taptuna, "the seal harvest is central to the Inuit, and Canadian, way of life, [and] the misrepresentation of the seal hunt has an effect on our local economies".[44] Thus, in spite of the EU's nominal exception for Indigenous-hunted seal products, the ban still serves to weaken this core aspect of Inuit identity and thus implicates their rights to subsist as Indigenous peoples on their traditional territories.[45]

The relationship between the environment, Inuit identity, and insecurity is also demonstrated by other harmful social phenomena in the North that are exacerbated by climate change. Terry Audla links "the insecurities that Inuit face as a result of our living, over three or four generations, in what has been a firestorm of cultural change," with the ongoing economic modernization of Arctic life, noting that "while some insecurities have abated, new ones have arisen and some old ones have taken on new forms".[46] One such insecurity is the extraordinary level of suicide in Northern Canada, particularly among Inuit youth. Rates of suicide among Inuit are more than 11 times higher than the Canadian average, over 85% of these are young men, and the rate is increasing, having more than doubled in the past decade.[47] The causes of such a high suicide rate are complex, but "this pattern has been associated with a view of young males not seeing a future for themselves as hunters and contributors to their community and at the same time not fitting into the cash employment structures that are becoming the dominant lifestyle".[48] Practices such as hunting and traveling on the land require traditional knowledge that is being lost as the older generation dies, or is being undermined as the land it is based upon radically alters.

44 Hopper, Tristin, "Europe's unfair ban on Canadian seal products can stay to 'protect public morals,' WTO rules," *National Post,* May 22, 2014. Accessed March 21, 2015. http://news.nationalpost.com/2014/05/22/europes-ban-on-canadian-seal-products-can-stay-to-protect-public-morals-wto-rules/.

45 Hossain, Kamrul, "The EU Ban on the Import of Seal Products and the WTO Regulations: Neglected Human Rights of the Arctic Indigenous Peoples?" *Polar Record* 49 (2013).

46 Audla 2013, *supra* note 35, 8.

47 ITK, "Inuit Approaches to Suicide Prevention," 2014. Accessed December 22, 2014. https://www.itk.ca/inuitapproaches-suicide-prevention.

48 Kirmayer, Laurence J. *et al., Suicide Among Aboriginal People in Canada.* Ottawa: Aboriginal Healing Foundation, 2007, 157.

By undermining the health and viability of cultural practices and the land, climate change fuels the erosion of traditional knowledge and lifestyles that is vital to Inuit identity, which is in turn vital to individual and collective wellbeing. According to one study of Inuit views of climate change, "there is an expression of fear of loss of traditional knowledge and connection to the land… expressions of concern of the dire impacts of climate change on Inuit culture is a common theme".[49] Worsening climate change and its impacts on subsistence ways of life will thus likely aggravate what is already an Inuit suicide epidemic. According to Sheila Watt-Cloutier: "human-induced climate change is undermining the ecosystem upon which Inuit depend for their cultural survival…[which] threatens our ability far to the North to live as we have always done in harmony with a fragile, vulnerable, and sensitive environment." As a result, "the changes to our climate and our environment will bring about the end of the Inuit culture".[50]

Autonomy

Finally, Inuit have identified their political autonomy as a self-determining Indigenous people as vital both *to* their security and to ensuring the agency necessary to provide *for* their security. In this respect, the central challenge is reconciling the Arctic sovereignty claims of the Canadian settler state with the prior claims of Inuit over their traditional territories. *Canada's Northern Strategy* acknowledges the important contribution of Inuit political claims, noting "Canada's Arctic sovereignty is longstanding, well-established and based on historic title, founded in part on the presence of Inuit and other Aboriginal peoples since time immemorial",[51] with similar language repeated in *Canada's Arctic Foreign Policy.*[52] Inuit leaders emphasize that if Canada invokes Inuit as part of the basis for its Arctic sovereignty, then it must also respect transnational legal instruments such as the *Circumpolar Inuit Declaration on Sovereignty in the Arctic*, *Circumpolar Inuit Declaration on Resource Development Principles*, and *Declaration on the Rights of Indigenous Peoples* that afford Inuit rights over their territories, natural resources, and self-determination. Inuit and non-Inuit

49 Smith, Heather A. and Brittney Parks, "Climate Change, Environmental Security, and Inuit Peoples," in *New Issues in Security #5: Critical Environmental Security: Rethinking the Links Between Natural Resources and Political Violence*, ed. Matthew A. Schnurr and Larry A. Swatuk, 1–18. Halifax: Centre for Foreign Policy Studies, 2010, 8.

50 Ibid., 7–8.

51 Canada, *Canada's Northern Strategy: Our North, Our Heritage, Our Future.* Ottawa: Government of Canada, 2009b, 9.

52 Canada, *Statement on Canada's Arctic Foreign Policy: Exercising Sovereignty and Promoting Canada's Northern Strategy Abroad.* Ottawa: Government of Canada, 2010.

analysts note that since Canada's Arctic sovereignty draws upon the legal justification of prior Inuit occupation, it raises complicated normative questions if the Canadian government continually fails to reflect Inuit political views.[53]

Many Inuit thus identify Canada's limited implementation of self-government through Inuit-federal land claim agreements – including the *James Bay and Northern Quebec Agreement, Nunavik Inuit Land Claims Agreement, Labrador Inuit Land Claim Agreement,* and especially the *Nunavut Land Claims Agreement* (*NLCA*) – with infringing on both their rights and security. Rosemarie Kuptana asserts that Canada's "failure to consult Inuit on all matters affecting Inuit, including sovereignty and security," is illegal under domestic and international law, and could be subject to constitutional challenge. She claims "Inuit are suffering from a want of dialogue even though this dialogue is constitutionally mandated… This manner of governing is not working for Inuit in Canada, particularly on the issue of arctic [sic] sovereignty and security".[54] James Arreak, CEO of Nunavut Tunngavik Incorporated, the organization mandated to implement the *Nunavut Land Claims Agreement*, also identifies the link between colonialism, the *NLCA*, and Canadian sovereignty over its Arctic territory: "Notwithstanding the colonialism that marred the historic interaction of Inuit and the Canadian state, Inuit are proud Canadians. For years we have been holding up the Canadian flag over disputed waters of the Northwest Passage. Full and fair implementation of the *NLCA* must be part of our continuing to do so".[55] Inuit leaders view land claim agreements as crucial for ensuring Inuit representation within Canadian Confederation, and as a bulwark against Southern pressures for social change, economic modernization, and cultural assimilation. This link between autonomy and security is succinctly identified by Kirt Ejesiak, a former official with ITK and the Government of Nunavut, who asserts that, for Inuit, "the security part comes in when our governments don't respect our way of life".[56]

53 Fenge, Terry, "Inuit and the Nunavut Land Claim Agreement: Supporting Canada's Arctic Sovereignty," *Policy Options* 29 (2007/2008). 84–88; Loukacheva, Natalia, "Nunavut and Canadian Arctic Sovereignty," *Journal of Canadian Studies* 43 (2009); Simon, Mary, "Inuit and the Canadian Arctic: Sovereignty Begins at Home," *Journal of Canadian Studies* 43 (2009).

54 Kuptana 2013, *supra* note 18, 10–11.

55 Canada. Parliament. House of Commons. Standing Committee on Foreign Affairs and International Development. *Evidence.* 1st sess., 41st Parliament, Meeting No. 73, 2013. http://www.parl.gc.ca/HousePublications/Publication.aspx?DocId=6066687&Language=E&Mode=1&Parl=41&Ses=1.

56 *Nilliajut* 2013, *supra* note 20.

A central point of contention has therefore been the approach of the Conservative Government towards articulating and asserting Canada's Arctic interests. Under Prime Minister Stephen Harper, Canada has pursued a vision of Arctic security that emphasizes militarism and natural resource extraction,[57] and has implemented policies detrimental to Inuit interests and contrary to their understanding of their own security. Mary Simon has repeatedly criticized the Government's approach to the Arctic as inappropriate for contemporary realities. She views current Canadian policy as an "outdated model" unable to justly or effectively address the complex issues confronting Northerners.[58] She and other leaders dismiss the Government maxim that Canada must "use it or lose it" when it comes to its Arctic sovereignty. For Inuit, the implicit claim that Canada's Arctic sovereignty is threatened should it fail to promote military or industrial activities is met "with a certain level of irony. Inuit have been living in…and using…[sic] the Arctic for millennia, and we have no intention of 'losing it'".[59] In 2009, John Amagoalik, of Qikiqtani Inuit Association, testified before Parliament that:

> We were disappointed with the first two or three times [Prime Minister Harper] was up there [in the Arctic]. He never met with Inuit leaders. He never mentioned the Inuit in his speeches. We were curious as to why that was happening. Then he came out with this line of "use it or lose it". That to us was very painful. It was a hurtful thing. It was insulting. We do use and occupy the Arctic every day, and we have been doing that for thousands of years. We feel that the Government of Canada has to stop using that line. It doesn't work.[60]

James Arreak reiterated the point before Parliament four years later, following little change in government rhetoric towards the Arctic: "Whatever its political appeal, this statement does not accurately reflect or respect the history

57 Beauchamp, Benoit and Rob Huebert, "Canada's Sovereignty Linked to Energy Resources in the Arctic," *Arctic* 61 (2008); Dodds, Klaus, "We are a Northern Country: Stephen Harper and the Canadian Arctic," *Polar Record* 47 (2011); Greaves, Wilfrid, "For Whom, From What? Canada's Arctic Policy and the Narrowing of Human Security," *International Journal* 67 (2012).

58 Simon, Mary, "Inuit and the Canadian Arctic: Sovereignty Begins at Home," *Journal of Canadian Studies* 43 (2009): 258.

59 Ibid., 252.

60 Canada. Parliament. House of Commons. Standing Committee on National Defence. *Evidence*. 2nd sess., 40th Parliament, Meeting No. 37, 2009b. http://www.parl.gc.ca/HousePublications/Publication.aspx?DocId=4199141&Language=E&Mode=1&Parl=40&Ses=2.

or demography of the Arctic or relevant Canadian and international laws"[61] Rosemarie Kuptana is also explicit in her view that Canada's current conduct towards Inuit constitutes "an immoral and shameful exercise of out-dated and discredited colonialism".[62]

Arguments invoking the colonial history of Inuit in Canada emphasize that, in many respects, the security of Inuit has been negatively affected by contact with, and subordination to, colonial and federal authorities. Zebedee Nungak describes the "decimation of Inuit security" which has resulted from colonial contact and imposition of Southern Canadian policies, citing "the pattern of behavior of European monarchs and their successor governments...through the centuries to assault and decimate the security and wellbeing of indigenous people, including Inuit, the world over".[63] In recent history, the actions of the Canadian state have profoundly contributed to the insecurities facing Inuit, particularly related to the disruption caused by forced permanent settlement:

> The settlement of Inuit in hamlets has resulted in many people being unskilled in hunting and the ways of life on the land. This settlement was government policy...[and] resulted in a society which is resettled with some of the amenities of the south but also in a society devoid of the economy which sustained it...The on-going results of this government policy have robbed the Inuit of a viable economy. The government policy of residential schools too worked to this end: it ensured, as best it could, that the traditional ways would not be transferred to a new generation. It can be argued, therefore, that ongoing government policy and actions are working to deprive the Inuit of a basic right to life.[64]

Key historical episodes in the relationship between Inuit and Canada are consistent with a pattern of Indigenous peoples' wellbeing undermined by the policies pursued by the colonial state in the assertion of its sovereignty. Such episodes are often documented as instances of colonial insensitivity, arrogance, oppression, and attempted assimilation, but they also profoundly affected the individual and collective security of Indigenous people. For Inuit, this includes the mass slaughter of Inuit sled dogs by RCMP and provincial police forces in

61 Canada 2013, *supra* note 55.

62 Kuptana 2013, *supra* note 18, 11.

63 Nungak, Zebedee, "The Decimation of Inuit Security," in *Nilliajut: Inuit Perspectives on Security, Patriotism, and Sovereignty*, ed. Scot Nickels. Ottawa: Inuit Tapiriit Kanatami, 2013, 14.

64 Kuptana 2013, *supra* note 18, 12.

the 1950s and 1960s,[65] and the forced relocation of Inuit families to Ellesmere Island in the 1960s to serve as "human flagpoles" in support of Canada's Arctic sovereignty.[66] If Inuit view autonomy as integral to their security – namely their survival and wellbeing as Indigenous people – the actions of the Government of Canada have consistently served to undermine Inuit security claims and subordinate them to the interests of the Canadian state. Taken together, the evidence suggests that security for Inuit has been negatively affected by the historical and contemporary policies of Canada. On their own terms, it seems clear that "Inuit have yet to find true security in Canada".[67]

Conclusion: Inuit and In/Security in the Canadian Arctic

Two principal conclusions can be drawn from the Inuit views of Arctic security assessed in this chapter. First, there is ample empirical support for the argument that Inuit in Northern Canada discursively construct a holistic, human-centred understanding of what Arctic security means. For Inuit, security is primarily concerned with protecting the Arctic environment from degradation and radical climate change; preserving their identity through the maintenance of Indigenous cultural practices; and asserting and maintaining Inuit autonomy as self-determining, rights-holding political actors whose claims to their traditional territory precede and underpin the sovereignty of the Canadian settler state. In terms of securitization theory, Inuit are securitizing actors who employ the grammar and language of in/security to identify threats to the continued wellbeing of valued referent objects linked to their survival as an Indigenous people. On the basis of the threat-referent relationships they articulate, Inuit are primarily concerned over threats to the Arctic environment, their Indigenous identity, and their political autonomy, but emphasize the interrelated nature of these security issues. Overall, however, human-caused

65 Croteau, Jean-Jacques, *Final Report of the Honourable Jean-Jacques Croteau, Retired Judge of the Superior Court, Regarding the Allegations Concerning the Slaughter of Inuit Sled Dogs in Nunavik (1950–1970)*, 2010. Accessed November 24, 2014. http://thefanhitch.org/official reports/Final%20Report.pdf; QIA, *Qikiqtani Truth Commission Final Report: Achieving Saimaqatigiingniq*. Iqaluit: Qikiqtani Inuit Association, 2010.

66 Makkik, Romani, "The High Arctic Relocations," *Naniiliqpita*. Iqaluit: Nunavut Tunngavik Incorporated, 2009. Accessed November 25, 2014. http://www.tunngavik.com/documents/publications/Naniiliqpita%20Fall%202009.pdf; Tester, Frank and Peter Kulchyski, *Tammarniit (Mistakes): Inuit Relocation in the Eastern Arctic, 1939–63*. Vancouver: UBC Press, 1994.

67 Nungak 2013, *supra* note 61, 15.

environmental change permeates Inuit understandings of Arctic security; as a contributing factor to many longstanding challenges to Indigenous peoples, and as a cause of many new security hazards confronting Inuit and other Northerners, environmental change is the backdrop against which all other insecurities in the Arctic are occurring.

Inuit understandings of in/security in the Arctic stand in stark contrast to the perspective that informs Canada's current Arctic policy. While Inuit leaders and organizations have performed numerous securitizing moves identifying the compounding threats posed by rapid cultural change, political disempowerment, and ecological transformation, Canada's understanding of Arctic security emphasizes military defence of its territorial claims and the northward expansion of an extraction-based natural resource economy. Canada insists on seeing climate change as an economic opportunity while "choosing not to see" the dangers it presents,[68] whereas Inuit perceive climate change as foreclosing future opportunities to exist *as* Indigenous peoples in their traditional territories. In effect, Canada's Arctic policies prioritize the very practices causing the ecological changes that Inuit identify as threatening. As such, the second conclusion of this chapter is that the security concerns of Inuit are virtually absent from the official Arctic security discourse employed by the Canadian state. Despite the significant political achievements made by Inuit, their views of security in their own lands remain marginalized. In this respect, Canada's Arctic security discourse and its current Arctic policy framework remain fundamentally colonial.

To the extent that Inuit understandings are not included within official Arctic security discourse in Canada, it suggests there are limitations upon the capacity of Indigenous peoples, and other non-dominant social groups, to successfully transform hazards threatening them into security issues acknowledged and addressed by the state. Though a full theorization of this phenomenon is beyond the scope of this chapter, closer examination of the role of identity in the securitization process may cast light on the exclusion of certain groups' views from official security discourse. Building on the discussion of securitization theory in the first section of this chapter, I propose that Indigenous identity operates as a barrier that obstructs the success of Indigenous peoples' securitizing moves. Since the facilitating conditions of securitization reflect conditions of unequal social power, it seems reasonable that Indigenous peoples making security claims within the context of settler-colonial states that have historically and contemporarily generated the conditions of

68 Smith, Heather A., "Choosing Not to See: Canada, Climate Change, and the Arctic," *International Journal* 65 (2010).

insecurity for their Indigenous populations would be analytically significant. Indigenous peoples – as an example of non-dominant societal groups with oppositional, antagonistic, or threatening identities to the authoritative audience of the sovereign state – may thus experience their identities as an *inhibiting condition* that impedes, rather than facilitates, acceptance of their security claims. Understood as reflecting the historical and contemporary relationships between Indigenous peoples and the settler-colonial states in which they reside, Indigenous identity may result in structural limitations on the capacity to speak security to the authoritative audience of the state and thus to successfully securitize. This does not mean that dominant groups will always succeed in securitizing their issues, or that non-dominant groups will always fail to securitize theirs. But it does suggest that identity may determine why some securitizing moves fail: not because of the relative seriousness of the danger or the value of a referent object, but because of the speaker making the security claim and their relationship to the audience whose acceptance is required to mobilize the power of the state in response to the specified threat.

In the case of Inuit in Northern Canada, securitizing moves are clearly, repeatedly, and powerfully expressed in multiple fora, by authoritative and legitimate Inuit political actors, and invoke high stakes: the survival and wellbeing of Inuit in the face of serious material threats. These claims are often made using the language and grammar of in/security, and would seem to rate favourably in terms of the three facilitating conditions for securitization success. Yet, Inuit securitizing moves appear to be consistently rejected by the Canadian state in favour of a conception of Arctic in/security explicitly rejected by Inuit because it undermines their rights and interests, and because it is all but certain to worsen the very hazards they are attempting to defend themselves against. Sadly, this situation is not new: contemporary Inuit views of Arctic security as linked to holistic human wellbeing, and the role of government policy in undermining that wellbeing, echo words written by Mary Simon in 1989: "Arctic security includes environmental, economic and cultural, as well as defence, aspects," but has been subordinated to state security discourse that "too often serve[s] to promote our *insecurity*".[69] Thus, the very priorities of the Canadian state remain the identified by Inuit as threatening their interests and survival, such that the greatest threat to their security originates from or is exacerbated by their own government. This is the essence of settler-colonialism, and lies at the heart of contemporary government policy in the Canadian Arctic.

69 Simon, Mary "Security, Peace and the Native Peoples of the Arctic," in *The Arctic: Choices for Peace and Security*, ed. Thomas R. Berger. Vancouver: Gordon Soules, 1989, 67, 36. Emphasis in original.

Securitization theory provides a set of analytical tools with which to engage and deconstruct security discourses, exposing the role of identity and other variables in structuring securitization outcomes, and exposing the unequal opportunities of different groups to securitize issues threatening their communities. This discussion of non-dominant identities and securitization, though brief, provides some direction for future research into how the meanings of in/security are constructed in specific political contexts, whose interests those meanings serve, and whose interests are obscured or undermined. Indigenous peoples – along with other groups experiencing conditions of settlement and occupation, or otherwise disempowered within their respective polities – have not typically been objects of security analysis, with the predictable implication that their security interests have usually been overlooked, ignored, or denied. Given the stakes of rapid environmental and social change occurring in a transforming Arctic, the security claims of Inuit and other vulnerable communities in the face of seeming indifference from their own states, including Canada, poses analytical and normative challenges for security analysts. An analytical approach sensitive to the role of identity and power in shaping and constraining securitization outcomes may help bring such voices into mainstream security discourse, contributing to the (re)production of new understandings of what in/security means.

CHAPTER 3

The Narrated 'Other' – Challenging Inuit Sustainability through the European Discourse on the Seal Hunt

*Nikolas Sellheim**

Abstract

With the adoption of EU Regulation 1007/2009 on trade in seal products in September 2009 the EU effectively shut down its markets for products from commercial seal hunts. Products from Inuit and other indigenous hunts are exempt from this ban. Given the ineffectiveness of this 'indigenous exemption' Inuit organizations and others launched several unsuccessful legal proceedings before the EU Courts to overturn the ban.

The indigenous exemption is built on the discursive notion of 'good' indigenous versus 'bad' commercial seal hunts. This paper examines what narratives prevail in the discourse surrounding the seal hunt and how far they are built on knowledge of hunting and living conditions of Inuit communities. It further examines how far these narratives are built on stereotypes and clichés, and constitute a paternalistic paradigm. Parallels are drawn between Inuit seal hunts and commercial seal hunts in Newfoundland where non-indigenous hunters engage in seal hunts discursively labelled as 'bad'. While both hunts contribute to community sustainability, only selected elements are considered, are narrated, by the discourse on the seal hunt.

1 Introduction

For many decades the hunt for seals has led to numerous campaigns, which aim to expose its perceived cruelty. Further, a lack of necessity has underscored a need for its cessation. While in the early years no clear-cut distinction was drawn between the commercial hunts in Atlantic Canada and the hunts in

* Nikolas Sellheim holds a PhD in law from the University of Lapland. His research examines the interconnection between the EU seal products trade ban and living conditions in seal hunting communities. He works furthermore as Editor for *Polar Record,* the journal of the Scott Polar Research Institute, University of Cambridge, UK. Nikolas holds a master's degree in Polar Law from the University of Akureyri, Iceland. He has been working for the CAFF Working Group and the University of the Arctic International Secretariat and has been involved in several Arctic research projects.

 | DOI 10.1163/9789004314399_005

Inuit communities, more recent campaigns have explicitly excluded the Inuit, or 'subsistence', hunt from any desired goals to shut down the trade.

In September 2009 the European Union, adopted Regulation 1007/2009 on trade in seal products (Basic Regulation),[1] followed by Commission Regulation 737/2010 on implementing measures (Implementing Regulation)[2] for the Basic Regulation. This occurred also due to the influence of animal welfare organizations.[3] This EU seal regime has barred the European internal market from all products stemming from the commercial seal hunts. It nevertheless holds an exemption for Inuit and other indigenous communities, aiming at not affecting indigenous hunts by this trade measure.

This paper discusses the indigenous exemption taking into account some narratives that this exemption is based on. It argues that the implementation has not created a regime which benefits the Inuit people due to economic circumstances that go beyond the notion of pure 'subsistence'. To the contrary. The understanding of the Inuit as being economically distinct from the commercial seal hunts has created a trade environment which negatively affects all trade in seal products, irrespective of its origin.

2 The EU Seal Regime

The current EU seal regime was preceded by the Council Directive 83/129/EEC of 1983, the 'Seal Pups Directive',[4] which prohibited the trade in products stemming from harp and hooded seal pups. While initially drafted to be in force for two years, in 1989 the Directive was extended indefinitely.[5] Legally it is still in force today, but has since 2009 been effectively replaced by Regulation

1 Regulation (EC) No 1007/2009 of the European Parliament and of the Council of 16 September 2009 on trade in seal products (OJ L 286, 31.10.2009, 36–39).

2 Commission Regulation (EU) No 737/2010 of 10 August 2010 laying down detailed rules for the implementation of Regulation (EC) No 1007/2009 of the European Parliament and of the Council on trade in seal products (OJ L 216, 17.8.2010, 1–10)

3 Sellheim, Nikolas, "The Neglected Tradition – The Genesis of the EU Seal Products Trade Ban and Commercial Sealing," in *The Yearbook of Polar Law* 5 (2013), ed. Gudmundur Alfredsson and Timo Koivurova, 417–450. (Leiden: Martinus Nijhoff, 2013).

4 Council Directive 83/129/EEC of 28 March 1983 concerning the importation into Member States of skins of certain seal pups and products derived therefrom (OJ L 91, 9.4.1983, 30–31).

5 Directives 85/444/EEC of 27 September 1985 amending Council Directive 83/129/EEC concerning the importation into Member States of skins of certain seal pups and products derived therefrom *OJ L 259*, 1.10.1985, 70–70, http://eur-lex.europa.eu/legal-content/en/ALL/?uri=CELEX:31985L0444 and 89/370/EEC of 8 June 1989 amending Directive 83/129/EEC concerning the importation into Member States of skins of certain seal pups

1007/2009. Contrary to the Seal Pups Directive which was concluded primarily over conservation concerns of harp and hooded seals,[6] the EU seal regime was concluded over claims of cruelty in predominantly the Canadian commercial seal hunts as the Parliamentary Declaration of 2006, which set the policy-making process in motion shows. In Paragraph D the Declaration reads that "a team of international veterinarians concluded that 42% of the slaughtered seals [...] may have been skinned whilst still conscious" and in Paragraph H.1 that it "[r]equests the Commission to immediately draft a regulation to ban the import, export and sale of all harp and hooded seal products."[7]

The narrative of cruelty of commercial seal hunts spanned throughout the drafting process of the seal regime. To this end the European Commission commissioned the European Food Safety Authority (EFSA) to conduct an assessment of animal welfare aspects of different killing methods of seals.[8] The EFSA report concluded that "seals can be, and are, killed rapidly and effectively without causing avoidable pain" while this "effective killing does not always occur."[9] Also skinning methods were assessed and resulted in the recommendation of a legislative inclusion and practical, systemic application of the so-called three-step-process, i.e. stunning, checking, bleeding, before the skinning of a seal.[10] In March 2009, Canada made the three-step-process mandatory, also based on the EFSA recommendations.[11] The Canadian amendments notwithstanding, the European Parliament overwhelmingly voted in favour for the adoption of a trade ban on *all* seal products in early May 2009. This is despite the final regulation being contrary to the rejected legislative proposal that aimed at opening the European markets for seal products stemming from hunts with high animal welfare standards. Thus, the adopted regime does not include any clause that effectively improves animal welfare in the commercial

and products derived therefrom *OJ L 163*, 14.6.1989, 37–37, http://eur-lex.europa.eu/legal-content/EN/TXT/?uri=CELEX:31989L0370, respectively.

6 Council Directive 1983, *supra* note 4, chapeau.

7 EP (European Parliament), Declaration P6-YA (2006) 0369, Banning seal products in the European Union.

8 The assessment included the *hakapik* (a wooden club with a metal hammer head), clubs, firearms and netting.

9 EFSA (European Food Safety Authority), "Animal Welfare Aspects of the Killing and Skinning of Seals. Scientific Opinion of the Panel on Animal Health and Welfare," *The EFSA Journal 610* (2007): 1–122, 94.

10 Ibid., 94.

11 Canada (Department of Fisheries and Oceans, Canada). ARCHIVED – Amendments to the Marine Mammal Regulations (Ottawa, DFO, 2009). Accessed April 7, 2015, http://www.gazette.gc.ca/rp-pr/p2/2009/2009-03-04/html/sor-dors66-eng.html.

seal hunts. This has raised different interpretations over the objectives and goals of the seal regime.[12]

3 The Genesis and Implementation of the 'Indigenous Exemption'

Throughout the drafting process of the regime the aim to protect Inuit populations from a possible trade ban was verbalized consistently. The Parliamentary Declaration explicitly stated that any policy measures were not to affect the Inuit.[13] While the Seal Pups Directive noted in art. 3 that "[t]his Directive shall only apply to products not resulting from traditional hunting by the Inuit people", its effects on Arctic livelihoods were drastic and have been widely documented.[14] Therefore, the Basic Regulation in its Chapeau in paragraph 14 and in article 3 make the ban not applicable for Inuit and other indigenous communities that hunt seals for their subsistence.

In order to reduce possible negative impacts of the regime on the Inuit, the Implementation Regulation specifies the scope of the indigenous exemption based on several initiatives. The European Commission initiated two Arctic Dialogue Workshops in 2010 and 2011 in Brussels and Tromsø respectively with representatives of the Arctic's indigenous peoples in order to include the indigenous peoples in all decisions affecting them. The European General Court refers also to a meeting of 21 January 2009 after which the Inuit exemption was introduced.[15] This cannot be verified as the only documented stakeholder meeting was held on 18 November 2009.[16] Notwithstanding, two factors stand

12 See for example EUGC (European Union General Court), Judgement of the General Court, *Inuit Tapiriit Kanatami and others v European Commission.* Case T-526/10 (2013), paras. 64, 83; WTO (World Trade Organization), European Communities – Measures prohibiting the importation and marketing of seal products. WT/DS400/AB/R, WT/DS401/AB/R, Reports of the Appellate Body, 22 May 2014, para. 5.16. Accessed November 18, 2014, http://www.wto.org/english/tratop_e/dispu_e/400_401abr_e.pdf; Sellheim, Nikolas, "The Goals of the EU Seal Products Trade Regulation – From Effectiveness to Consequence," *Polar Record* 51 (2014): 274–289, doi:10.1017/S0032247414000023.

13 EP Declaration 2006, *supra* note 7, para. H.2.

14 See for example Royal Commission on Seals and the Sealing Industry, *Seals and Sealing in Canada.* Ottawa: Minister of Supplies and Services Canada, 1986; George Wenzel, *Animal Rights, Human Rights – Ecology, Economy and Ideology in the Canadian Arctic.* Toronto: University of Toronto Press, 1991; Kalland, Arne and Frank Sejersen, *Marine Mammals and Northern Cultures.* Edmonton: Canadian Circumpolar Institute Press, 2005.

15 EUGC 2013, *supra* note 12, para. 114.

16 EC (European Commission). *Trade in seal products* (not dated). Accessed November 18, 2014, http://ec.europa.eu/environment/biodiversity/animal_welfare/seals/seal_hunting.htm; Sellheim 2014, *supra* note 12, 12.

out. First, the Commission-commissioned study on the impacts of measures constituting a blanket ban on trade in seal products identified Inuit as adversely affected by these[17] although Regulation 1007/2009 clearly exempts Inuit from any trade measure. Second, since the measure adopted was indeed of a blanket character, the report on the implementing regulation aimed at specifying who can after all be exempted from the ban. Here, the study carried out as part of the drafting of the Implementing Regulation refers to five characteristics that are of relevance for trade in seal products and an Inuit exemption. Namely: a "distinct identity; Historical continuity; Basic rights (specifically the rights to natural resources); Respect for the integrity and non-discrimination; and Non-dominant part of society."[18] In combination with the Basic Regulation's undefined notion of 'subsistence', the study clarifies that this is to be understood as the intention of the hunt not being purely commercial, that the killing of seals does not occur in order to market the products for commercial benefit and that the hunts contribute to the economic and social maintenance of a community.[19]

To this end, the Implementing Regulation in article 3 frames the indigenous exemption as follows:

1. Seal products resulting from hunts by Inuit or other indigenous communities may only be placed on the market where it can be established that they originate from seal hunts which satisfy *all* [own emphasis] of the following conditions:
   (a) seal hunts conducted by Inuit or other indigenous communities which have a tradition of seal hunting in the community and in the geographical region;
   (b) seal hunts the products of which are at least partly used, consumed or processed within the communities according to their traditions.
   (c) seal hunts which contribute to the subsistence of the community.
2. At the time of the placing on the market, the seal product shall be accompanied by the attesting document referred to in Article 7(1).

17 COWI (Consultancy within Engineering, Environmental Science and Economics). *Assessment of the Potential Impact of a Ban on Products derived from Seal Species.* April 2008. (Copenhagen: COWI, 2008), 99. Accessed November 18, 2014, http://ec.europa.eu/environment/biodiversity/animal_welfare/seals/pdf/seals_report.pdf.

18 COWI (Consultancy within Engineering, Environmental Science and Economics). *Study on Implementing Measures for Trade in Seal Products.* Final report. (Copenhagen: COWI, 2010), 8. Accessed November 18 2014, http://ec.europa.eu/environment/biodiversity/animal_welfare/seals/pdf/study_implementing_measures.pdf.

19 Ibid., 10.

Although this exemption at first sight seems rather clear-cut and a trade ban should therefore not affect Inuit hunts, Inuit and others nevertheless challenged the EU seal regime before the European Courts in several cases.[20] Adverse effects of the ban on their livelihoods and the *de facto* ban from the European markets triggered these legal responses. Indeed, Hossain notes that the indigenous exemption is rooted in outdated notions of 'subsistence' and 'tradition'.[21] From a technical perspective, articles 6 and 7 of the Implementation Regulation require the existence of 'recognized bodies' that provide documentation for the compliance with the indigenous exemption. At the time of writing, only Greenlandic Inuit are able to place their products on the EU's markets as the Greenland Department of Fisheries, Hunting and Agriculture (APNN) has been recognized as an appropriate body.[22] Trade in products from

20 See for example Cambou, Dorothée, "The Impact of the Ban on Seal Products on the Rights of Indigenous Peoples: A European Issue," in *The Yearbook of Polar Law* 5 (2013), ed. Gudmundur Alfredsson and Timo Koivurova, 389–415. (Leiden: Martinus Nijhoff, 2013); Julinda Beqiraj, "The Delicate Equilibrium of EU Trade Measures: The Seals Case," *German Law Journal* 14 (2013): 279–320.

21 Hossain, Kamrul, "The EU ban on the import of seal products and the WTO regulations: neglected human rights of the Arctic indigenous peoples?" *Polar Record* 49 (2013): 154–166, 162–163, doi:10.1017/S0032247412000174.

22 EC (European Commission). Commission Decision of 25.4.2013 Recognising the Greenland Department of Fisheries, Hunting and Agriculture (APNN) for the purposes of Article 6 of Commission Regulation (EU) No 737/2010 of 10 August 2010 laying down detailed rules for the implementation of Regulation (EC) No 1007/2009 of the European Parliament and of the Council on trade in seal products (2013); Given the recognition of the APNN as a recognised body for the labelling of Greenlandic seal products these are allowed to enter the market. The presumption is that the primary objective for the hunt is of a non-commercial nature and that the hunt's products are at least partly used in the respective communities. The Greenlandic sealing industry, however, is a government-supported, centralized industry with a processing plant owned by Great Greenland A/S in Qaqortoq on the southern tip of the island. Around half of the skins from the hunts are processed there and traded in commercially by Great Greenland A/S while the company operates around 40 trading stations all over Greenland that hunters can sell their skins to. The revenues from the commercial trade constitute a significant economic pillar for the hunters while with the declining international markets also the Greenlandic hunters had to suffer significant economic losses (Government of Greenland. *Management and Utilization of seals in Greenland.* (Nuuk: Ministry of Fisheries, Hunting and Agriculture, 2012), 25–28. Accessed November 18 2014, http://dk.vintage.nanoq.gl/Emner/Landsstyre/Departementer/Departement_for_fiskeri/~/media/nanoq/DFFL/Departementet/Udgivelser/Hvidbog%20om%20s%C3%A6ler_april2012_eng.ashx). With regard to its size hunts in Greenland now outnumber the Canadian commercial seal hunt: while in Canada in 2013 around 90.000 seals were landed, in the first 9 months of 2013 almost 105.000 seals

Canadian Inuit is therefore in practice not possible. Since Greenland is still part of the Kingdom of Denmark, Danish political initiatives have by and large supported the Greenlandic seal hunt. To this end, Denmark abstained in the Council of the European Union's vote on the Basic Regulation.[23] Also in its Arctic strategy, Denmark emphasises that it "will work internationally for the Arctic indigenous peoples' right to conduct hunting and to sell products from seal hunting, as long as it is based on sustainable principles."[24]

In order to ensure that Canadian Inuit seal products are also able to enter the European market, the European Union and Canada issued a joint statement for this purpose in August 2014. The joint statement clarifies that an expert group that represents both sides will in particular work on the attestation system for Canadian Inuit seal products pursuant to article 3 of the Implementing Regulation. At the same time, the European Commission will take further steps to ensure that customs and other authorities do not prevent indigenous seal products from entering the EU market. Therefore, the statement aims to effectively remove barriers for Canadian indigenous seal products o enter the European markets. Canada, on the other hand, lifts its opposition to EU observership in the Arctic Council. The joint statement was approved in October 2014.[25]

Given that the EU seal regime is a trade regime that directly impacts Canadian and Norwegian trade in seal products, both countries made use of the WTO's Dispute Settlement Process (DSP) in order to overturn the ban based on international trade law with an emphasis on the General Agreement on Tariffs and Trade (GATT).[26] As the last instance, the Appellate Body (AB)

---

were landed in Greenland (Grønlands Statistik, "Tabell 11. Fangst av pattedyr og fugle." Nuuk: Grønlands Statistik, 2014. Accessed November 25, 2014, http://www.stat.gl/dialog/main.asp?lang=da&version=201407&sc=SA&subthemecode=t11&colcode=t; Grønlands Statistik, e-mail to author, November 20, 2014; Sellheim 2014, *supra* note 12, 11).

23 Council of the European Union. Interinstitutional File: 2008/0160 (COD), 12406/09. Voting Result. Brussels, 27 July 2009. (Brussels: Council of the European Union, 2009). Accessed February 6, 2015, http://data.consilium.europa.eu/doc/document/ST-12406-2009-INIT/en/pdf.

24 Denmark, Greenland and the Faroe Islands, *Kingdom of Denmark Strategy for the Arctic 2011–2020.* (Copenhagen: Ministry of Foreign Affairs, 2011), 32. Accessed February 6, 2015, http://ec.europa.eu/enterprise/policies/raw-materials/files/docs/mss-denmark_en.pdf.

25 EC (European Commission), "Commission Decision of 18.8.2014 on the Joint Statement by Canada and the European Union on Access to the European Union of Seal Products from indigenous communities in Canada".

26 On all documentation regarding the case, see WTO (World Trade Organization), "European Communities – Measures prohibiting the importation and marketing of seal products." Accessed February 6, 2015, http://www.wto.org/english/tratop_e/dispu_e/cases_e/ds400_e.htm.

adjudicates international trade regimes. With regard to the indigenous exemption, the AB considers it as not in compliance with international trade law since, as the EU has argues, opposition towards the seal hunt as such on moral grounds serves as the main background of the regime. Since there is a disconnect between animal welfare-based argumentation and whether or not the hunts are conducted by indigenous peoples, a logical fallacy exists, which creates a discriminatory trade regime that does not follow the main objective of the regime: addressing public morals with regard to the seal hunt. Since the so-called 'moral exception' of GATT art. XX (a) can only be accepted if it does not create a discriminatory trade environment, the EU is now required to bring its legislation in conformity with WTO law.[27] Upon agreement with Canada the EU is now required to enact legislative changes by 18 October 2015.[28]

It remains questionable what kind of legislative changes the EU is going to implement or whether the EU will apply non-compliance with the recommendations of the DSB. The agreement with Canada was concluded irrespective of the legislative steps the EU takes with regard to the WTO, but in how far an opening of the European markets will directly benefit Inuit communities in Canada cannot be ascertained and needs to be determined over time. A direct comparison with Greenlandic Inuit cannot be drawn due to the special relationship between Greenland and Denmark and the support by the Danish government that make especially the Danish markets available for Greenlandic seal products.[29] In how far the general opposition towards seal products plays a role in the marketing of Inuit seal products must be determined empirically.

On 6 February 2015 the European Commission proposed amendments to the seals regime. In order to comply with the ruling of the Appellate Body, the exception for products stemming from marine resource management should be removed. Moreover, the indigenous exemption is to be tightened to ensure that "the hunt is conducted in a manner which reduces pain, distress, fear or other forms of suffering."[30]

---

27 WTO (World Trade Organization), "European Communities – Measures prohibiting the importation and marketing of seal products". AB-2014-1, AB-2014-2, Reports of the Appellate Body, 22 May 2014. (Geneva: World Trade Organization, 2014), 5.167, 5.338.

28 WTO, European Communities – Measures prohibiting the importation and marketing of seal products. Agreement under article 21.3 (b) of the DSU (2014 (b)). Accessed November 18 2014, https://docs.wto.org/dol2fe/Pages/FE_Search/FE_S_S009-DP.aspx?language=E&CatalogueIdList=126897,126239,125339,124826,124807,124760,123564,122179,122111,121006&CurrentCatalogueIdIndex=0&FullTextSearch=.

29 Government of Greenland 2012, *supra* note 22, 25–28.

30 European Commission, "Proposal for a Regulation of the European Parliament and of the Council amending Regulation (EC) No 1007/2009 on Trade in Seal Products. 2015/0028 (COD)." Brussels: European Commission, 2015.

4 Narrating the 'Other'

Throughout the drafting process of the current EU seal regime certain narratives can be found that render an objective dealing with the issue of cruelty and cultural sustainability unlikely. In essence, the question of whom to exempt from a trade measure that prohibits the trade in seal products boils down to the question who is considered to be a legitimate seal hunter and why. On the contrary, this implies an answer to the question of who is not a legitimate seal hunter and why. The European Union has answered the question by imposing a ban on all seal products, irrespective of the hunting methods applied. This implies that as such all seal hunting is considered inappropriate for the maintenance of a market for seal products. As shown above, the primary reason for this is the allegation of policy-makers that the seal hunt is inherently cruel.[31] Indigenous, and in particular Inuit, hunts and economies do not fall within the debate of 'necessity' and 'cruelty'. As this section shows, indigenous peoples are still discursively accepted to hunt animals which non-indigenous are not. The linking of seal hunting as a 'necessity' for maintaining livelihoods with a stereotypical perception of Inuit economies constitute the main background for the indigenous exemption.

a *Narrating Indigenous Peoples and the Hunt of Charismatic Megafauna*

Problematic in the context of legal responses to the seal hunt is that of a solid knowledge base. Interestingly the EU seal products trade ban is by no means exceptional, with national and international agreements dealing with the hunts of 'charismatic megafauna' such as polar bears, whales or seals, always including an exception from any hunt or trade bans for indigenous peoples. The US Marine Mammal Protection Act (MMPA) of 1972 or the International Convention for the Regulation of Whaling (ICRW) of 1946 stand as prominent examples for this. Already article 8 of the Award by the Tribunal of Arbitration following the Treaty for Submitting to Arbitration the Questions Relating to the Seal Fisheries in the Bering Sea of 29 February 1892, which was concluded between the United States and Great Britain over the seizing of ships resulting in a ban on commercial sealing in the Bering Sea, holds an exemption for "Indians dwelling on the coasts of the territory of the United States or of

31 The claim of cruelty is the most commonly found narrative in the discourse on the seal hunt. As shown in the EFSA report, this claim cannot be upheld satisfactorily and requires large-scale assessments which do not exit. Consideration of the narrative of cruelty shall therefore not be part of this paper due to the author's lack of expertise in this matter.

Great Britain [...]."[32] Contrary to the EU seal regime, however, the indigenous exemptions were not included over the opposition towards the commercialization of products stemming from these hunts, but were rather based on the minor impact of indigenous hunts on the population statuses of the respective species. This means that human impacts on the respective population status were the incentive behind these regulatory regimes.

In the case of the EU seal regime the issue of animal welfare and not the population status of seals has been the trigger for the legislative process.[33] One might therefore be compelled to think that irrespective of the reason to hunt seals or the processing of the products derived from the hunts animal welfare stands at the fore of the legislation. Here, the narrative of 'good' indigenous hunts and 'bad' commercial hunts, however, expounds the problems to an objective approach to animal welfare in the seal hunts. In the EFSA study, for example, an often applied killing method in the Arctic – harpooning – is not considered for two reasons: first, the mandate by the European Commission for the EFSA study clarifies that EFSA is to issue an opinion on "the animal welfare aspects of the methods currently being used, *particularly non-traditional*."[34] Second, presumably as a result of the first point, the methodology of the EFSA study is based on observer reports which focus predominantly on the Canadian and Namibian seal hunts. Since the focus is indeed on non-traditional hunting methods, any further inquiry concerning the animal welfare aspects of harpooning is not necessary. It seems therefore that the narrative of a 'good' indigenous hunt reflects into the knowledge base and creates an epistemology which does not circle around animal welfare aspects of seal hunts in general, but which excludes elements surrounding the narrated 'good' hunts.

b *Narrating Inuit Economies*

The complex economic systems in Arctic communities have been discussed widely and shall not be reproduced here.[35] It suffices to say that with regard to the Inuit, continuous interaction with non-indigenous economies for several decades have created economic systems which can no longer be categorized as

32 Robb, Cairo A.R., *International Environmental Law Reports. Vol. 1. Early Decisions.* (Cambridge: Cambridge University Press, 1999), 71.

33 Sellheim, Nikolas, "Policies and Influence – Tracing and Locating the EU Seal Products Trade Regulation," *International Community Law Review* 17 (2015): 3–36.

34 EFSA 2007, *supra* note 9, 10. Own emphasis.

35 See for example Glømsrod, Solveig and Iulie Aslaksen, ed., *The Economy of the North 2008.* (Oslo: Statistics Norway, 2009).

clearly market- or subsistence-based. Instead, the ability to conduct hunts for local consumption depends on monetary income for fuel and other equipment. Therefore, for example Inuit seal products are sold through established market chains. Consequently, with a reduction in market demand for seal products in general or declining prices, the subsistence dimension is affected directly. This notwithstanding, seal hunting narratives paint a picture that distinguish between a hunt for seals which is either solely driven by market, commercial, forces or solely driven by subsistence needs without a commercial dimension. If the latter were the case, an inclusion of an indigenous exemption would not be necessary as a subsistence economy by and large implies that the products do not enter the market sphere. Instead it would rather remain on the community sphere of exchange.[36] Yet, as I have argued elsewhere, the notion of a purely commercial hunt, in reference to the Canadian seal hunt, must be challenged based on the high cultural, as well as on the social values attached to it.[37]

The narratives prevailing in the European political discourse are well reflected in the European Parliament debate prior to the vote on the approval of a regulation banning the trade in all seal products on 5 May 2009. Here, Members of Parliament (MEPs) often merely express that given the indigenous exemption Inuit communities are not to be adversely affected given the subsistence-based dimension of sealing in these communities. One MEP even goes so far as to state:

> If the Inuits [*sic*] want to continue selling these products, then they can only do this if it is quite clear that the products have nothing to do with the usual method of hunting seals. Only if a clear distinction is made will the Inuits [*sic*] have the opportunity to sell anything.[38]

36 For a discussion on the different spheres or circuits of exchange, see Gudeman, Stephen, *The Anthropology of Economy. Community, Market, and Culture.* (Malden: Blackwell Publishing, 2001).

37 Sellheim, Nikolas, "Direct and Individual Concern for Newfoundland's Sealing Industry? – When a Legal Concept and Empirical Data Collide," in *The Yearbook of Polar Law* 6 (2014), ed. Gudmundur Alfredsson and Timo Koivurova, 466–496. (Leiden: Martinus Nijhoff, 2014); Sellheim, Nikolas, "The Right Not to be Indigenous: Seal Utilization in Newfoundland," in *Arctic Yearbook 2014*, ed. Lassi Heininen, Heather Exner-Pirot and Joël Plouffe. (Akureyri: Northern Research Forum, 2014).

38 Rühle, Heide, European Parliament, Debates – Monday, May 4 2009 – Strasbourg, 21. Trade in seal products. Accessed November 19, 2014, http://www.europarl.europa.eu/sides/getDoc.do?pubRef=-//EP//TEXT+CRE+20090504+ITEM-021+DOC+XML+V0//EN&language=EN.

Interestingly, at the time of the vote for the ban the difficulties of implementing the indigenous exemption were already known, both because Inuit representatives had repeatedly expressed their concerns over the ban and because the impact assessment also notes that irrespective of the measure taken "policy measures that have adverse impacts on the image of the seal skins and other seal products will have a negative impact on the Inuit population anyway."[39] Therefore, even if the main driver behind the Inuit seal hunt was to be of a non-commercial nature, the complex economic environment that makes Inuit seal hunters also dependent on the sale of seal products as well as the reputational losses of seal products in general would have direct and individual effects on Inuit sealers. A report by the Government of Nunavut of 2012 clarifies this issue and notes that "the ringed seal industry in Nunavut benefits from the harp seal industry by 'piggy packing' on markets that are created and maintained by the much larger harp seal industry."[40]

From a political perspective the narrative of a subsistence hunt that is confined to a specific community or region without regard to the complex economic systems in the Arctic makes the inclusion of an Inuit exemption a choice that follows an easy political "distinction between 'good' and 'bad' seal products"[41] and therefore does not touch upon the realities of Arctic life. Rafia Zakaria writes with regard to development help in Africa and the associated 'volontourism':

> Typically other people's problems seem simpler, uncomplicated and easier to solve than those of one's own society. [...] Unlike the problems of other societies, the failing inner city schools in Chicago or the haplessness of those living on the fringes in Detroit is connected to larger political narratives. In simple terms, the lack of knowledge of other cultures makes them easier to help.[42]

While the adoption of the seal regime was not aimed to help the Inuit, it is nevertheless aimed to not affect them and their livelihoods. Therefore,

39 COWI 2008, *supra* note 17, 117.

40 Government of Nunavut, *Report on the Impacts of the European Union Seal Ban,* (EC) *No 1007/2009,* in *Nunavut.* (Iqaluit: Department of Environment, 2012): 9.

41 COWI 2008, *supra* note 17, 5.

42 Zakaria, Rafia "The white tourist's burden", *Al Jazeera America,* April 14, 2014. Accessed November 19, 2014, http://america.aljazeera.com/opinions/2014/4/volunter-tourismwhit evoluntouristsafricaaidsorphans.html.

Zakaria's statement in so far fits the debate as the simplistic perception of Inuit and the highly mixed economies leads to a simplistic political and ultimately legal outcome which, however, had caused a significant stir in Canadian–European relations with regard to the EU's observership in the Arctic Council. To legally consider the larger issues surrounding the seal hunt and in particular local and Inuit economies would have placed a significant burden on policy-makers, bearing in mind that the parliamentary elections were taking place only about one month after the vote in Parliament concerning the seal regulation.

c *Narrating the Inuit Seal Hunt*

A simple Google search with the keywords 'Inuit seal hunt' reveals a clear picture of the prevailing narrative concerning the hunt on seals by Inuit hunters: an individual, historical hunt. Whether or not this corresponds to empirical facts shall not be of issue here. More interesting is the question in how far this narrative is reflected in the political discourse in the European Union and in how far this is considered the 'good', 'real' or legitimate Arctic seal hunt.

As pointed out, a key concept applied in the political discourse concerning seal hunting is that of 'tradition' and 'traditional hunting'. As I have shown, however, the criteria applied to frame this concept throughout the drafting process of the seal regime can equally be applied to non-Inuit, commercial seal hunting activities in Newfoundland.[43] Campaigns by animal welfare organizations to end the seal hunt have by and large excluded any indigenous hunts due to their 'traditionality' and socio-economic and socio-cultural relevance for the communities. Parallels in narrating Inuit livelihoods can be found in the tourism sector which paint certain images of 'other' cultures and which contribute to revitalizing the museified understanding of Inuit cultures.[44]

In a similar vein, the organization Sea Shepherd states on its website that it does not oppose aboriginal sealing as long as they do not hunt seals when they are not dependent on them for survival. Also, the organization notes that it opposes export from these communities.[45] Similarly, yet less radical, the organization International Fund for Animal Welfare (IFAW), without further specification, supports aboriginal sealing as long as it is sustainable, without unnecessary suffering and the products of which are processed used and traded in within aboriginal communities.[46]

---

43 Sellheim 2013, *supra* note 3.

44 Ibid,

45 "Frequently Asked Questions about Canadian Seals and Sealings [*sic*]", Sea Shepherd. Accessed November 19, 2014, http://www.seashepherd.org/seals/seals-faq.html#16.

46 International Fund for Animal Welfare. "Aboriginal Seal Hunts." Accessed November 19, 2014, http://www.ifaw.org/united-states/our-work/seals/aboriginal-seal-hunts.

The 'museification' of culture in the context of the EU seal products ban implies the protection of fragile Arctic livelihoods. Former vice-president of the European Parliament, Diana Wallis, in aforementioned parliamentary debate notes that "the Arctic is not some sort of theme park or museum: it is a living, breathing community with its own modern economy."[47] This statement thus calls for recognition of the opened Arctic economies contrary to the narrated and implicitly imagined economically isolated subsistence systems. The seal hunt therefore, following Wallis' line of thought, cannot be perceived through a lens that isolates it from other economic activities. Considering the Inuit seal hunt, or the 'traditional' seal hunt, as a part of the Inuit cultural heritage, a narrative of the aboriginal seal hunt which is being treated independently from any other discourse on animal welfare and seal economy may be considered insulting and patronizing by Inuit.[48] Moreover, the isolated treatment of a 'museified' seal hunt does not recognise heritage as a mode of adaptation to changing circumstances beyond the modi of conservation, recovery or protection. Heritage, in general terms, is consequently "a mode of cultural production in the present that has recourse to the past."[49]

5 The Narrated 'Other' – Narratives, Self-Determination and Sustainability

Indigenous peoples' adaptation to modern times beyond the museification of cultures has been legally accepted by the United Nations. In *Länsman v Finland No. 1*[50] the Human Rights Committee adopted the view that traditional livelihoods and their adaptation to modern times still enables them to be protected under article 27 of the International Covenant for Civil and Political Rights (ICCPR). This article reads:

> In those States in which ethnic, religious or linguistic minorities exist, persons belonging to such minorities shall not be denied the right, in

47 Wallis, Diana, European Parliament, Debates – Monday, 4 May 2009 – Strasbourg. 21. Trade in seal products. Accessed November 19, 2014, http://www.europarl.europa.eu/sides/getDoc.do?pubRef=-//EP//TEXT+CRE+20090504+ITEM-021+DOC+XML+V0//EN&language=EN.

48 Sellheim 2013, *supra* note 3, 446.

49 Kirshenblatt-Gimblett, Barbara, "Theorizing Heritage," *Ethnomusicology* 39 (1995): 370.

50 *Ilmari Länsman et al. v. Finland* (Communication 511/1992), Views adopted: 26 October 1994, Report of the Human Rights Committee, Vol. II, GAOR, Fiftieth Session, Suppl. No. 40 (A/50/40), 66–76.

> community with the other members of their group, to enjoy their own culture, to profess and practise their own religion, or to use their own language.

The inclusion of the indigenous exemption into the EU seal regime was decided to avoid negative impacts of any trade measures regarding trade in seal products for Inuit and other indigenous peoples. Although the negative impacts were known, the regime was voted in favour with overwhelming majority. The political reasons for the outcome of this vote shall not be examined here. Focus shall be laid on the impacts of narratives on the sustainability of livelihoods and the right to self-determination as manifested in common article 1.1 and 1.2 of the 1966 Covenants which reads:

> 1. All peoples have the right of self-determination. By virtue of that right they freely determine their political status and freely pursue their economic, social and cultural development.
> 2. All peoples may, for their own ends, freely dispose of their natural wealth and resources without prejudice to any obligations arising out of international economic co-operation, based upon the principle of mutual benefit, and international law. In no case may a people be deprived of its own means of subsistence.

The indigenous exemption, albeit meant well, must be considered ineffective, otherwise the tremendous financial efforts to launch several court cases before the European Courts by Inuit and others would not have been necessary. In other words, despite the indigenous exemption, the pressures put on the sustainability of seal-related activities and economies must have been so significant that they had rendered these efforts necessary.

Looking at the prevailing narratives presented in this paper, the problem appears manifold. An underlying characteristic of animal welfare organizations as well as EU policy makers, as reflected in the indigenous exemption, is that of cultural relativism. As a principle it was established by the early ethnographer Franz Boas who in 1887 noted that "civilization is not something absolute, but that it is relative, and that our ideas and conceptions are true only so far as our civilization goes"[51] resulting in a perception of "internally integrated, self-contained, and analytically isolable cultures."[52] The insertion

51 Boas, Franz, "Museums of Ethnology and Their Classification," *Science* 9 (1887), 589.

52 Laidlaw, James, *The Subject of Virtue: An Anthropology of Ethics and Freedom* (Cambridge: Cambridge University Press, 2014), 27.

of an indigenous exemption as the main tool for shielding Inuit seal hunting from adverse effects of the ban indeed reflects an understanding of contemporary Inuit society which is, at least to some degree, isolated from non-Inuit trade systems.[53]

Although in the regime's drafting process reference was made to the incentive behind the seal hunt which is to be considered when speaking of 'subsistence', and not the *actual* degree of the seal products' contribution to the Inuit's subsistence, this seems not to have found its way into the narratives on an ongoing mode of cultural and therefore economic production. The Implementing Regulation, however, does indeed seem to take the external dimension of the 'traditional' seal economy into consideration: in article 3 (b) it refers merely to the *partial* utilization, consumption and processing in the respective community. Problematic in this context is the cumulative approach the Implementing Regulation takes: apart from the partial utilization it furthermore requires a tradition of seal hunting in the community or the geographical region as well as a contribution to the subsistence of the community, which can be understood here as an immediate-return economy.[54]

Questions concerning sustainability and self-determination emerge here: in light of the changing climate that may result in relocation of entire communities in the Arctic, some of which may or may not have a tradition in seal hunting, would the indigenous exemption still be applicable if the geo-economic systems change?[55] That is, if environmental pressures make a community formerly eligible to trade in seal products with the European Union no longer eligible, would this community still fall under the indigenous exemption? At the same time, the dwindling of the markets for seal products changes the economic situation in communities fully or partly dependent on

---

53 Bernard Williams argued, "[f]or standard relativism [...] it is always too early or too late. It is too early, when the parties have no contact with each other, and neither can think of itself as 'we' and the other as 'they'. It is too late, when they have encountered one another: the moment that they have done so, there is a new 'we' to be negotiated" (Williams, Bernard, *In the Beginning was the Deed: Realism and Moralism in Political Argument.* (Princeton: Princeton University Press, 2007), 69).

54 Barnard, Alan, "The Foraging Mode of Thought," in *Self- and Other-Images of Hunter-Gatherers,* ed. Henry Stewart *et al.* (Osaka: National Museum of Ethnology, 2002), 7; Tim Ingold, *The Perception of the Environment – Essays on Livelihood, Dwelling and Skill* (London and New York: Routledge, 2011), 66.

55 On the acuteness of this question, see for example Hastrup, Kirsten and Maris Louise B. Robertson, "Fixed and Fluid Waters. Mirroring the Arctic and the Pacific," in *Living with Environmental Change – Waterworlds*, ed. Kirsten Hastrup and Cecilie Rubow. (London and New York: Routledge, 2014).

their commercialization. Important remedies stemming from the sale of seal products that are relevant for the conduct of other 'traditional' activities dry out, necessitating, as a worst case scenario, relocation, potentially altering the status of this community under the indigenous exemption.

But narratives that reflect into a legal regime such as the EU seal regime hold implications for self-determination. Would an indigenous community that fulfilled all criteria in the regime still be eligible to fall under the exemption if it decided to shift the incentive towards hunting seals for commercial gain with locally-used seal products as by-products of the commercial hunt? Discursively the answer is a likely 'no' as it is the commercialization of seal products that the EU seal regime aims to tackle and the discourse opposes. However, self-chosen economic shifts towards discursively more unpopular activities than small-scale (seal) hunting are not unknown in the Arctic.[56] Legally, on the other hand, especially article 27 ICCPR would take hold as indeed a potential shift from a subsistence-incentive to a commerce-incentive could be considered an adaptation to prevailing, 'modern', markets. The legal challenge therefore lies in the elaboration whether or not self-chosen adaptation (a positive will) or outside pressures necessitating adaptation (*force majeure*) generate differences in the applicability of article 27 ICCPR. Irrespective of potential future changes in the conduct of the hunt and the marketing of the products, the narratives upon which the indigenous exemption is built generate discursive as well as legal problems pertaining to self-determination and sustainability.

6 Conclusion

The way in which the EU seal regime was adopted does not to make use of the epistemic basis it could have, and as it had been, commissioned by the European Commission. It therefore contradicts underlying principles which led, for example, to the conclusion of the Northern Fur Seal Treaty between Russia, Japan, Great Britain/Canada and the US and which was in force from 1911 until the 1980s to protect the fur seal populations in the Bering Sea. Here, shared knowledge stemming from different stakeholders merged and formed the regime, meaning that the regime aimed at identifying and resolving a specific set

56 For example shown by Sejersen, Frank, "Water as Power and Destroyer," in *Living with Environmental Change – Waterworlds*, ed. Kirsten Hastrup and Cecilie Rubow. (London and New York: Routledge, 2014).

of problems.[57] In the case of the EU seal regime, narratives and not knowledge have influence the outcome of the basic regulation. In many respects this has created a *sui generis* legal regime which does not correspond to other international regimes.[58]

The insertion of an exemption for indigenous peoples was based on good will and the wish not to impact the livelihoods of the Arctic's indigenous peoples. Yet, as this paper shows the culturally relativistic approach this exemption has taken based on rather unsubstantiated narratives has not led to the best possible outcome and has in essence continued or even reinvigorated the problems caused by the Seal Pups Directive which it aimed to avoid. For example, given the interwoven economies in Inuit communities, a decline in the market value of seal products has direct impacts on Inuit seal hunts irrespective of whether or not an indigenous exemption is built into the regime. While in the past the indigenous exemptions were in so far justified as they were based on the little impact of aboriginal hunting on the population statuses of certain species, given the trade dimension of the current seal regime and the mixed economic systems of subsistence and commerce, an exemption of indigenous peoples is difficult to implement.

The perception of the Inuit people in the discourse surrounding the seal hunt is shaped by specific narratives, first and foremost that the hunt is 'necessary' and therefore tolerable. To this end also the indigenous hunt of charismatic megafauna is not faced with opposition provided a large-scale commercialization does not take place. This narrative, which excludes considerations of cruelty or animal welfare, neglects the embedment of indigenous cultures in the global economic systems and contradicts provisions in international law pertaining to self-determination and sustainability. Instead, a rather stereotypical, museified view on Inuit and Inuit culture is applied which renders the Inuit seal hunt a 'good' seal hunt, carried out first and foremost for local consumption. The utilized narratives have thus created a regime which does not correspond to empirical circumstances. Despite the indigenous exemption, the EU seal regime in practice challenges the sustainable trade in indigenous seal products.

57 Mirovitskaya, Natalia S., Margaret Clark and Ronald G. Purver, "North Pacific Fur Seals: Regime Formation as a Means of Resolving Conflict," in *Polar Politics: Creating International Environmental Regimes,* ed. Oran R. Young and Gail Osherenko. (Ithaca and London: Cornell University Press, 1993).

58 Sellheim 2015, *supra* note 33

CHAPTER 4

Economic Security in the Canadian Arctic

*Heather Exner-Pirot**

Abstract

The most acute human security threats facing Canadian Arctic indigenous peoples are related to economic insecurity – the social, cultural and physical ills that result from poverty. These include poor health outcomes as a result of the social determinants of health; pervasive unemployment; crowded and limited housing; dependency; low educational attainment; food insecurity; and anomie. Arctic indigenous peoples are often depicted as privileging environmental protection over economic development, particularly since the majority of economic activity in the Arctic is a product of natural resource exploitation. This chapter will critically assess the dichotomy that sees Arctic indigenous peoples as overwhelmingly opposed to resource development opportunities. It will use as case studies the economic development experiences of Alaskan Native Corporations beginning in the 1970s; the profusion of Canadian Impact Benefit Agreements in the past 2 decades; and the Greenlandic opening to oil exploration drilling and uranium mining, all in attempts to regain economic self-sufficiency and self-determination. The chapter will provide an appreciation of the complexities and sometimes competing demands of human security objectives as Arctic indigenous peoples adapt to globalizing forces.

Introduction

Economic security is an integral but often overlooked facet of human security in the Arctic region, where environmental and cultural threats, particularly those arising from climate changes, tend to dominate analysis.

Part of the challenge in discussing and addressing economic security in the Arctic are the many conflicting interpretations of what a desired state is and how it can be achieved. Is the transition to a market economy focused on resource development perpetuating economic insecurity – or is it the means to eliminate it? Are economic and environmental security in the region

* Heather Exner-Pirot, Strategist for Outreach and Indigenous Engagement at the University of Saskatchewan.

 | DOI 10.1163/9789004314399_006

fundamentally at odds with one another? Can development in the Arctic be sustainable and benefit the peoples who inhabit the land?

These are difficult questions for which consensus has not emerged. But they are posed, in one way or another, every day, and Arctic communities are tasked with finding answers.

This chapter will assess the multiple interpretations of economic security in the Arctic, and identify some of the cases in which Arctic communities are attempting to address it. Examples include the economic development experiences of Alaskan Native Corporations beginning in the 1970s; the profusion of Canadian Impact Benefit Agreements in the past two decades; and the Greenlandic opening to oil exploration drilling and uranium mining, all in attempts to regain economic self-sufficiency and self-determination.

Overall, this chapter attempts to provide an appreciation of the complexities and sometimes competing demands of human security objectives as Arctic indigenous peoples adapt to globalizing forces.

Human Security Discourses in the Arctic

Whereas traditional, Westphalian conceptions of security focus on the protection of the state, human security seeks to "safeguard the vital core of all human lives from critical pervasive threats, in a way that is consistent with long-term human fulfillment".[1] The notion of securing people instead of states became prominent in the 1980s, when activists questioned the wisdom of obscene military spending amid pervasive poverty, and on privileging the state when so often it acted as the source of insecurity and violence rather than a protector for its citizens against such abuses. The human security narrative in the Arctic similarly traces its roots to a repudiation of the media and political obsession with sovereignty and military security in the region, particularly in the Canadian context, and the rise in attention to the far-ranging impacts of climate change in the region.

In academia, the concept of human security became much more prominent in the 1990s as a means in which to address security and insecurity from the point of view of referents other than the state. 'Broadeners' (versus 'Narrowers') further accepted non-traditional or non-military applications of the concept of security as legitimate.

1 Alkire, Sabina, "A Conceptual Framework for Human Security," CRISE Working Paper, Working Paper #2 (Queen Elizabeth House, University of Oxford, 2003), 2. Retrieved from http://www3.qeh.ox.ac.uk/pdf/crisewps/workingpaper2.pdf, July 13, 2015.

In the Arctic, the concept of human security was articulated and applied by a number of scholars beginning in the late 2000s[2] as a useful way to frame some of the challenges facing inhabitants of the Circumpolar North, in particular indigenous peoples. Although the Arctic is not an arena for state-led physical violence, there are serious identified human security threats, particularly in the environmental and cultural spheres, that are urgent and require governmental intervention – i.e. that are worthy of securitization.

The subsequent focus on Arctic human insecurity as primarily a consequence of climate changes has had the effect of monopolizing contemporary policy discussions, much as the sovereignty debate did in the early 2000s. Climate change has become a – arguably *the* – starting point for scholarly discussion of human security, with a subsequent focus on environmental threats to traditional ways of life. This focus conveniently supports advocacy efforts to allocate resources to the mitigation of and adaptation to climate change, not only in the policy sphere but in the region's scientific network research priorities as well.

While few disagree that climate change is a huge issue that has had real impacts on the quality of life and well-being of Northerners, there is legitimate concern that it is overshadowing other, equally important, issues. In particular, global perspectives of the Arctic are frequently filtered through a lens of climate change, whereas regional perspectives often prioritize human development, self-determination, and cultural integrity. Human security in the Arctic is not, and cannot, just be about environmental security.

Economic Security is Human Security, Too

Economic security is somewhat of an amorphous concept, and straddles the fine line between human security, which focus on narrow and urgent threats,

2 Hoogensen, G., D. Bazely, J. Christensen, A. Tanentzap and E. Bojko, "Human Security in the Arctic–Yes, it is Relevant!" in *Journal of Human Security* 5 (2009): 1–10.; Forrest, P., L. Heininen, M. Sfraga, R. Virginia and K. Yalowitz, "Final Report and Main Findings", *Climate Change and Human Security*, 3rd Workshop of the UArctic Institute for Applied Circumpolar Policy, 2010, Rovaniemi.; Greaves, Will, "For whom, from what? Canada's Arctic policy and the narrowing of human security," in *International Journal*, 67 (2012): 219–240.; Exner-Pirot, Heather, "Human Security in the Arctic: The Foundation of Regional Cooperation," in *Working Papers on Arctic Security No. 1* (2012), Munk-Gordon Arctic Security Program.; Hoogensen, G., D. Bazely, M. Goloviznina, and A. Tanentzap, *Environmental and Human Security in the Arctic*. (Routledge: Oxon, 2013).; Hossain, Kamrul, "Securing the Rights: A Human Security Perspective in the Context of Arctic Indigenous Peoples" in *The Yearbook of Polar Law* 5 (2013): 493–522.

and human development, which focuses on general and long term goals. However it has a long pedigree in the human security literature, with the pioneering 1994 United Nations Development Programme (UNDP) Human Development Report including economic security among its seven categories of human security.[3] It described economic security as "an assured income – usually from productive and remunerative work, or in the last resort from some publicly financed safety net".[4] Acharya, assessing the differences in Western and Eastern interpretations of human security, famously characterized as freedom from fear versus freedom from want, describes the latter as addressing widespread poverty, unemployment and social dislocation, which were felt particularly acutely in Asia with the economic crises of the 1990s.[5]

Most Arctic peoples do not experience the same level of abject poverty as found in the Global South due to the relatively generous social safety nets of the Arctic states, and income is relatively high – according to the Arctic Human Development Report II, per capita household disposable income for the combined Arctic region is US$21,900, and per capita GRP is US$45,400.[6] However, living costs are generally also very high and as Sen articulates, relative deprivation in terms of incomes can yield absolute deprivation in terms of capabilities.[7] In other words, being relatively poor in a rich country can be a capabilities handicap, leading to social exclusion. Here, Sen defines poverty in terms of capabilities deprivation – the ability to do things, and the freedom to lead lives, that individuals have reason to value.[8] He highlights unemployment, which is particularly problematic for Arctic indigenous peoples in the context of a transition of a traditional to a wage economy, as one prominent example. There, the forgoing of income is just one of many negative impacts that also includes psychological harm; loss of motivation, skill and self-confidence; an increase in ailments and morbidity; disruption of family relations and social life; hardening of social exclusion; and accentuation of racial tensions and gender asymmetries.[9]

3 United Nations Development Programme. (1994). *Human Development Report: New Dimensions of Human Security*. New York & Oxford: Oxford University Press, 25.
4 Ibid.
5 Acharya, Amitav, "Human Security: East Versus West," in *International Journal*, 56 (2000–01), 450.
6 Huskey, Lee, Ilmo Mäenpää and Alexander Pelyasov, "Economic Systems," in *Arctic Human Development Report II* (Nordic Council of Ministers: Denmark, 2015), 173.
7 Sen, Amartya, *Development as Freedom*. (New York: Oxford University Press, 1999), 89.
8 Ibid, 85.
9 Ibid, 94.

Food Security

One particular consequence of economic underdevelopment in the Arctic has been food insecurity. Although feast and famine cycles were prevalent in the pre-contact hunter gatherer societies of the North, the transition from a subsistence to a wage economy is having a drastic impact on families' abilities to plan and prepare adequate supplies of food. Across the Circumpolar North, imported foods are on the rise,[10] however they are generally much more expensive than groceries in southern locales due to higher transportation, labour, spoilage and other overhead costs. Concomitantly, traditional harvesting is declining, due to factors such as environmental dispossession, loss of traditional knowledge, and a lack of time to devote to hunting given the shift to formal education and wage employment.[11] In fact, hunting in many places is an activity that needs to be subsidized by wage employment given the high cost of snowmobiles/snowmachines, rifles, bullets, and gasoline used by modern hunters. Better economic security would not only address food security, it would address cultural security by supporting continued practices of hunting and gathering.

Housing

Overcrowded housing and homelessness is another consequence of economic insecurity in the Circumpolar North. For Canadian Inuit for example, inadequate housing has been a reality since permanent settlement began in the 1950s and 60s, and persists today due to limited local economic opportunity, a virtually non-existent private housing market, high building and heating costs, costly shipping and transportation of materials, insufficient public resources, and geographic remoteness.[12] The young age of the population and high teenage pregnancy rates also contribute to overcrowded housing as the dependency ratio is very high. The crisis in housing has become an acute public health issue, with high levels of respiratory and digestive disease, mental illness, and physical and sexual abuse.

The economics are daunting. A 2004 study found that it cost about $330 a square foot to build a house in Nunavut, compared to an average of $104 in

10 Rasmussen, Rasmus Ole, Grete K/Hovelsrud, and Shari Gearheard, (2015). "Community Viability and Adaptation," in *Arctic Human Development Report II*, ed. Fondahl, Gail and Joan Larsen (Nordic Council of Ministers: Denmark, 2015), 467.

11 Council of Canadian Acadamies, 2014. Aboriginal Food Security in Northern Canada: An Assessment of the State of Knowledge. Ottawa, ON. The Expert Panel on the State of Knowledge of Food Security in Northern Canada, Council of Canadian Academies.

12 Knotsh, Cathleen and Dianne Kinnon, "If Not Now...When? Addressing the Ongoing Inuit Housing Crisis in Canada," (Ottawa: National Aboriginal Health Organization, 2011), ii.

southern Canadian communities,[13] even though household income and employment rates are significantly lower for Inuit. On top of that, the costs of maintaining and operating homes are very expensive, even for the homeless: Knotsch and Kinnon cite one family living in a plywood shelter near the beach who racked up $1000 in monthly heating bills with their electric heater.[14]

Human Security Priorities

All of this is by way of saying that economic security can be considered one of, if not the most, important human security issue facing Arctic indigenous peoples. Yet the scholarly human security literature has focused almost exclusively on environmental and cultural security issues, framed largely within a climate change discourse.[15] Interestingly, in a 2011 survey conducted by EKOS for the Walter and Duncan Gordon Foundation, both Southern and Northern Canadians themselves identified environmental security as their top priority when identifying definitions of security "when it comes to protecting the Arctic",[16] ahead of social and economic security, with national security concerns coming last.

That said, when Northern respondents were confronted with scenarios where they had to allocate resources to different policy options, health care, infrastructure, housing, and better access to post-secondary education were consistently selected ahead of protection for the environment.[17] Within the scholarly community, we need to determine whether economic security is about jobs and development, or if it's about meeting basic nutritional, shelter and educational needs. Practically, it seems fairly impossible to resolve the latter without improving the former.

Environmental Protection versus Sustainable Development?

Unfortunately there has been a severe dichotomization between the economic and the environmental in the Arctic, a distinction that has been exasperated in

13 Nunavut Housing Corporation and Nunavut Tunngavik Inc., Nunavut Ten Year Inuit Housing Action Plan (Government of Nunavut: Nunavut, 2004).

14 Ibid, 35.

15 See Exner-Pirot, "Human Security in the Arctic: The Foundation of Regional Cooperation" and Greaves, "For whom, from what? Canada's Arctic policy and the narrowing of human security".

16 EKOS Research Associates, 2011, 35.

17 Ibid, 48.

recent years. Some Southern environmentalists see development in the Arctic as such an unmitigated evil that it cannot be conducted in any form or under any circumstances – thus the position by some to impose bans and moratoriums, for example on oil drilling, commercial fishing, or uranium mining.[18] While no serious observer or stakeholder will deny the need for environmental regulation, it is regrettable that some environmentalists have adopted extreme positions when it clearly compromises the ability of Northerners to make progress towards economic self-sufficiency and autonomy.

Politically, the 2013–15 Canadian Arctic Council Chairmanship became a lightning rod for many environmentalists due to its theme of "Development for the People of the North", which many saw as a thinly veiled threat to promote non-renewable resource development.[19] But the Arctic Council – the preeminent international forum for the region, established in 1996 and comprised of the eight Arctic states as members, six indigenous organizations as Permanent Participants, and several state and non-state Observers – has always had a mandate for both environmental protection and sustainable development. There has been dissonance in the fact that environmentalists saw the historic focus on environmental protection as a reason to continue that focus; Canada, under the Harper Conservative government, instead saw an opportunity to provide balance to the Arctic Council's activities. The key outcome has been the establishment of an Arctic Economic Council (AEC) in January 2014, a circumpolar business forum established consensually by all members of the Arctic Council to foster business development, engage in deeper circumpolar cooperation, and provide a business perspective to the work of the Arctic Council.[20] However many have viewed the AEC suspiciously, worried it provides corporate interests with preferential access to national governments[21] and even "sets the frame for a new era of exploitation of the Arctic".[22] These same critics have also alternately accused the AEC of causing confusion by adopting a mandate that

18 See Greenpeace (N.D.), *Save the Arctic*. Accessed from https://www.savethearctic.org/, March 31, 2015.

19 See for example Quaile, Irene, "Arctic Economic Council – and the Environment?" *Eye on the Arctic*. (September 2, 2014). Accessed from [http://www.rcinet.ca/eye-on-the-arctic/2014/09/02/ice-blog-arctic-economic-council-and-the-environment/] April 3, 2015; and Greaves, Will, "When the Ice is Gone," in *OpenCanada.Org* (Canadian International Council: Ontario, December 11, 2013).

20 Arctic Council (website), Arctic Economic Council, (January 28, 2014). Accessed from http://www.arctic-council.org/index.php/en/arctic-economic-council, March 31, 2015.

21 Axworthy, L. and M. Simon, "Is Canada Undermining the Arctic Council?" in *Globe and Mail* (Toronto, March 4 2015).

22 Neil Hamilton, as quoted in Quaile, "Arctic Economic Council – and the Environment?".

"is virtually the same as that of the Arctic Council"[23] and "negating its prime function" of protecting the environment.[24] Needless to say, the very idea of business development in the Arctic provokes disquiet among many.

The United States, which took over the Arctic Council Chairmanship in April 2015, initially favoured a return to the status quo of prioritizing environmental protection and renewing the Council's focus on climate change, consistent with the values and objectives of the Obama Administration.[25] However it very soon confronted opposition from stakeholders in Alaska, who supported the work of the Arctic Economic Council and prioritized economic development over climate change mitigation. Alaska Arctic Policy Commission Co-Chairs Bob Herron and Lesil McGuire, for example, wrote in an open letter to US Special Representative to the Arctic Admiral Robert Papp Jr. and Ambassador David Balton that they were "very concerned that our number one priority, jobs and economic opportunity for Arctic residents, is being ignored" and that "Alaskans' voices in this matter of promoting resource and economic development are being overlooked".[26]

Similarly, Alaskan Senator Lisa Murkowski, questioning Papp on his policy priorities at a Senate Energy Committee hearing, declared that: "an economy that allows for the people of the North to not only exist but to thrive is critical".[27] The Alaskan Senate even made the unprecedented move of passing a resolution articulating support for, and recommendations to, the Arctic Economic Council, over which it has no authority.[28]

While the American State Department was initially lukewarm to the idea of the Arctic Economic Council in particular, and to economic security in general, it has seemed to evolve to respond to the Alaskan concerns: to whit, "improving economic and living conditions" in the Arctic has become a more prominent feature and one of three pillars of its Chairmanship agenda.

23 Axworthy and Simon, "Is Canada Undermining the Arctic Council?".

24 Neil Hamilton, as quoted in Quaile, "Arctic Economic Council – and the Environment?".

25 Papp, Robert, Remarks made at "Passing the Arctic Council Torch", event held in Washington D.C., September 30, 2014. Center for Strategic and International Studies.

26 Herron, Bob and Lesil McGuire, "An Open Letter to Admiral Papp and Ambassador Balton," The Bristol Bay Times, October 17, 2014. Retrieved from http://www.thebristolbaytimes.com/article/1442an_open_letter_to_adm_papp_and_ambassador, July 13, 2015.

27 Bennett, Mia, "Senate Energy Committee Exposes Irony of Arctic Opportunities," Eye on the Arctic, Radio Canada International: Montreal, (March 9, 2015). Retrieved from http://www.rcinet.ca/eye-on-the-arctic/2015/03/09/blog-senate-energy-committee-hearing-exposes irony of arctic opportunities/, July 13, 2015.

28 Alaska State Legislature, 2015. ARCTIC ECONOMIC COUNCIL: Bill SJR 16, April 2, 2015. http://www.legis.state.ak.us/basis/get_bill.asp?session=29&bill=SJR016.

In fact, the Arctic Council is generally seen as having found a good balance between the two ideals of environmental protection and sustainable development – or rather, it seeks balance between the two, without privileging one over the other. But some environmentalists remain unimpressed, wondering if development can be sustainable in the Arctic.

Can Development be Sustainable?

Of course, promoting sustainable development in the Arctic has begged the question of whether non-renewable resource extraction, from oil and gas to iron and nickel, can ever be considered sustainable. When environmentalists criticize development in the Arctic, it is almost always non-renewable resource extraction, in particular oil and gas drilling and mining, though fisheries and forestry can also be subject to criticism. The Arctic is described as a particularly vulnerable ecosystem, where slow growth rates and extreme weather conditions make it difficult for flora and fauna to adapt quickly to anthropogenic disruptions; where climate change is already wreaking havoc on growing and living conditions; where many animal migratory routes cover extraordinarily long distances that can be compromised by even isolated activities along its path; and where humans have limited capacity to mitigate and react to spills and pollution.

At the same time, options for economic development in the underdeveloped (non-Nordic) regions of the Circumpolar North that are not resource-based are very limited.[29] The resource sector comprises well over a third of the economy in the region encompassing Alaska, Yukon, Northwest Territories, Nunavut, Greenland and northern Russia, and is even more significant that the ubiquitous public sector.

Tourism in the Arctic – which at any rate is not always sustainable – attracts a very niche audience and is generally expensive, limiting market opportunities. The labour force is relatively unskilled, and despite high unemployment, is poorly matched to the northern jobs market. Infrastructure is limited and expensive, and inhibits cost-effective transport of goods to market. Indeed the costs for almost every input in the Arctic is more expensive than in other markets. Resource development thus marks the most likely – and sometimes the only – viable opportunity to create jobs, raise public revenues, and create some economic security for Northerners.

29 See Table 4.1.

TABLE 4.1 *Distribution of gross regional product in arctic regions, 2005 (%)*

	USA	Canada	Finland	Iceland	Norway	Russia	Sweden	Denmark	Arctic	Non-Nordic incl. Greenland
Fishing	6	0	0.1	4.7	5	0.6	0	10.5	3.36	4.3
Mining and petroleum	33.2	27.7	0.8	0.1	1	56.9	7.5	3.2	16.3	30.3
Other resources	0.1	0.4	4.7	1.4	0.9	1.3	3	2.4	1.8	1.1
Resource processing	2	0	13.3	4.8	5.2	4.4	7.2	5.8	5.3	3.1
Construction	5.4	8	6.8	9.6	6.9	5	5.4	7.2	6.78	6.4
Public sector	26.9	28.7	24.8	23.8	40.5	9.1	32.6	29.9	27	23.7
Other services	31.3	34.8	37.7	50.1	37.4	22.1	36.6	38.9	36.1	31.8
Remainder	0.5	0.4	11.8	5.5	3.1	0.6	7.7	2.1	4	0.9

SOURCE: HUSKEY, MÄENPÄÄ AND PELYASOV, "ECONOMIC SYSTEMS," 151.

Still, many resource development projects have had a terrible social and environmental impact in the North, with jobs and profits flowing south to negligible economic benefit to Northerners. As a result, many Northerners, especially indigenous inhabitants, continue to be suspicious and even hostile to prospects for greater resource development, as they have often borne all of the risks and received none of the benefits. In those cases, resource development has clearly compromised human security.

However evolving regulative and legislative improvements have made the environmental impact of resource development less deplorable, and new governance arrangements, such as the proliferation of Impact and Benefit Agreements (IBAs) in Canada, mean local communities, including indigenous ones, have much to gain from new projects. Canada's legal "duty to consult" Aboriginal stakeholders since 2008 and Norway's 2005 Finnmark Act also provide some ability to reject resource developments in traditional territories.

Profits do not guarantee economic security and have the potential to compromise social stability. But for many Northerners, the only options are to focus on improving the economic, social and environmental impacts of resource development or continue to depend on transfers from central governments to support minimum standards of living – a state of affairs which many blame for the high levels of unemployment, addictions and family break-down. The rejection of a wage economy and a return to traditional lifestyles is no longer possible nor, for many, desirable at a societal level.

Concern over the outsized role of the public sector and the economic dependence on federal transfers in many parts of the Arctic are also contributing to greater acceptance, and indeed promotion of resource development, where revenues and profits contribute to northern communities, economies and governments. Some stakeholders in Greenland for example have heralded the potential of an offshore oil and gas boom – as well as mineral extraction from rare earths to uranium – as a means to achieve full independence from Denmark, which currently provides more than US$11,000-capita in annual transfers. The Government of Nunavut, which is seeking devolution of governing authorities that have already been granted to Yukon and NWT, receives an astonishing CAN$40,352/capita in federal transfers to the territorial government,[30] exclusive of federal spending from other ministries. First Nation reserves across Northern Canada receive up to 95% of their revenue from federal transfers.[31] It is difficult to proclaim or practice self-determination under these circumstances.

Resource development is the most obvious solution to the challenge of generating alternative sources of revenue. Efforts towards this end have been ongoing across the Circumpolar North where traditional occupancy has resulted in legal rights to manage and benefit from land use. However finding balance and consensus on the question and scope of resource development has been difficult to obtain, as the cases of Alaska, northern Canada and Greenland demonstrate.

Case Studies

Alaska

One of the earliest comprehensive efforts at northern economic self-sufficiency came in 1971, when the Alaska Native Claims Settlement Act (ANCSA) was enacted. The objective of ANCSA was to settle Aboriginal land claims in the State, spurred by the granting of statehood to Alaska in 1959 and the subsequent transfer of over 100 million acres of federally owned lands to the State; the

30 Finance Canada. Federal Support to Provinces and territories. Accessed from [http://www.fin.gc.ca/fedprov/mtp-eng.asp#Nunavut] on June 3, 2015.

31 Campbell, Rob, "Spoken Remarks", *Saskatchewan First Nations Economic Development Annual Forum*, September 18, 2013, Saskatoon SK.

discovery of oil at Prudhoe Bay in the 1960s; and the growing political engagement and capacity of Alaskan Native activists.[32]

ANCSA came into law in December 1971, and legislated the transfer of 44 million acres of land, or about 10% of Alaska, and a monetary payments totaling $962.5 million. This was transferred to twelve regional and 200 village corporations established under ANCSA, with any living person with at least one-quarter Alaskan blood eligible to be a shareholder in either or both a regional and village corporation.[33] A thirteenth regional corporation was also established for non-resident Alaskan Natives.

The Settlement brought unprecedented economic and political power to Alaska Natives and promised greater independence and prosperity. Although many shortcomings to the legislation were identified, including criticism of the corporate structuring, there was general consensus that ANCSA represented the best deal Alaska Natives were likely to get; as Inupiat Charlie Edwardsen Jr., drawing comparisons between Native corporations to innovations required by an Eskimo whaling crew, declared at the time: "the Eskimo has a new harpoon".[34]

As might be expected, Native corporations have had a mixed history in Alaska. It transformed traditional tribal areas into corporate properties, disrupting traditional land management practices and imposing an often incongruent capitalistic economic system on Alaskan Native communities.[35] It has not solved the problems of poverty, addictions, health and education, indicators of which are still poorer for Alaskan Natives than for other Alaskans.

However the ANCSA legacy has also provided an incredible success story. In 2011, for example, Alaska Native Corporations occupied eight spots of the top ten Alaska businesses and generated US$11.89 billion in revenues. Some 62.4% of the 25,138 jobs provided by the 'Top49' Alaskan businesses, as identified by Alaska Business Monthly, were provided by ANCSA businesses.

Many of these revenues have arisen from non-renewable resource extraction, and ANCSA businesses have entered into partnerships with large multinational corporations. Environmental security has not taken precedence over economic security as a principle for development amongst Alaskan Natives.

32 See Anders, Gary, "The Role of Alaska Native Corporations in the Development of Alaska," in *Development and Change*, 14 (1983): 555–575.

33 See Summit, Ben, "The Alaska Native Claims Settlement Act (ANCSA): Friend or Foe in the Struggle to Recover Alaska Native Heritage," in *Thomas M. Cooley Law Review* 14 (1997): 607–632.

34 As quoted in Huhndorf, Roy M. and Shari M. Huhndorf, "Alaska Native Politics since the Alaska Native Claims Settlement Act," in *The South Atlantic Quarterly* 110:2 (2011): 385–401.

35 Ibid.

Canada

Canada has been progressively devolving governance rights and responsibilities to First Nations, Inuit and territorial governments over the past four decades. This has set a stage in which Aboriginal and northern communities have significant roles in decisions about whether large resource development projects go forward – or increasingly, how the projects go forward.

Since the 1990s, the establishment of Impact and Benefit Agreements (IBAs) have become commonplace to define the frameworks and obligations under which resource development may occur on or adjacent to traditional indigenous territory. IBAs are negotiated, private agreements that serve to document in a contractual form the benefits that a local community can expect from the development of a local resource in exchange for its support and cooperation. As of 2012, there were more than 180 such agreements in Canada. They have become de facto, if not de jure, requirements for resource development in the Canadian North.

Common provisions in IBAs include environmental impact assessment, mitigation and remediation clauses – although federal and provincial/territorial legislation also requires these; indigenous employment quotas or targets; local training programming; social programming and/or community investment in e.g. roadway infrastructure, educational facilities, recreational facilities; revenue sharing; and preferential access to sub-contracts.

IBAs have quickly become popular in Canada because they have afforded a degree of autonomy and self-determination that has previously been unavailable due to overreliance on federal funding for community investments. They allow those communities that are most impacted by resource development to benefit directly from it, and lend legitimacy to Aboriginal land rights by providing space in which Aboriginal communities negotiate directly with industry as opposed to via the federal government. On the economic side, these agreements can spur economic development and improve training and employment prospects, and provide stability and predictability for corporations engaging in risky and expensive extractive projects.

However, like the ANCSA corporations, their success has been mixed. IBAs often contain confidentiality clauses, or explicit requirements for public support, and can stymie community debate or dissent, in particular over environmental impacts of development. Because they are private deals, there is a lack of comprehensive regulatory oversight and there is an argument to be made that they allow the state to vacate its responsibilities by shifting some of the burden of social and community programming onto industry. Finally, reliance on large scale resource development has a long history of producing rentierism and the associated poor governance.

There is no guarantee that economic success from resource development will translate into social development, as the example of Bigstone Cree Nation demonstrates.[36] And not all communities are interested in resource development, however great the economic incentive, as the unanimous rejection for environmental reasons by northern British Columbia's Lax Kw'alaams eligible voters of a $1-billion cash offer from Pacific NorthWest LNG to export liquefied natural gas through their territory demonstrated.[37] However both of these cases appear to be exceptions. Future trends look far more likely to focus on improving IBA processes and First Nations societal benefit from resource development than on rejecting them.

Greenland

Greenland achieved Home Rule status in 1979, thereby gaining control over most domestic functions of government as well as establishing a Greenlandic Parliament (the Landsting, or Inatsisartut).[38] Greenland's autonomy was further extended in June 2009, when it assumed Self-Rule. This occurred following a referendum in which over 75% of Greenlanders voted to have greater independence from Denmark, a move that was later approved in the Danish Parliament.

Greenland's Self Rule Act recognizes that the people of Greenland are a people under international law with the right to self-determination. It further devolved responsibility from Denmark to Greenland over judicial affairs and established a new formula by which Greenland's subsidy would be reduced as its mineral and hydrocarbon revenues increased (*Act on Greenland Self-Government*, 2009). The implication is that if enough revenues are generated by resource exploitation, Greenland could become independent.

Greenland has had successive democratically elected, primarily Inuit governments expressing support to exploiting, as sustainably as possible, the island's hydrocarbon and mineral resources in order to reduce its dependence on Denmark. However many others have been opposed to this economic path,

36 MacMahon, Tamsin, "Bigstone's Lost Opportunity," Maclean's, Maclean's (Ontario), November 24, 2014.

37 Jang, 2015.

38 Responsibilities that were eventually assumed by the Greenland Home Rule included internal administration, taxation, social welfare, education, cultural affairs, environmental and natural resource management, health services and housing. Self Rule extended responsibility over criminal, legal and judicial areas, but excluded the Constitution, foreign policy, monetary policy and exchange rates, defense and security policy, the Supreme Court, and nationality.

and the poor results of offshore oil drilling in the past four years have quelled optimism that independence is on the horizon.

Culturally, though, a shift is apparent. Greenlandic stakeholders increasingly see resource exploitation as a strategy for self-determination rather than an externally imposed burden with the primary consequence of environmental degradation.

Finding Consensus

Two clear, if perhaps incompatible, lines of argument have emerged in northern indigenous circles in the past decade. The first is that development should only transpire if it is sustainable and environmentally sensitive, linked to conceptions of indigeneity as representing a particular connection and respect for the land and the natural world. The second is that resource development is necessary in order to achieve material well-being and economic self-sufficiency.

One of the best articulations of the intersection of these often competing objectives – sustainability and development – is found in the May 2011 *Circumpolar Inuit Declaration on Resource Development Principles*. It came at a time when the debate over Greenlandic resource development was particularly divisive and public, for example between Greenland Prime Minister Kuupik Kleist and ICC President Aqqaluk Lynge,[39] and a normative framework to guide future activities was seen as desirable. The document is conservative, prioritizing environmental protection over improving living standards and well-being in its Section 9 hierarchy of priorities. And strictly speaking, it is contradictory, accepting non-renewable resource extraction including offshore oil and gas, but insisting upon sustainability and "not exacerbat[ing] the climate change-related stresses on the survival of Arctic wildlife".

What seems clear is that greater self-determination and governance are opening up opportunities for Arctic indigenous peoples to benefit from resource development in ways that have not been possible before. This makes the position of objecting across the board to resource development increasingly untenable. The struggle to find balance between development and sustainability, and between environmental and economic security, is universal, and the Arctic is not immune.

39 George, Jane, "Inuit Leaders at Odds over Oil and Gas Emissions," in *Nunatsiaq News*, December 13, 2009. Accessed from http://www.nunatsiaqonline.ca/stories/article/86455_inuit_leaders_at_odds_over_oil_and_gas_emissions, June 1, 2015.

Conclusions

Scholarly analyses of human security in the Arctic have traditionally focused on environmental security. Economic security has been comparatively ill-defined and applied, despite the prevalence of disparate living conditions and poorer health outcomes in the Arctic as a result of poverty, unemployment, food insecurity and homelessness.

If we accept that economic conditions in the Circumpolar North are as worthy of securitization as the environment, there is a responsibility to also conceive and advocate for economic development activities. In many cases, the opposite has occurred, with the very idea of economic development in the Arctic being viewed with suspicion and contempt by some environmentalists from the South.

Such judgment is flawed. Those who advocate for environmental protection above all else must be able to offer alternative means to addressing economic insecurity in the Arctic. But options for significant revenue generation separate from large scale resource exploitation are negligible. Unable to govern under those tenets, northern sub-national governments and indigenous nations are now tasked with finding balance between environmental and economic security within their own communities. This is a challenging task and consensus will be difficult to obtain as indigenous societies rapidly transition from a subsistence to a capitalist economic system. But not appreciating that economic security is just as important to human well-being in the Arctic as environmental security is an indulgence that the North can no longer afford.

CHAPTER 5

Threats to Human Security Imposed on the Ainu in Biratori, Hokkaido, Japan

*Hiroshi Maruyama**

Abstract

In recent decades, the livelihood of indigenous peoples across the world has been affected by the exploitation of nature, more so than by earlier assimilation policies. The Ainu in Japan are no exception. In March of 1997, the Sapporo District Court ruled against the construction of the Nibutani Dam on the basis that the Ainu have the right to enjoy their own culture as an indigenous people in Hokkaido, and that the construction is illegal because the authorities did not take into consideration how much of an impact it would have on Ainu culture. However, the Nibutani Dam was almost completed at that time, so, in the public interest, the Court permitted the dam to operate. Despite the ruling on the Nibutani Dam, the construction of another dam named the Biratori Dam is now underway in the heart of Ainu territory in Biratori, home to a higher percentage of Ainu than any other area. Ainu culture is shaped by a history of hunting, gathering, and fishing in harmony with nature, and the treatment of all things in nature as gods. Ainu culture and identity are therefore essentially connected to the land and their way of life. In other words, Ainu cultural identity is especially vulnerable to environmental degradation. In order to protect and empower the Ainu, this chapter attempts to discuss threats to the human security of the Ainu in Biratori, specifically the threats to the community security or the security of cultural identity that are caused by the construction of the Biratori Dam as well as the Nibutani Dam on the same Saru River System.

Introduction

Modernization, which brought about tremendous increases in human productivity, goes hand in hand with a centrally administered state that promotes a policy of "one nation, one people and one language". As a consequence, ethnic minorities such as indigenous peoples have been coercively assimilated into

* Hiroshi Maruyama, Professor Emeritus, Muroran Institute of Technology in Japan and Guest Professor at the Hugo Valentin Centre, Uppsala University.

 | DOI 10.1163/9789004314399_007

mainstream society in many countries. In Japan, the Ainu were deprived of their lands, culture and language under the colonization and modernization of Hokkaido and other northern islands, including Sakhalin and the Kuril Islands. After WWII, progress was made by the United Nations in the way of establishing core human rights, which resulted in the protection of indigenous peoples' rights, or indigenous rights, as defined by the Human Rights Committee:

> The Human Rights Committee (HRC), in interpreting article 27 of the International Covenant on Civil and Political Rights (ICCPR), has expressed the positive duties on States to protect indigenous peoples' cultural rights, including their rights in relation to their lands, territories and resources as well as in relation to their traditional activities, the need to include indigenous peoples in decisions affecting them, the requirement to interpret the right to culture consistently with the right to self-determination in the context of indigenous peoples' issues.[1]

Furthermore, in its general comment No. 21 on the right of everyone to take part in cultural life, the Committee on Economic, Social and Cultural Rights for the International Covenant on Economic, Social and Cultural Rights (ICESCR) recognizes:

> the collective element of indigenous peoples' right to culture, noting that "the strong communal dimension of indigenous peoples' cultural life is indispensable to their existence, well-being and full development, and includes the right to lands, territories and resources which they traditionally owned, occupied or otherwise used or acquired".[2]

In recent decades, the exploitation of nature caused by the rapid advancement of globalization, including deforestation, mining and damming, has seriously affected the livelihood and violated the rights of indigenous peoples around the world. Even if these peoples live in industrialized countries that formally recognize indigenous rights to some extent, in accordance with international human rights instruments, they still struggle to maintain, develop and revitalize

1 Expert Mechanism on the Rights of Indigenous Peoples: Study on the role of languages and culture in the promotion and protection of the rights and identity of indigenous peoples. UN Human Rights Council Expert Mechanism on the Rights of Indigenous Peoples, Fifth Session, 9–13 July 2012, 5. Accessed June 10 2015, http://daccess-dds-ny.un.org/doc/UNDOC/GEN/G12/160/52/PDF/G1216052.pdf?OpenElemen.

2 Ibid, 5.

their own culture. For instance, in the northern part of Alaska near the Canadian border, the extraction of oil has put the Arctic National Wildlife Refuge at risk, a critical habitat for the migratory Porcupine caribou herd. The caribou is a principal resource of subsistence for indigenous peoples such as the Inupiat and the Gwichi'in.[3] As another example of such exploitation, in Gallok, on the outskirts of Jokkmokk, Sweden, the British company Beowulf Mining is exploring the opportunity to mining iron ore. A Sámi reindeer herder who is concerned about the potential negative impact of the mining on his livelihood has said the following to a BBC correspondent:

> In the summer time we're with the reindeer up in the mountains but in the winter we need to go down to the forest. The reindeer need to find food in nature so they need a big area to graze. We take many things from the reindeer into our culture so I think if reindeer herding dies then our culture also dies.[4]

The Ainu in Japan are also under a similar threat of exploitation. In March of 1997, as a result of three Ainu landowners' eight-year court battle against the authorities over the expropriation of their lands for the construction of the Nibutani Dam, the right to enjoy their own culture in the ruling of the Sapporo District Court was legally recognized. This was the first time that such a case was won in the history of Japan. At the same time, the Nibutani Dam itself, which was almost completed before the ruling, was left alone, though the Ainu plaintiffs as well as the experts of Ainu studies testified that Ainu culture in the Saru River System Catchment Area was endangered by the construction of the Nibutani Dam. Two months later, the Japanese government finally replaced the Hokkaido Former Aborigines Protection Act, which represented the attitudes of colonization by Japan in the name of modernization, with the Ainu Culture Promotion Act (CPA). However, the indigenous rights of the Ainu are not guaranteed by the CPA. It can therefore be argued that the government enacted the CPA in order to repeal the above-mentioned ruling. In June of 2008, the government recognized the Ainu as an indigenous people in the northern part of the Japanese archipelago and its surroundings, including Hokkaido, in the wake of its voting in favor of the 2007 United Nations Declaration on the Rights of Indigenous Peoples (UNDRIP). Nevertheless, the

3 Nuttall, Mark, "Alaska's Arctic National Wildlife Refuge Debate," in *Indigenous Affairs* 2–3 (2006): 8. Accessed March 24 2015, http://www.iwgia.org/iwgia_files_publications_files/IA_2-3-06.pdf.

4 BBC, 30 July 2014.

CPA still remains intact as of December of 2015. As a result, the Biratori Dam is being built today on the upper reaches of the Saru River System, where the Nibutani Dam was also built, on the grounds that the authorities must at least take into consideration the preservation, transmission and promotion of Ainu culture. Additionally the specifications of the Nibutani Dam are enormous; the dam's height is 35 meters and the crest's length is 550 meters, with an affected catchment area of 1,215 square kilometers. In comparison, the Biratori Dam has a height of 56.5 metres and the crest length is 600 metres. It is clear simply by looking at these numbers that the colonization of Hokkaido still continues.

In order to protect and empower the Ainu in their pursuit of decolonization, this chapter attempts to shed light on how the exploitation of nature in the name of development affects Ainu culture in terms of threatening human security, more specifically the security of cultural identity for the Ainu in the Saru River System Catchment Area in Biratori. The catchment area, which has the above-mentioned two dams (the Nibutani Dam and the Biratori Dam) is well-known as the home of Ainu culture given its dense population of the Ainu. At present, around 20% of the population in Biratori (1,100 residents) descend from the Ainu.[5] In addition, the latest official figure of the Ainu population in Hokkaido as a whole is 16,786 (based on self-identification).[6]

In essence, human security is meant "to protect people against a broad range of threats to individuals and communities and, further, to empower them to act on their own behalf."[7] The broad range of threats corresponds to the seven categorized components of human security: economic, environmental, personal, communal (e.g., cultural identity) and political security, along with security of food and health.[8] A guiding principle of the human security approach "requires understanding the particular threats experienced by particular groups of people, as well as the participation of those people in the analysis process."[9] Therefore, in order to understand the threats faced by the Ainu, it is

5 No city in Hokkaido discloses the official figures for the Ainu population in its territories. In November of 2014, however, the municipality told me by phone that approximately 1,100 of the total population in Biratori Town are descendants of the Ainu.

6 The Hokkaido Prefectural Government has carried out a questionnaire survey on the actual conditions of life for the Ainu every seven years since 1972. The latest survey was done in 2013. The figure is far from the reality.

7 Commission on Human Security, "Outline of the Report of the Commission on Human Security", 2003, 2. Accessed May 24, 2015, http://www.icbjapan.org/humansecurity_outline.pdf.

8 UNDP, "A Thematic Guidance Note for Regional and National Human Development Report Teams," 2. Accessed March 24, 2015, http://hdr.undp.org/sites/default/files/human_security_guidance_note_r-nhdrs.pdf.

9 Ibid, 2.

important to first understand the culture itself. In this chapter, Ainu culture and its background are described through the testimony of experts on Ainu studies and the Ainu plaintiffs themselves in the above-mentioned Nibutani Dam Case. Secondly, Ainu culture and its heritage in the predetermined area of the Biratori Dam, and the potential loss of Ainu culture caused by the construction, are discussed with reference to research that some local Ainu residents have been involved in. Finally, an account of the lack of security of the Ainu in Biratori is used as a means of supporting the pursuit of decolonization of the Ainu island, Hokkaido, in the name of human security.

Ainu Culture and Its Background Information as Revealed in Court Testimony in the Nibutani Dam Case

In March of 1997, the Sapporo District Court made the following ruling on the Nibutani Dam Case:

> The state should have paid the maximum attention to culture of the Ainu, a minority and indigenous people. However, it failed to judge whether or not benefits from the construction of the Nibutani Dam exceed costs caused by the construction, including the violation of the Ainu right to enjoy their own culture, for the expropriation of Ainu lands for the construction. As a consequence, the state wrongfully dismissed such Ainu right, which should be attached the greatest importance to, and went ahead with the construction. The expropriation of Ainu lands was, therefore, illegal.[10]

At the same time, the court legitimized the construction of the Nibutani Dam on the pretext that the Nibutani Dam was already completed before the ruling and, consequently, the abolition did not accord with public interest concerns. The ruling was able to account for what was stated in court by the three experts of Ainu studies, in addition to the two Ainu plaintiffs, Kayano Shigeru and Kaizawa Koichi (who succeeded his father Tadashi as the plaintiff after his death). The experts consulted in this case were: Ohtsuka Kazuyoshi, then Professor of Ethnology at the National Museum of Ethnology; Tabata Hiroshi, then Professor of History at Hokkaido University of Education; and Aiuchi Toshikazu, then Professor of Politics and International Human Rights Studies

10 Nibutani Damu Saiban Hanketsubun [Judgement Document on the Nibutani Dam Case], Accessed December 10, 2015, http://www.geocities.co.jp/HeartLand-Suzuran/5596/.

at Hokkaido University of Education. Ethnology, history, politics and international human rights studies were combined in the ruling that recognized the right of the Ainu to enjoy their culture as an indigenous people, as mentioned above. In addition, their statements substantiated the legitimacy of the Ainu plaintiffs' claims for the protection of Ainu culture and the environment, as shown below.

Before appearing in court as the first witness among the Ainu plaintiffs in May and July of 1995, Ohtsuka Kazuyoshi made a statement to the court. The statement began with an emphasis on Nibutani's significance for Ainu culture as follows:

> Nibutani in Biratori Town is a community with the highest proportion of Ainu residents in Hokkaido and consequently, Ainu traditional culture is well preserved and transmitted from generation to generation. The Saru River System Catchment Area, including Nibutani, has attracted many researchers, including international ones, for the centre of the field work of Ainu studies since the 1870s. It is no exaggeration to say that Nibutani is the birthplace of Ainu studies. Since around the 1970s, a political campaign for the restoration of Ainu ethnic rights and the improvement in their status by the Ainu Association of Hokkaido and a cultural movement for the revitalisation of Ainu culture by the Ainu themselves in every corner of Hokkaido have emerged. The Nibutani Resource Centre for Ainu Culture, which was established by Kaizawa Tadashi and Kayano Shigeru for the first time in Ainu history, played a significant role in leading the revitalisation of Ainu culture. In the 1980s and 90s, Nibutani was also a place for cultural exchange between the Ainu and other peoples in Japan and the world. Nibutani hosted the World Council of Indigenous Peoples in 1989 and the Nibutani Forum in 1993, led by Kaizawa Koichi.[11]

Ohtsuka moved on to identify the core of Ainu culture in Nibutani and the impact of the construction of the Nibutani Dam on Ainu culture as follows:

> The Saru River and its surroundings such as topography, air and wind have nurtured rich oral epics. In general, the connection between culture and nature ensures sustainability of indigenous culture. The Ainu have been dispossessed of their right to fish salmon since the colonization of

11 Ohtsuka, Kazuyoshi, "Chinjutsusho [Letter of Representation]," In *Nibutani Dam Saiban no Kiroku* [*Documentation of the Nibutani Dam Case*], ed. Kayano, Shigeru and Tanaka Hiroshi (Tokyo: Sanseido, 1999): 335–343.

> Hokkaido by Japan in the late 19th century. As a result, Ainu culture, in relation to salmon, including words offered to salmon as prayers, skills necessary for the production of tools for rituals of harvesting salmon and the spiritual world of the Ainu, was distorted or lost. Each community where the Ainu had lived had its own common land called *Iwor*, which includes places to produce everything for their life, cemeteries to pray, and mountains and rivers in relation to mythical transmissions. *Iwor*, or Ainu traditional livelihood zones, are worthy not only to be considered as cultural heritage from the viewpoint of history, but also to be preserved for the sustainable development of Ainu culture in the future. Three historical remains called *Chashi*, which are interpreted to be fortifications, were destroyed by the construction of the Nibutani Dam, though it was not clear how those *Chashi* were built. Also, the place for Ainu launching ceremony called *Chipsanke*, to celebrate the creation of a new canoe, was forcibly changed to an alternative place by the construction of the Nibutani Dam, though the original place is of great significance.[12]

Kayano Shigeru testified in court as a plaintiff twice: once in December of 1995 and again the following February. The main points of his testimony are as follows:

> In my childhood, my father was arrested on suspicion of "poaching" salmon for us. Ethnic Japanese, who came to Hokkaido later than the Ainu, have deprived the Ainu of salmon, the principal food for the Ainu, by forcing Japanese regulations onto the Ainu, who did not read Japanese. The Ainu in our community utilised salmon not only for food, but also clothing and shoes. The construction of the Nibutani Dam is likely to have negative impacts on the survival of salmon in the Saru River System even if a fish ladder is created. The construction will also inundate a lot of mountain streams where edible wild plants have been harvested by the Ainu. *Chipsanke*, a launching ceremony which gives the Ainu an opportunity to make a tool for rituals called *Inau*, and to make millet dumplings called *Inakibi*, will disappear in the future due to the construction of the Nibutani Dam. There are three *Chinomisir*, sacred place for the Ainu in Nibutani, of which two were destroyed by the construction. The same is true with historical remains called *Chashi*. Japan should recognise the

12 Ohtsuka, "Chinjutsusho [Letter of Representation]," 340–343.

> Ainu as an indigenous people and return the right to fish salmon to the Ainu.[13]

Kaizawa Koichi complemented Kayano's testimony, as another plaintiff on behalf of his late father, with the following statement in December of 1995:

> Originally, the Ainu were a hunting people, so that every aspect of topography has its own meaning, while ethnic Japanese have levelled the land for fields or paddy fields as an agricultural people. The construction of the Nibutani Dam modifies such topography and damages natural resources that are closely linked to Ainu culture. The reason why my father continued a court battle against the expropriation of his land conducted by the authorities until his death is that the Japanese government had never listened to voices of the Ainu about anything affecting them. The least Japan can do is to recognise the Ainu as an indigenous people and to take responsibility for the losses the Ainu have suffered as a result of the construction of the Nibutani Dam.[14]

In addition, Tabata Hiroshi testified in support of the Ainu plaintiffs that the Ainu have been proven to be the indigenous people of Hokkaido, and that they had been marginalized in the course of colonization in the name of development.[15] Aiuchi Toshikazu provided additional evidence in support of the Ainu plaintiffs' testimony as the last witness. Japan as well as China and Bangladesh keep insisting that a universal definition of indigenous peoples is imperative for the establishment of the UNDRIP. The other countries, however, recognise that no universal definition of indigenous peoples is able to represent the diversity of their historical backgrounds, cultures and languages. In Australia, the

13 Kayano, Shigeru, "Honnin Chosho [Plaintiff Examination Record]," In *Nibutani Dam Saiban no Kiroku [Documentation of the Nibutani Dam Case]*, ed. Kayano, Shigeru and Tanaka Hiroshi (Tokyo: Sanseido, 1999): 438–481.

14 Kaizawa, Tadashi, "Kensetsusho niokeru Ikenchinjutsu [Letter of Representation at the Ministry of Construction]," In *Nibutani Dam Saiban no Kiroku [Documentation of the Nibutani Dam Case]*, ed. Kayano, Shigeru and Tanaka Hiroshi, (Tokyo: Sanseido, 1999): 173–183.; Kaizawa, Tadashi, "Shuyo Iinkai niokeru Chinjutsu [Letter of Representation at the Land Expropriation Committee in Hokkaido]," In *Nibutani Dam Saiban no Kiroku [Documentation of the Nibutani Dam Case]*, ed. Kayano, Shigeru and Tanaka Hiroshi (Tokyo: Sanseido, 1999), 487.

15 Tabata, Hiroshi, "Shonin Chosho [Witness Examination Record]," In *Nibutani Dam Saiban no Kiroku [Documentation ofthe Nibutani Dam Case]*, ed. Kayano, Shigeru and Tanaka Hiroshi (Tokyo: Sanseido, 1999): 369–406.

Aborigines' right to land came into effect. In Canada, the government has declared that the Inuit will have the right to self-determination in Nunavut in 1999. Japan, however, has yet to recognise the Ainu as an indigenous people.[16]

The Potential Loss of Ainu Culture by the Construction of Dams on the Saru River System

In 1971, the Biratori Dam was originally planned along with the Nibutani Dam to supply water for the future industrial development in the neighbouring city of Tomakomai. In 1978, the purpose for the construction of those dams was changed behind closed doors, and instead they were to focus on flood control, because the planned industrial development had collapsed.[17] The year 1997 gave rise to the following three historical events that could have led to a watershed for the Ainu plaintiffs who struggled for the protection of Ainu culture and the environment in the Nibutani Dam Case: (1) The River Act was revised to some extent in terms of allowing local residents to participate in the decision-making process; (2) The CPA replaced the notorious Hokkaido Former Aborigines Protection Act of 1899; and (3) The court of the controversial Nibutani Dam Case ruled in favour of the Ainu, legally enforcing their cultural rights. In 1999, the Saru River Committee was established in an attempt to represent the opinions of the local residents in the planning of the Biratori Dam in accordance with the revised River Act. However, there was no option to abandon the Biratori Dam project. In 2002, the Saru River Committee devised a new plan for the Biratori Dam such that the preservation, transmission and promotion of Ainu culture was to be taken into consideration. In order to satisfy this requirement, a research project for environmental and cultural assessment was launched in 2003.

The municipality of Biratori was commissioned to carry out the research project at the nation's expense in preparation for the construction of the Biratori Dam by the Hokkaido Regional Development Bureau, which was responsible for the construction of the Nibutani Dam and the Biratori Dam as a local branch of the Ministry of Land, Infrastructure, Transport and Tourism.

16 Aiuchi, Toshikazu, "Shonin Chosho [Witness Examination Record]," In *Nibutani Dam Saiban no Kiroku [Documentation of the Nibutani Dam Case]*, ed. Kayano, Shigeru and Tanaka Hiroshi (Tokyo: Sanseido, 1999): 407–426.

17 Maruyama, Hiroshi, "Ainu Landowners' Struggle for Justice and the Illegitimacy of the Nibutani Dam Project in Hokkaido Japan," in *International Community Law Review* 14 (2012), 65.

The research project was hierarchically organized into two groups: a research committee and a research office. The research committee has led the research project and has explained how alternative means for the conservation of Ainu culture could be adopted in order to minimize the potential loss of Ainu culture caused by the construction of the Biratori Dam. The discussion has been based on the research conducted by the research office under the guidance of the research committee. The research office has mainly performed fieldwork, such as collecting data on Ainu cultural heritage, interviewing Ainu elders about their traditional knowledge of natural resources, and harvesting wild edible plants based on traditional Ainu knowledge. It is worth mentioning that the majority of the research committee's members are ethnic Japanese, while the Ainu, and in particular the local Ainu, comprise a majority of researchers in the office. The following paragraphs briefly show part of the research results in relation to Ainu culture and its heritage within the planned dam site.[18] The potential loss of Ainu culture due to the construction of dams on the Saru River System is also discussed in the results.[19]

The Nukabira River, a tributary of the Saru River on which the Biratori Dam is to be built, is a place to celebrate the many *Yukar*, the eposes of the Ainu.[20] For example, around the planned dam site is the peak named *Echinanke*, where *Kueran*, one of the goddesses on Mount Poroshiri, the most sacred mountain for the Ainu, is believed to live. Also, there are the *chashi*, or fortifications for the god *Okikurukamui*, the mountain of *Pekunchi* or another god of water, and the cliff of *Apekunchi* or a god of fire. The catchment area of the Nukabira River therefore reminds the Ainu of their oral literature, and scores of memory keepers of their oral literature have been educated and nurtured here. Furthermore, with respect to the archaeology of the area, 47 ruins have been found so far in the Nukabira River Catchment Area, and seven ruins have been found within the planned dam site. With the continuation of the research project into the future, it is most likely that more remains will be found. The catchment area is also famous for its greenschist. This stone was used for stone axes across Hokkaido and in the northern part of mainland Japan in the Neolithic Period. Furthermore, in pre-modern times, Matsuura Takeshiro, an explorer who contributed to the development of one of the earlier maps of Hokkaido, recorded 11 Ainu place names within the planned dam site, and more than 100

18 Biratori Municipality, "Ainu Bunka Kankyo Hozen Taisaku Chosa Sokatsu Houkokusho [Comprehensive Report on the Environmental and Cultural Assessment for the Saru River Development]," (Biratori Town: Biratori Municipality, 2006): 127–240.

19 Ibid, 427–535.

20 Ibid, 127–128.

Ainu place names in the catchment area. Through the interviewing of Ainu elders by the research office, the number of historically-documented Ainu place names in the Nukabira River Catchment Area rose to 204.

The research committee confirmed that 19 Ainu persons have hunted, fished and harvested in the planned dam site and its surroundings. According to an Ainu elder in Nibutani, a specific place to hunt bears was assigned to each hunter, which means the concept of *Iwor*, or the traditional land management of the Ainu for their subsistence, was transmitted from generation to generation at that time. *Iyomante*,[21] a ceremony performed in order to send back the spirits of the bears to *Kamuimosir*, or the world of gods, was held in the planned dam site until the 1930s. The research committee also reported that there are 59 species of trees and 69 species of grasses used for natural resources by the Ainu in the predetermined area for the Biratori Dam and its immediate surroundings. Those plants were used for food, medicine, daily commodities, and rituals, among other possible uses. A fact-finding survey based on interviews shows that 39 out of the 51 objectified Ainu residents in Biratori Town harvest edible wild plants there to this day. Prayers for ancestors called *Shinurappa* and prayers for gods called *Kamuinomi* were said in specific locations around the Nukabira River that overlap with the area of the dam. According to an Ainu belief, a variety of gods inhabit every part of a river. For example, one god lives in a rapid, while another lives in the whirlpools near a cliff. Every spring was revered as the location of a god of war. The meeting point of two rivers was also the object of prayer for the Ainu.

The research office collected information of the likely influence of the construction of the Biratori Dam on Ainu culture. It is likely that places that are important in the Ainu belief system, including three *Chinomisir*, three other objects of prayer, a spring, and a place to remember ancestors, will be submerged by the construction of the Biratori Dam. Fourteen Ainu places that were named will also be sunk under the water by the dam's construction. Even the lowest water level in the planned reservoir is most likely to submerge a large amount of habitat for the nine species of plants that were linked to the livelihood of the Ainu. Climbing plants, which usually grow along the river, and which were used by the Ainu for food, medicine and daily living utensils, will likely die because of submersion. Plants are also thought to play a key role in maintaining the quality and quantity of the river water, providing habitats for animals and controlling water shortages and floods. As a result of the loss of plants in the planned dam site, the brown bear's scope of activities will

21 The Ainu believe in the tradition that the god in the mountain appears in bears to give them meat and fur.

be negatively influenced. The potential loss of brown bears in the Saru River System Catchment Area could harm Ainu culture in the future, because the brown bear is revered by the Ainu as the god of the mountains. Not only brown bears but also snow owls, Hokkaido deer, sables, Hokkaido squirrels, and red foxes will surely be affected by the dam construction.

The report compiled by the Municipality of Biratori on the environmental and cultural assessment of the Biratori Dam points out that there are three main problems with fish in the Saru River caused by the construction of the Nibutani Dam.[22] First, although a fish ladder was provided for the Nibutani Dam, only several cherry salmon per year were reported to swim upstream over the dam between 1997 and 2002. This contradicts the claim made by the Hokkaido Regional Development Bureau based on its fundamental policy for the construction of the Biratori Dam in 1999, such that the salmon and the cherry salmon were to be conserved in the Saru River System. Second, it is said that the large reservoir prevents cherry salmon fry from swimming downstream. Although no full-scale investigation has been carried out, authorities have concluded that almost no cherry salmon fry remain in the reservoir. Third, it has also been suggested that the majority of the experimentally-released smolt in the reservoir could not swim downstream by the fish ladder. Research conducted in 2004 found only 17 cherry salmon in June and 11 in September in the Nukabira River, though the spawning grounds of cherry salmon were confirmed in the upstream tributaries. Thus, the Nibutani Dam has had an irreversible impact on the population of fish in the Saru River System. The same result is anticipated to be occur with the construction of the Biratori Dam.

Concluding Remarks

In March of 1991, Kaizawa Tadashi, in spite of illness, issued a formal objection to the administrative decision to build the Nibutani Dam in his fields which was delivered to the Ministry of Construction in Tokyo (the predecessor of the Ministry of Land, Infrastructure, Transport and Tourism), stating that:

> Japanese timber dealers, who were gifted with a large area of more than a million hectares by the Colonial Office in accordance with the 1897 Act on Use of Undeveloped National Land in Hokkaido, made a huge profit on logging timbers in the Saru River Catchment Area. In contrast the mountains in the Catchment Area were stripped of all vegetation, so that the

22 Ibid, 476–483.

> lands in the Catchment Area allotted to the Ainu by the Hokkaido Former Aborigines Protection Act suffered flood damages. Those lands were also devastated by logged timbers that were transported on the river. The 1968 completion of an embankment of the Saru River made the Ainu free from floods. The Japanese government, however, furthered alterations of the Saru River System. The planned construction of the Nibutani Dam in the wake of the unsustainable deforestation by Japanese colonisers will exploit nature more.[23]

It seems that the construction of those dams on the Saru River System is likely to pose a threat to the environmental security of the Ainu, as Kaizawa mentioned in his statement. The construction may also pose a threat to the security of the cultural identity of the Ainu as the aforementioned Ainu plaintiffs and others had warned. Unfortunately, the research project for the environmental and cultural assessment of the construction of the Biratori Dam is now confined to "recording Ainu place names and empirically transplanting plants in the predetermined area to unaffected places by the construction."[24]

The history of the Saru River Development suggests that the Ainu have been excluded from the decision-making process. Before the 1997 amendment of the River Act regulating river development in Japan, the authorities concerned had no obligation to consult local residents, including the Ainu, regarding their plans to build the Nibutani Dam and the Biratori Dam. Nevertheless, the Saru River Committee, which was established in order to represent local voices in the construction of the Biratori Dam, had only one Ainu among the 11 members. As mentioned previously, local Ainu residents were recruited for the research office for environmental and cultural assessment which is under the control of the research committee. The research office, therefore, has no role in the decision-making process. Furthermore, Japan has already ratified the ICCPR and the ICESCR, as well as other international human rights treaties that legally bind State parties. The Japanese government, however, does not adequately recognize any human rights of the indigenous Ainu, as the CPA shows, though Article 98 (2) of the Constitution of Japan states that the treaties signed by Japan and the established international laws should be faithfully observed.

23 Kaizawa, "Kensetsusho niokeru Ikenchinjutsu [Letter of Representation at the Ministry of Construction]," 179–180.

24 It was reported by Kaizawa Koichi, who has been working for the research office for environmental and cultural assessment of the Biratori Dam as the leader since the outset, in an interview on March 7, 2015 at his home.

It is a plain fact that the on-going construction of the Biratori Dam is threatening the political security of the Ainu.

The construction of the Nibutani Dam can also have a negative impact on the economic security of the Ainu. The expropriated lands for the construction of the dam were originally allotted to the Ainu, including Kaizawa Tadashi and Kayano Shigeru, by the Hokkaido Former Aborigines Protection Act. According to Kaizawa's statement, in the process of formally opposing the administrative decision,[25] some of the Ainu landowners, who had accrued a large amount of debt from the Agriculture Cooperative due to the shift from soybean cultivation to rice growth, sold their lands to rich Japanese farmers in the lower reaches. Other Ainu landowners in the planned dam site accepted the expropriation of their lands to offset loans against debts to the Agriculture Cooperative. Kaizawa and Kayano were the only two Ainu who could afford to fight against the authorities in court over the construction of the Nibutani Dam. In fact, even the questionnaire survey on the living conditions of the Ainu conducted in 2013 by the Hokkaido Prefectural Government made it clear that the Ainu are still suffering from the gap between themselves and the ethnic Japanese in terms of their standards of living. For example, the Ainu youth are less likely to go to university than the ethnic Japanese. It can be said that the economic insecurity of Ainu landowners in the planned dam site has allowed the authorities to easily advance construction work for the Nibutani Dam and the Biratori Dam.

Historically, the food and health of the Ainu were threatened during the colonization of Hokkaido. At first, the Colonial Office justified its disposition of Hokkaido by regulations, including the 1897 Act on Use of Undeveloped National Land in Hokkaido, which led to an increase in the number of Japanese immigrants from mainland Japan.[26] Secondly, the Office strengthened restrictions on traditional means of living, such as hunting and fishing across Hokkaido. The changes in Ainu traditional food in the Saru River Catchment Area caused by the immigration of the Japanese in the late-nineteenth century had serious effects on everyday life for the Ainu.[27] In 1883, the Ainu were prohibited from fishing salmon in the Tokachi River, though they relied on salmon

25 Kaizawa, Tadashi, "Shuyo Iinkai niokeru Chinjutsu [Letter of Representation at the Land Expropriation Committee in Hokkaido]," 132–133.

26 Ibid.

27 Iwasaki, Goodman Masami et al., "Traditional Food Systems of Indigenous Peoples: the Ainu in the Saru River region, Japan," In *Indigenous Peoples' Food Systems: the many dimensions of culture, diversity and environment for nutrition and health*, ed. Kuhnlein, Harriet V., Bill Erasmus, and Dina Spigelski (Rome: FAO, 2009), 145.

for food in the winter. As a result of the authorities keeping an eye on "illegal fishing", some Ainu in the Tokachi River Catchment Area were found to have starved from the prohibition of salmon fishing coupled with bad harvests in the fields.[28] For their survival under colonization, the Ainu have had to change their eating habits to a great extent. This might be why the construction of the two dams in the Saru River Basin (the Nibutani Dam and Biratori Dam) seems to impose no direct threat to the food and health security of the Ainu.

Considering human security could bring to light a variety of insecurities faced by the Ainu in relation to the exploitation of their land and natural resources which is supported by the Japanese government. It may be helpful to question the idea that benefits from the construction of the Nibutani Dam should be weighed against the costs of construction before the expropriation, as was the basis of the court's decision in 1997. It is impossible to compare benefits with costs here, because benefits are gained by the majority, while costs are borne by the minority (the indigenous Ainu people). Furthermore, economic and social benefits for the majority lead to the threatened security of the Ainu's cultural identity, as well as their environmental, economic and political security. It can be argued that the construction of the Biratori Dam conflicts with the assurance of human security, which "seeks to protect people against a broad range of threats to individuals and communities",[29] in addition to violating international human rights norms, including ICCPR and ICESCR. In principle, human rights are, at their core, to be secured for *all* individuals. On the basis of equality, positive measures to ensure the human security of indigenous peoples facing uncertainties over the exploitation in their communities should be adopted, since positive measures for the protection of the human rights of indigenous peoples are required by international law.

28 Sasamura, Ichiro, "Tokachi no Rekishi wo Tsutaete [In Search of Transmitting the History of the Ainu in Tokachi to Posterity]." Accesssed March 24, 2015. http://www.frpac.or.jp/about/files/sem1314.pdf. Sasamura is the former president of the Ainu Association of Hokkaido.

29 Commission on Human Security, "Outline of the Report of the Commission on Human Security", 2003, 2. Accessed May 24, 2015, http://www.icbjapan.org/humansecurity_outline.pdf.

CHAPTER 6

Is it Possible to Hear the Voices of Ainu Women? Silence and Empowerment

*Masumi Matsumoto**

Abstract

This chapter focuses on the life stories of Ainu women. The Ainu, an indigenous ethnic group who live in Hokkaido, has faced social discrimination particularly since the Meiji Restoration period. Many Ainu are not proud of being Ainu, and some even strived to erase their ethnic identity in order to avoid discrimination and social exclusion. The stipulation of the Act of the Promotion of Ainu Culture in 1997 seemed to promote ethnic pride, but fostering young culture bearers of both genders is hard. Since 1997, the government has financed various Ainu culture projects and dispatched Ainu to Japanese and overseas districts to provide introductions to Ainu cultural activities, such as dancing, playing music, carving, embroidery, and so on. Although these performers included women, they never confessed during the "performance" how Ainu women were discriminated against and their voices were muted in front of audiences and male Ainu leaders. After listening to several old women's life stories, the author points out how Ainu women were undereducated and low-paid and had low self-esteem because of the structural violence. They are still "subordinate" in postcolonial theory (Spivak). However, some Ainu women have empowered themselves by teaching the Ainu language and traditional culture and have begun to tell their life stories. The author describes how sisterhood among Ainu women and teaching their language to others, including the next generation, empowered them and discusses the difficulty of hearing their muted voices.

Introduction

Ainu issues are very difficult for Japanese (*wajin*)[1] who live outside Hokkaido to understand. First, "Japanese" in general know that Japanese society is

* Masumi Matsumoto, Professor, Muroran Institute of Technology.

1 In this paper, "Japanese people" are called *wajin*, which indicates immigrants from the Honshu Island, Shikoku Island, and Kyushu Island. It was commonly believed that *wajin* and the Ainu had not only linguistic differences but also racial differences. In terms of nationality,

 | DOI 10.1163/9789004314399_008

heterogeneous. The In 2006, the Ainu population in Hokkaido was 23,767. However, Ainu also live on the Honshu island and other islands. The precise population is not known because of the lack of demographic statistics in Japan. Presumably, 99% of the main Japanese population will answer that they have never seen real Ainu. Within the realm of public education, Ainu issues are touched upon only in modern Japanese history, such as the colonization of Hokkaido Island by Japan and the island's development by Japanese settlers. Despite the recent description of indigenous Ainu characters in textbooks, the majority of "Japanese" do not know or are not interested in what Ainu history was like before the modern period, how their lifestyle was forcibly changed by the assimilation policy, what kind of rights the Ainu have, or how their livelihood has improved since the Ainu Cultural Promotion Act (CPA) was enacted in 1997.

Most "Japanese" in Hokkaido are almost the same as the residents of the other islands of Japan in terms of their knowledge and understanding of Ainu issues. Hokkaido has a population of 5.4 million, and the majority of "Japanese" on this island are the descendants of settlers who arrived after the Meiji Restoration. However, only a few recognize that the name of Hokkaido appeared as a new colony of Japan and that the Meiji government confiscated the Ainu's homeland by force and subterfuge. In other words, students have less opportunity at school to learn about the modern history of Hokkaido, including the expropriation of Ainu lands, the loss of their fishing and hunting rights, the forced assimilation policy, and uncontrolled discrimination. Therefore, the Ainu's ethnic rights as indigenous people are still invisible to the majority of "Japanese."

However, in the wake of the 2008 Parliament resolution to seek the possibility of recognizing the Ainu as an indigenous people, Ainu indigenous status will be recognized formally in the hope of inaugurating the National Ainu Museum and the Symbolic Space of Ethnic Harmony in Shiraoi in 2020, when the Olympic Summer Games will be held in Tokyo. Over the last two decades, the opening ceremonies of the Olympic Games have presented elements of the indigenous people's cultures of the host country, and we predict that the Ainu culture will be also highlighted during the 2020 Summer Games. Some Ainu still want to hide their ethnicity for fear of discrimination, while the government is in the process of recognizing the Ainu as an indigenous people in accordance with the global movement to recognize indigenous people's rights. There are contradictions between the government's will and some Ainu's will.

---

both *wajin* and the Ainu had Japanese nationality. Therefore, pressure upon Ainu to be authentic Japanese was very strong.

The Hokkaido Ainu Association has upgraded the Ainu's social status, provided subsidies and loans, introduced stable jobs and improved education, preserved and developed Ainu culture, fostered relationships between the Ainu and other indigenous people not only in Japan but also all over the world, and conducted research on race and ethnicities.

Concerning Ainu issues, the most invisible phenomena are the voices of Ainu women, which were ignored frequently even in the Ainu Association's requirements to the government and thus in decision-making regarding Ainu policies. Ainu women have only recently started to tell their own stories to resolve many problems. It is difficult to grasp the reality because the issues are due to complex discrimination based on gender, ethnicity, and class.

This chapter consists of two sections. In the first section, general images of Ainu women are discussed based on travel writings and postcards that represented curiosity about sightseeing and folklore. In addition, an overview of temporary marriages called *otsunenkon*, women's roles in childcare, including adopted "Japanese" (*wajin*) children, domestic violence and harassment by male partners, and inferior education is provided. In the second section, the voice of an elderly woman, who began to feel proud of her Ainu heritage after learning the Ainu language and practicing Ainu culture after she retired, is introduced. She can be assessed as a new woman who has found another horizon by reencountering Ainu culture and acquiring a positive Ainu ethnic identity.

1 Who are Ainu Women?

1.1 *Exceptional Female Writers: Chiri Yukie and Bachelor Taeko*

The most famous Ainu woman in the modern history of Japan is Chiri Yukie (1903–1922), who is mentioned in the textbook on understanding Ainu history and culture distributed to every elementary school and junior high school in Hokkaido by the Foundation for the Promotion of Ainu Culture. She came from Noboribetsu, the southern part of Hokkaido, and published *Ainu Shinyoshu* (1923), a bilingual Ainu – Japanese version of the oral Ainu epic *Kamuy Yukar*. *Kamuy Yukar* was very important in transferring Ainu values, ethics, and traditional culture among young Ainu. Chiri's grandmother was an important guardian of Ainu traditions, and Chiri Yukie was raised in an atmosphere surrounded by Ainu culture, which attracted Dr. Kindaichi Kyosuke, a prominent linguistic scholar. Chiri Yukie and Dr. Kindaichi collaborated in translating the Ainu language into Japanese, and they preserved the *Kamuy Yukar* in letters. However, after Chiri had completed her work, she passed away at the age of nineteen. *Ainu Shinyoshu* became a best-selling book in the 1920s. It gave

Japanese readers culture shock because they were ignorant about the existence of Ainu language and culture, which stressed harmony between human beings and nature. However, despite the popularity of the book, the official Japanese assimilation policy did not change.

The second most famous Ainu woman is Bachelor Yaeko (1884–1962). A daughter of a local Ainu strong man in Usu in southern Hokkaido, she became familiar with Christianity through John Bachelor, an Anglican Church missionary. She was adopted by Bachelor at the age of twenty-two to take care of John Bachelor's elderly wife. Yaeko became accustomed to a Western lifestyle and served as a female Christian missionary to the Ainu, while writing *waka* short poems in Japanese. Dr. Kindaichi Kyosuke also supported the 1931 publication of her anthology of *waka* poems, *Wakaki Utari ni* (For Young Ainu Brothers and Sisters).

There are similarities between the two women. First, both used Japanese literature to express discrimination against the Ainu, and both recorded oral epics. These two women were exceptional, as most Ainu women were illiterate or semi-illiterate in Japanese, being deprived of the rights to appreciate ethnic values and the opportunity to go to school in normal conditions. Second, both had close male collaborators such as Kindaichi and Bachelor, who were exceptional intellectuals and appreciated and respected the Ainu culture. Third, both women maintained their virginity. Yukie passed away when she was only nineteen, and Taeko remained unmarried until her death at the age of seventy-eight. They were free from the victim status of Ainu women. In general, Ainu women suffered from discrimination regarding marriage, sexual harassment, domestic violence, reproduction, child-raising, child adaption, hard work, poverty, and so on. From this perspective, these two famous Ainu women became excellent symbols of Ainu purity and generosity. Moreover, their virginity (implying their infertility) was utilized to propagate the misery of the dying Ainu race, without implicating the "Japanese" (*wajin*) guilt of colonization. Both women also used the logic of the happy and free Ainu life before the coming of Japanese settlers, who brought "civilization" and competition. In the preface to *Ainu Shinyoshu*, Chiri Yukie wrote:

> Ainu shining beautiful souls are lost and are anxious and complain that we are going rusty and losing the goal, as we depend on others' charity. Dying race is our saddest name. Our ancestors would never have imagined our land would go to rack and ruins as the loser of the competitive principle. Our desire is to have a couple of strong men to compete with the advanced world.[2]

2 Chiri, Yukie, *Ainu Shinyoshu* (Tokyo: Iwanami bunko 1923), 3–4.

Bachelor Yaeko wrote the following poems:

> Ainu people, is there any choice but dying after much anxiety?
> Until you become the last Ainu, live and fight with the ethnic spirits.
> Even though we have lost our country's name, houses and field, we will not lose our spirit.[3]

When these two Ainu-language books were published in the 1920s and 1930s, the 1899 Hokkaido Former Natives Protection Act had been in full effect for more than twenty years. Moreover, Taeko's book was published when anti-government speech and press were suppressed because of the enactment of the Public Order and Police Law (1925). The 1899 Hokkaido Former Natives Protection Act aimed to assimilate Ainu and turn them into "civilized" Japanese who would cultivate the land and teach modern knowledge. The Ainu were "given" farming land and agricultural instruments by the local Japanese government after it banned traditional hunting and fishing. At the same time, the law regulated the promotion of assimilative education. However, the allocated land was in bad condition, and many Ainu who did not have farming skills became impoverished. From a cultural perspective, the assimilation policy included a ban on tattoos and piercing, promoted the creation of Japanese surnames and forenames in place of Ainu names, and enforced the teaching of the Japanese language at school.

1.2 *The Meaning of* Ainu-menoko (*Ainu Young Girls*)

Young Ainu women called *Ainu-menoko* were represented on many picture postcards and travelogues, and were depicted in such a way to serve as a sexual metaphor. *Ainu-menoto* was also a taunting word associated with the Ainu's weakness and their "backwardness." In general, the postcards were effective tools for educating ordinary "Japanese" that Japan controlled overseas colonies and different people with different cultures and folklore. The Japanese had implanted national pride that their nation was superior enough to give such "backward" people "civilization." In accordance with the development of the Japanese postal system, the rising literacy rate, and migration from inland to outland due to the development of capitalism, Japanese became familiar with the colorful picture postcards. The "common sense" of backward Ainu-ness was fixed with a "savage" image.

3 Kakegawa, Gen'ichiro, *Bachelor Yaeko no shogai* [*A Life of Bachelor Yaeko*] (Sapporo: Hokkaido Shuppan Kikaku Centre, 1988), 108–109.

The Lafayette College East Asia Digital Collection has 32 sheets of Ainu picture postcards published before 1945.[4] The Sapporo Central Library has uploaded 73 sheets of Ainu postcards.[5] The postcards in the collection that depict Ainu women emphasize tattoos around the lips and show a "peculiar" method of giving piggyback rides to a child, dancing, and weaving. The aim of these pictures was obviously to satisfy the curiosity about "backward" people's strange customs. The representations of the colonized residents of Hokkaido became the standard for representations of other groups residing in Japanese colonies such as Taiwanese aborigines, Koreans, Mongolians and nomads in Manchukuo, and aborigines on the Southern Ocean Islands.

The Ainu women depicted on the picture postcards were shown smiling less frequently than the colonized women's broad smiles after the Japanese occupation and the establishment of Manchukuo in 1932. In the Japanese occupied area, women with smiles represented a colony's submission to Japanese men, implying a gender order between a colony and Japan, the suzerain state. The "Japanese" already knew that the Ainu were not willing to accept settlers who treated Ainu like barbarians. Therefore, the smiles of Ainu women were not evident. However, their "stubborn" character was also imagined as their unchanged "savageness" vis-à-vis Japanese curiosity and the desire for further conquest.

In contrast, the picture postcard (Figure 1)indicates that Ainu women could be "civilized" through attire. The postcard is entitled "Ainu women dressed-up." The woman in the center is wearing traditional Ainu clothes, while the woman on the left wears Western clothes, and the woman on the right is wearing a kimono (traditional Japanese attire). This postcard might be used to suggest that Ainu women in traditional clothes had almost been completely exterminated and could attain civilized status with kimono and Western clothes, symbols of advancement. That is to say, assimilation was the only way to civilization.

The picture of the Toyosaka Dojin (Aborigine) School near Asahikawa indicates all Ainu children wore kimono. What does this mean?, (Figure 2)[6] At the four-year Ainu Aborigine schools that continued from 1899 to 1937, Japanese educational boards and teachers banned the traditional Ainu way of life, including wearing traditional clothes called *attus* and speaking the Ainu language. The children were taught the Japanese language (*kokugo* – national

4 https://digital.lafayette.edu/islandora/search/foxml.all.text%3A%28%22ainu%22%29?f%5B0%5D=cdm.Relation.IsPartOf%3A%22East%20Asia%20Image%20Collection%22.

5 http://gazo.library.city.sapporo.jp/searchResult/searchResult.php?pageId=1.

6 Sasaki, Chouemon, *Hokkaido Asahikawa-shi Ainu Shashin-cho* [*Photo Album of the Ainu of Asahikawa, Hokkaido*] (Asahikawa: Sasaki Hoeido, 1929).

FIGURE 6.1 *Ainu Women with Dress Clothes*

FIGURE 6.2 *Pupils and Graduates of the Toyosaka Dojin (Aborgine) School, 1929*

language) at school, moral training, and mathematics. History, geography, and science were not included in the curriculum. This meant that the Ainu children could not continue their education at higher-level schools.

Hokkaido was the first Japanese inner colony after the Meiji Restoration and became the place to resolve poverty problems in inner Japan. Those who came from inner Japan were poor, and many single men also came to Hokkaido seeking their fortune and opportunities. However, land cultivation and development were very difficult because of the freezing temperatures in the winter, barren land, decreased investment, disease, and the lack of welfare and medicine. The Ainu supported these settlers by teaching them how to survive the winter, build houses, and find food.

However, from a gender perspective, Ainu women were convenient outlets for the sexual desires of male Japanese. *Otsunen-muko*, or an over-the-winter husband, was often seen in Ainu society after the Meiji period. Before winter arrived, men visited young Ainu women at their houses. The men remained during the winter, and the women became pregnant. After spring came, the men left the Ainu women's houses, and the women were left behind with children. These men often had wives in inner Japan or in other places.[7] These Ainu women were treated as concubines. Married Ainu women's families were sometimes destroyed because "Japanese" men wished to have an Ainu concubine when an Ainu husband was absent for long periods as a guest fishing and forestry worker.[8] Furthermore, during the course of the increase in male "Japanese" migrants, brothels multiplied, syphilis became rampant, and the Ainu birth rate decreased.[9] According to a travel record in the 1920s, many beautiful Ainu women were sold into prostitution at brothels at the age of fifteen and sixteen.[10] At the same time, small pox, tuberculosis, and syphilis were brought by Japanese settlers, and the non-resistant Ainu died one after another. The poverty of the Ainu accelerated the spread of these epidemic diseases.[11]

To avoid discrimination, the Ainu even wanted to have their children intermarry with Japanese. In the 1930s, male Ainu leaders believed that through intermarriage the Ainu could be reborn as homogeneous *Yamato minzoku* (the

---

7 Sugawara, Kosuke, *Gendai no Ainu* [*Contemporary Ainu*] (Tokyo: Genbunsha, 1966), 69–77.

8 Takakura, Shin'ichiro, "Ainu Hika [Elegy of the Ainu]," in Vol 4 of *Nippon Zankoku Monogatari* [*Japan's Brutal Stories*], ed. Miyamoto, Tsuneichi et al. (Tokyo: Heibonsha, 1960), 230–231.

9 Ibid, 224–226.

10 Ogasawara, Shiroya, *Isoganu tabi* [*A slow travel*] (Osaka: Osaka Mainichi Shinbunsha, 1924), 218.

11 Takakura 1960, 239–249.; Shirukushii, *Matsurowazaru mono* [*Those who don't obey*] (Sappporo: Jurousha, 2010), 87–134.

Japanese pure blood nation) in accordance with the ideal nation-state.[12] Intermarriage took place broadly, but more intermarriage took place between Japanese men and Ainu women. It is/was a general phenomenon that a man of superior ethnicity marries a woman of inferior ethnicity in asymmetric power relationships.

In general, marriage brings happiness to women, but in the case of the Ainu, they experienced misery. It is very hard to hear their voices because marriage happens behind closed doors. In the 1970s, Takahashi Mieko, a female "Japanese" writer, interviewed twenty-nine Ainu women born at the end of the nineteenth century and the beginning of the twentieth century and portrayed their difficult lives in two books.[13] The women's experiences included bullying at school by "Japanese" classmates and even teachers, providing childcare for younger brothers and sisters and other families' children, love affairs with "Japanese" men, marriage discrimination, domestic violence by their husbands, drunken husbands, their husbands' adultery, gambling addiction, joblessness, repeated marriage and divorce, defamation upon reproduction, recusal of Ainu breed with hairy gene, contempt toward their illiteracy and semi-illiteracy, cheating by Japanese settlers who took full advantage of Ainu illiteracy, job discrimination, fear of continuous discrimination to the next generation, poverty, illness caused by poverty and hard work, and so on.[14] Complex discrimination based on poverty, ethnicity, and gender weighed heavily upon the women.[15]

This discrimination made Ainu women feel ashamed of their ethnicity and womanhood. In the belief that it was best to forget Ainu culture and assimilate

---

12 Kita, Koyo, *Ainu Hatashite Horobiruka* [*Will the Ainu perish?*] (Hokkaido Shiraoi Utari Kyokai [Hokkaido Shiraoi Utari Association], 1932), 52–53.

13 Takahashi, Mieko, *Hokkaido no Onna-tachi* [*Women in Hokkaido*] (Asahikawa: Hokkaido Joseishi Kenkyukai, 1976).; Takahashi, Mieko, *Zoku Hokkaido no Onna-tachi Utari-hen* [*Women in Hokkaido, an Ainu Women's volume*] (Asahikawa: Hokkaido Joseishi Kenkyukai, 1981).

14 Takahashi, 1976.; Takahashi, 1981.; Sugawara, 1966, 25–29.; Arai, Kazuko, *Sensei wa Ainu Desho – Watashi no kokoro no shi* [*You are Ainu, aren't you? A teacher of my heart*] (Sapporo: Hokkaido Shuppan Kikaku Centre, 2013), 220–221.; Kikuchi, Chinatsu, (2013) "Ainu no hitobito eno sabetsu no jituzou—Seikatsu ni kizamareta sabetsu no jittai [Real life images of discriminations against Ainu people—The Reality of the discriminations on life]," in *Gendai Ainu no Seikatsu no Ayumi to henyou* [*The Trades and Transformation of Contemporary Ainu People – A report for the survey on real life of the Ainu in Hokkaido, 2009*], 146–156.

15 Tahara, Ryoko, "Ainu josei no ookina jishin to hokorini – Ainu josei no jittai chousa wo jisshishite [For the confidence and pride of Ainu women – on the fact-finding survey on Ainu women]," in *Buraku Kihou* 579 (2007): 45–55.

into Japanese culture, the women tried to be good students in schools, but the majority were not successful because of daily bullying, discrimination after graduation, domestic violence, and moral harassment from their husbands. Many Ainu women lacked confidence and had low self-esteem. According to research conducted in 1960, 100 percent of the Ainu youths in the Hidaka district wanted to marry "Japanese," but 95 percent of "Japanese" did not want to marry Ainu. Because of the boom in Ainu tourism that emphasized freak shows, images of "old and backward Ainu" were disseminated with prejudice.[16] Cultural and ethnic assimilation with Japanese was considered and internalized as the only choice for Ainu men and women. In contrast, "Japanese" men took advantage of Ainu women's desire to marry Japanese. In many cases, "Japanese" men abandoned Ainu women mercilessly, leaving behind a child or children. Such Ainu women had no option but to become single mothers. They led lives accepting intolerance, poverty, and trouble.

1.3 *Complex Discrimination toward Ainu Women in Contemporary Japanese Society*

As the Ainu have not been recognized as an official nationality (*minzoku*), encouraging Ainu teachers has not been promoted as an educational policy.[17] This creates a clear contrast with other multi-ethnic countries' minority policies such as China, which has made efforts to foster ethnic minority teachers and cadres to be role models for ethnic minority children. The Hui Muslims and Koreans are typical examples.[18] In contrast, before the 1960s, "Japanese" (*wajin*) teachers in Hokkaido were ignorant about Ainu ethnic culture and language and sometimes even hostile to Ainu children. The teachers provided a uniform school education for Ainu children based on the conviction that Japanese culture and language had absolute and superior values. The teachers

16 Sugawara, 1966, 104–105, 107.

17 The exceptional pioneer is Ms. Arai Kazuko. She was appointed as an assistant teacher at an elementary school in Asahikawa in the center of Hokkaido in 1945. She felt humiliated on the very first day of her teaching when a four-grade "Japanese" boy growled, "Get out, Ainu! I don't want to be taught by an Ainu". After her appointment as a full-time teacher, she was covered by newspapers and TV programs frequently because of her ethnic rareness. She was furious when NHK (National Broadcasting Station) produced a drama on her life story and broadcast it in 1960 without her permission (Arai 2013:8, 176–183). In other words, people casted curious eyes upon a rare Ainu female teacher.

18 Matsumoto, Masumi and Shimbo, Atsuko, (2011) "Islamic education in China: Triple discrimination and the challenge of Hui women's madrasas," *The Moral Economy of the Madrasa—Islam and education today*, ed. Sakurai and Adelkhah (Routledge, 2011): 85–102.

sometimes criticized Ainu children who were absent from school due to school bullying. The teachers and educational boards had no intention of resolving ethnic discrimination.

After the 1960s, Japan experienced rapid economic growth after the country's complete defeat in World War II, and Japanese society seemed to become more modern and democratic with full attention given to the values of human rights. However, concerning Ainu issues, things changed only slightly.

In 1997, the CPA was enacted after the years-long movement by the Ainu Association, and finally, the preservation of Ainu culture was supported with financial aid. In spite of the act, during a study conducted in 2004 by female members of the Ainu (Utari) Association in Hokkaido, Ainu women in their forties, fifties, and sixties in various areas in Hokkaido observed in interviews and on questionnaires that they had experienced and felt inequality and disadvantages in daily life because of their gender, ethnicity, and lower socioeconomic status. However, most took the discrimination and even victimization for granted because they felt there was no resolution to these problems.[19]

According to this study, 17 percent of 241 Ainu female respondents answered that they had been frequent victims of domestic physical violence, while 20 percent answered "several times." More than one third of Ainu women were victims of domestic violence.[20] The frequent domestic violence can be attributed to men's feeling of humiliation caused by the official forced assimilation policy, poverty caused by the poor land conditions, and the generational chain of abuse. The women's husbands were forced to be in the bottom of the social strata in many cases. One point seven percent of Ainu women were still illiterate due to their absences from school apparently caused by bullying and poverty. The women's husbands were raised in almost the same circumstances. They faced discrimination in Japanese society, were not approved of socially, were deprived of human dignity, were not confident, and were labeled good for nothings. Their unspoken anger appeared in self-destructive behavior, such as drinking, violence toward others, and domestic violence involving their wives who did not take the situation seriously or blame their husbands. As "Japanese" society and Ainu society are patriarchal societies, women with less literacy and confidence took it for granted that women in general were beaten by men who were superior to women in terms of social power. Ainu women were neither able to speak out nor did they ever imagine that they were able

19 Hokkaido Utari Kyokai [Hokkaido Utari Association], ed., "A research on the current condition of Ainu Women," In *Ukopururuí-- Ainu Women's Empowerment* (Sapporo Branch, Hokkaido Utari Kyokai, 2007), 77–78.

20 Ibid, 81.

to claim their troubles toward others because of the twisted and complex discrimination against them based on lower socioeconomic status, ethnicity, and gender. These issues are similar to minority women's discrimination problems, which are often seen among African American women in the United States, Filipino wives in Japan, and ethnic Korean wives in Japan.

Ainu women suffered from trauma and an inferiority complex caused by school bullying and non-attendance at school. Many did not finish junior high school although they received their diploma. Ainu women born between 1945 and 1948 worked hard as little laborers to support their families when they were school age. Some remembered and are still tortured by their heartbreaking experiences and memories in school days when even teachers discriminated against Ainu, who were believed to be inferior in every aspect of their ability and biological essence.[21]

Furthermore, even though the government proclaimed the importance of education for the Ainu in order to improve their living standards after the enactment of the CPA in 1997, the Ainu language was still not taught in schools. As long as less-educated Ainu parents lacked a real image of future wealth or pride after receiving an education, they would not be passionate about their children's education because the parents were afraid that their children might also face discrimination in the workplace. Therefore, multiple types of discrimination led to the concealment of Ainu-ness, negative images of the Ainu, and the appearance of the discourse that poverty was the result of self-responsibility.[22]

In such circumstances, "coming out" as an Ainu is still avoided except by those who engage in producing woodcraft souvenirs and in tourism. In particular, contemporary middle-aged Ainu in their forties and fifties have had fewer opportunities to hear about their Ainu-ness from the older generation. Accordingly, they have no ethnic pride in being Ainu.[23]

Assimilation used to be the only and absolute national policy to "protect" the Ainu. Therefore, learning the Ainu language was constrained in private sectors. Even after the CPA was enacted in 1997, Ainu language study for Ainu

21 Ibid, 77.; Kikuchi, Chinatsu, "Ainu no hitobito eno sabetsu no jituzou – Seikatsu ni kizamareta sabetsu no jittai [Real life images of discriminations against Ainu people – the Reality of the discriminations on life]," in *Gendai Ainu no Seikatsu no Ayumi to henyou* [*The Trades and Transformation of Contemporary Ainu People – A report for the survey on real life of the Ainu in Hokkaido, 2009*] (2013): 146–156.

22 Hamada, Kunihiro, (2013) "Ainu shakai ni okeru sabetsu no mondai [On the discriminations in the Ainu society]," in *Gendai Ainu no Seikatsu no Ayumi to Henyou* [*The Trades and Transformation of Contemporary Ainu People – A report for the survey on real life of the Ainu in Hokkaido, 2009*] (2013): 157–168.

23 Kikuchi, 2013.

children was still prohibited in most public schools, although sub-textbooks are distributed to schools in Hokkaido. The sub-textbooks for the elementary and secondary levels, edited by the Ainu Cultural Promotion Foundation, explain the importance of appreciating the Ainu nature-preserving history to co-exist with bears, wolves, deer, trees and plants, culture and language. However, only a few lines are allocated to a description of Ainu women's experience as victims of multi-layered discrimination. Although Ainu Utari Kyokai (the Association of Ainu) continued promoting Ainu advancement, the group never considered women's particular issues until 2003 when the United Nations (UN) Committee on the Elimination of Racial Discrimination issued general advice on complex discrimination based on gender, ethnicity, and class.[24] The leaders of the Ainu Association were male, and it was very difficult for them to solve individual and private problems, particularly women's.[25]

2 Women's Empowerment through Learning the Ainu Language and Culture; the Case of Kibata Sachiko

2.1 *The Rebirth of a Proud Ainu Woman*

There have been many critiques of the CPA since 1997. For example, Ainu language learning is not promoted in the public school curriculum, and indigenous rights to lead and preserve traditional life are not respected. If the government allows indigenous rights, it should have given compensation for the confiscated land and lost fishing and hunting rights, and should have apologized for the forceful assimilation policy that destroyed Ainu pride and culture. However, the government has not done that thus far. In spite of many criticisms, the act should be evaluated because it provided the foundation for financing Ainu cultural activities.

At the end of the 1980s, Kibata Sachiko began to go to an Ainu language class run by Dr. Kayano Shigeru and Kaizawa Tadashi. She made several subsidized trips to Japanese regions other than Hokkaido, and she even traveled overseas in order to propagate Ainu culture and *Kamuy Yukar*. She has continued to introduce Ainu culture and languages not only as a teacher of the Ainu cultural class but also as a performer. Finally, she won the Ainu Culture Award in 2012. She has been empowered through learning Ainu culture and language, has overcome discrimination and difficulty, and retrieved human dignity through

24 Tahara, 2007.

25 Tin Tin Htum, "The Social identities of minority others in Japan: Listening to the narratives of Ainu, Buraku and Zainichi Koreans," in *Japan Forum* 24 (1) (2012): 1–22.

others' approval and applause. The interview was conducted on September 26 and 27, 2014, and April 22, 2015, at her house in Nukibetsu, Nibutani, Hokkaido.

Kibata Sachiko was born in Nukibetsu, Biratori, in southern Hokkaido in 1930. She was eighty-five years old in 2015. Her father was Ainu, and mother was *wajin*. Her father drank a lot. She was raised in a family with a paternal grandmother who regularly spoke the Ainu language to her. Her grandmother died when Sachiko was seven. She dared not talk about her schooldays when her mother ordered her to go to school every day despite frequent bullying and abuse. Sachiko preferred to engage in childcare as a part-time job for another family instead of studying at school because she loved to be given dresses as an allowance. She did not do well in school. After graduating from elementary school, she started to work very hard day and night. She had no opportunity to experience Ainu culture after her grandmother's death. She dared not speak out about her experiences of discrimination in the workplace, but she had a strong fighting instinct. After she married an Ainu, she worked in the forestry industry with her husband. In the 1950s and'60s, development boomed in Hokkaido, and she worked hard and even engaged in masculine work: operating various machine tools and driving ten-ton dump trucks daily. After the company closed, she opened a karaoke bar in the 1970s, and the bar prospered with many customers because she was attractive and cheerful. However, her husband hated the lifestyle of drinking late and asked her to stop. He intimated that he would divorce her if she did not close the bar. She decided to close the lucrative bar and began a third job as a door-to-door insurance sales woman after a friend suggested this to her. At first, her business results were excellent, and she sold insurance to ex-customers of the bar. However, when she became a boss at the branch business, her young employees did not do well, and she had to take responsibility for them. She had to quit the third job. She had already reached the end of her fifties, the age of retirement in general in Japanese society.

Then she heard about Ainu cultural classes that first began in 1987 through the passionate efforts of Dr. Kayano Shigeru.[26] She decided to learn Ainu language and culture after Dr. Kayano invited her. When she started attending the class regularly in 1988, she was fifty-nine years old. Even though she was born into an Ainu family, she had no Ainu identity. She had never worn *attus* (traditional Ainu clothing made from the bark of a specific tree). Her husband was

26 Kaizawa, Tadashi, "Biratori-cho Nibutani Ainu-go Kyoshitu no Kaisetsu to Keika nituite [On the opening and the development of Ainu language Class in Nibutani, Biratori town]", in *Nibutani Ainu-go Kyoshitu Kohoshi* [Bulletin of Nibutani Ainu language Class] (1) (1988). Dr. Kayano was the first Ainu member of the House of Councillors.

also Ainu, and he understood the oral Ainu language but did not speak it. The couple had adopted three *wajin* children, and after they had grown up and she had retired from various jobs, she now had free time for herself.

The class teacher was Dr. Kayano Shigeru, a great activist and preserver of Ainu culture.[27] Dr. Kayano later became the first Ainu member of the Upper House (1994–2000). It took about twenty minutes by car from her home to Nibutani, where the class was held. It was very hard to commute by car during the frozen winter, but she was rewarded for her perfect attendance. Because of her driving ability, her husband's appreciation of Ainu culture, Dr. Kayano's dedication to teaching Ainu culture and language, and her strong intention to complete something, she felt she was able to be rewarded. She had not been an ardent student during her younger school days. After she started to learn the Ainu language, she began to recall her grandmother's language.

She made every effort to learn the language. She listened to the cassette tape recorded by Dr. Kayano every day, even when she was driving. After ten years of effort to learn Ainu, she became a lecturer in the Ainu language class. In 2000, the Japanese music company JVC released the CD *Songs of Ainu* performed by the Biratori Ainu Culture Succession and Practice Group. Sachiko's *Kamuy Yukar* was also on the CD.

After the autumn of 2001, the group was subsidized by the Foundation of Ainu Culture Promotion and was sent to various places such as Niigata and Gunma on Honshu Island and performed various Ainu cultural activities, including reciting *Kamuy Yukar*, demonstrating embroidery, wood carving, and dancing. She recited *Kamuy Yukar* for the first time in 2001 at the large Niigata Prefectural Hall, where she trembled due to nerves but managed to finish the performance. She made some mistakes, but she relaxed because she realized that no one in the audience understood the Ainu language. Her first experience of seeing a female "professor" (that is to say, the writer) occurred when she visited Keiwa College in Niigata in the same year. After autumn 2001, the group gave many performances in various locations. The free travel and applause from audiences in places other than Hokkaido made her happy and increased her motivation to improve her Ainu language and cultural skills. Sachiko recognized herself as the only and dearest pupil of Dr Kayano Shigeru in terms of the Ainu language. When she was a child, she listened to the Ainu language. Thus, it was easier to learn the words. Lacking patience, most of the students left the class, and the majority of Ainu residents did not want to learn

27 Ainu language class was initiated by Dr. Kayano Shigeru and was financed by his pocket-money in 1983. After he acquired subsidies from the government of Hokkaido, it was re-started as Nibutani Ainu Language Class. Kaizawa, 1988.

Ainu. Dr. Kayano was a respectful man who made efforts to promote Ainu culture through the enactment of CPA. When he returned to Nibutani at the end of his last political term, he also worked hard for the enlightenment and promotion of Ainu culture not only in Japan but also in global society. When he died in 2006, Sachiko felt sadder than at her father's death. Dr. Kayano had been a benefactor.

In 2005, she received the Ainu Culture Incentive Award, with a prize of 100,000 yen, and in 2012, she received the Ainu Culture Award with a prize of 500,000 yen. She felt she had harvested the fruits of her efforts to learn about her Ainu heritage.

She brought up three adopted *wajin* children. One became the director of a non-profit organization (NPO) that promotes Ainu culture in Sapporo, Hokkaido. Her grandson is now a trainee leader of Ainu culture promotion in Shiraoi, where the Symbolic Space of Ethnic Harmony will be in place until 2020. Her daughter-in-law sewed *attus* with gorgeous embroidery. She wears them not only for special performances but also on casual occasions.

The characteristics of Sachiko's oral story are as follows. First, she seldom talked about the negative experience of discrimination. She emphasized her efforts to be a respected teacher of Ainu language and culture to live her second life after the retirement. Second, she retrieved the strong ethnic identity and pride of Ainu. Being Ainu used to be a cause of her inferiority complex, but now Ainu-ness has become her pride, partly because of her cheerful and positive outlook and partly because of the fortunate encounter with Ainu culture and language through Dr. Kayano Shigeru.

2.2 *The Meaning of Ainu Language Learning and Women's Empowerment*

According to a survey of Ainu women conducted in 2004, 85 percent perceived the importance of the inheritance of Ainu culture, 69 percent engaged in Ainu cultural preservation activities, and 13 percent had previously engaged in such activities. The activities included doing embroidery, dancing, wearing traditional clothing, and speaking the Ainu language. Thirty-five percent responded they had strong Ainu pride, 32 percent had Ainu pride, while 17 percent had negative feelings about being Ainu. Those who had some Ainu pride totaled 67 percent.[28] Those who engaged in Ainu cultural activities were proud of their Ainu-ness. In contrast, those who were not proud of their Ainu-ness would continue to hide their ethnicity due to the memory and anticipation

28 Hokkaido Utari Kyokai, 2007, 79.

of discrimination. As long as they try to hide their ethnicity, there will be no restoration of indigenous people's rights.

The example of Kibata Sachiko implies the following. Assimilation continued whether voluntarily or compulsorily. However, nothing positive happens to Ainu women through perfect assimilation as long as it is impossible to erase the racial gene. Then, they will take an essentialist strategy of using their ethnic characteristics to make their life and future better, taking advantage of the global trend of the restoration of the rights of indigenous peoples.

In Kibata Sachiko's case, the Ainu language class became a safety net for marginalized Ainu women. It became a vocational training institution and a place to proudly reconfirm their ethnic identity. By understanding the history and culture of Ainu ethnicity, she also recognized that her own life had been valuable. After mastering her ancestral Ainu language, her status within the community improved, and she engaged in respected professions, as a teacher and as a cultural performer.

Based on such essentialism of reawakening as an Ainu, she felt empowered to overcome every kind of past discrimination and humiliation. Emphasizing Ainu-ness can be the last tool for rethinking and reforming minority women's fragile social status. Such essentialism can be considered the strategy of the weak. Remaining within Ainu society, she tried to emancipate herself in Ainu and Japanese society by eliminating discrimination against women and the Ainu. At the same time, in the legal order that promotes the equality of the genders, her frequent appearances at meetings, performances, and school represent silent resistance against the patriarchy and assimilative power.

Whether she recognized it, it is another result of feminism. Ainu women have been undereducated due to their poverty, and they were not able to admit their own values. Ainu women such as Kibata Sachiko respond to the voiceless complaints of their grandmothers and great-grandmothers. Their offspring will inherit a passion for learning. "Ainu" in the Ainu language means "human beings," and the Ainu language represents humanity, they argue. Ainu women with such knowledge will be appraised and empowered with self-esteem.

Conclusion

In this chapter, the following issues were discussed. First, it is very difficult to hear the voices of Ainu women who have been the victims of complex discrimination based on gender, ethnicity, and poverty. The prominence of star poets such as Chiri Yukie and Batcher Taeko concealed the real facts of ordinary and deprived Ainu women. Adult Ainu women used to be the target of sexual interest. They were undereducated because of poverty and school bullying. They married men who were unfaithful, and in many cases, the women were beaten by their husbands. They loved their children but did not let them know their ethnic roots out of fear of discrimination that continued to the next generation. The problem was that because of negative feelings about Ainu-ness and womanhood, women accepted such harassment and violence stoically and even thought there was no way to resolve these problems but assimilation.

However, since the CPA was enacted, things have changed gradually, and Ainu women with Ainu knowledge have achieved empowerment by being cultural leaders. Kibata Sachiko studied her native language after retirement, which resulted in fame and confidence. In particular, without the Ainu language class conducted by Dr. Kayano Shigeru, a prominent leader of the Ainu movement, her post-retirement years might have been unrelated to Ainu life.

Needless to say, ethnic education is important in preserving indigenous culture. However, it is not always needed for children's schools. If Ainu language classes promote ethnic culture, they will become the location for those who are interested in the Ainu, and participants will feel comfortable learning the culture. It is possible that the Ainu culture movement will make progress, and Ainu offspring will follow their ancestors. Kibata Sachiko's son's and grandson's activities to inherit Ainu culture demonstrate this. It is very important to foster female leaders in Ainu cultural development. They will be the key to resolving discrimination against Ainu, particularly Ainu women.

Acknowledgement

This study was financially supported by the Grant for Cooperative Studies of the Muroran Institute of Technology. I am grateful for the generous allowance and for the cooperation of the Arctic Centre of the University of Lapland. I also thank Kibata Sachiko, who spared time for a long interview.

CHAPTER 7

The Common Threats to the Livelihood Security of the Nenets People

*Elena Tonkova**

Abstract

The Nenets are the biggest group of indigenous people in Russia and belong to the Samoyeds. They are nomadic people, reindeer herders living in the far north. Today, they inhabit some areas of the tundra and northern taiga of the European part of Russia and of Western Siberia. Their traditional lifestyle has become very fragile due to economic, ecological, and social reasons. Expansion of corporations harvesting raw materials (mainly oil and gas companies), climate change factors, and challenges of socio-cultural globalization have destroyed the environment for reindeer herding and ruined the world of the Nenets, both physically and psychologically. The traditional way of living has lost its basis, and it has become either impossible or rather hard and uncomfortable to follow. This chapter analyzes the common threats to the everyday life of the Nenets. Against the background of such threats, it also examines the attempts by the state and civil organizations, including those created by the Nenets themselves, to help the Nenets and other indigenous people overcome contemporary social and human security challenges and to continue with their traditional way of living.

The level of vulnerability for different livelihoods varies enormously, and one of the most vulnerable groups is indigenous people, to whom the concept of *livelihood security* means the opportunity to keep their traditional lifestyle. As stressed by S.N. Kharyuchi, the vice president of the Russian Association of the Indigenous People of the North (RAIPON), in his letter to president Putin: "The right to keep the traditional lifestyle for the indigenous peoples means the right to live."[1] And, together with this, the idea of livelihood security should presuppose the guarantees that all other possible choices of living strategies

* Elena Tonkova, associate professor at the Syktyvkar State University, Russia.

1 Tishkov, V.A., ed., *Sovremennoe polozhenie i perspektivy razvitiya korennyh malochislennyh narodov Severa, Sibiri i Dalnego Vostoka: Nezavisimy expertniy doklad* [Current situation and development perspectives of the indigenous small-numbered peoples of the North, Siberia and Far East: The independent expert report] (Novosibirsk: Izdatelstvo Instituta Arheologii i etnographii SO RAN, 2003), 10 (author's translation).

 | DOI 10.1163/9789004314399_009

are open for them too, such that the indigenous people are not tied by the society to follow the traditional lifestyle as the only option and that each of them can create their own life scenario.[2]

The principal aim of this paper is to analyze the life of the Nenets, an indigenous and primarily nomadic group of people inhabiting the Russian north, through the prism of the concept of livelihood security. And the key task is to present the main challenges that make the traditional lifestyle of the Nenets vulnerable, from their own perspective. This approach, based on the Nenets nomadic people's perception and evaluation of threats, seems to be rather promising and potentially fruitful: it takes into consideration the outlook of the indigenous people and the fact that it is the nomadic people who meet those threats and who deal with them. This approach can help discern what kind of threats to livelihood security are seen by the people, what kind of priorities are given to these threats, and what kind of steps are considered to be rational and worth while for stabilizing and optimizing the situation. Thus, it is logical to expect more cooperation from the side of the indigenous peoples if their perspective is to be followed. It allows an exploration of the strategies and solutions that are being implemented in real life by the people themselves and the expectations from all the other social agents involved.

The idea of livelihood security arises in discussions on topics devoted to the spectrum of characteristics of human and social well-being and can be explored based on both "apophatic" and "cataphatic" aspects. As the notion of health cannot be defined only as absence of disease, the notion of livelihood security includes the absence of economic, ecological, and social-cultural threats but it is not exclusive to this. The possibility of maintaining a specific lifestyle and to feel comfortable and satisfied with such a choice seems to be very important for personal and communal sustainability; that is, the chosen way of living must be economically profitable, socially inclusive, and culturally enlightening. In other words, the notion of livelihood security can be understood as a policy or set of measures aimed to ensure the basic needs and rights and to guarantee the maintenance of the capabilities and assets for human beings: both as individuals and as social entities.[3]

The economic aspects of livelihood security necessitate the absence of restrictions to keep a specific (e.g., traditional) lifestyle, which should bring a certain income. The social-psychological aspects include confidence in the

2 Ibid.

3 *CARE Household Livelihood Security Assessments: A Toolkit for Practitioners*, Prepared for the PHLS Unit by: TANGO International Inc., Tucson, Arizona 2002. Available at: http://www.careclimatechange.org/files/toolkit/CARE_HLSA_Toolkit.pdf.

social inclusion as based on the feeling of emotional comfort, together with health-related issues affecting the quality of life. The cultural aspects, in turn, are a combination of possibilities for an individual to gain knowledge on a specific lifestyle and to exercise it in a day-to-day way on a routine basis and be freely willing to follow it—be it the usage of language or practices of organizing a dwelling, cooking, housekeeping, clothing, herd stewarding, rearing and educating children, and so on.

Among all the indigenous peoples of the Russian Federation, the Nenets is the biggest group, with a growing population (according to the Census of 2010,[4] the number of the Nenets people is 44,640, and this number is steadily increasing). The Nenets ethnic group is qualified by the official Russian rhetoric as belonging to the so-called small-numbered indigenous peoples. Put differently, the very definition of indigenous people in the Russian political and legal systems includes a quantitative parameter—there must be fewer than fifty thousand people. The Nenets (*Nentsy* in Russian) belong to the Samoyedic branch of the Uralic-Yukaghir language family. They speak the Nenets language, existing in two dialects that belong to two rather different groups of Nenets people—the tundra Nenets and the taiga (or forest) Nenets. Whereas the first group historically has a nomadic way of living, and its economy is primarily based on reindeer herding, the taiga Nenets (a rather small-numbered group consisting of approximately 2,000 people[5]) mostly combine hunting, fishing, and foraging, and they have a sedentary lifestyle.

The Nenets spread along the Arctic coast in the seventeenth century, and they currently live mainly in Yamalo-Nenetsky (YNAO) and Khanty-Mansiysky, autonomous Okrugs (KHMAO) of Tyumen, Arkhangelsk (including the Nenets autonomous Okrug, NAO), and Krasnoyarsk regions. Some smaller groups also live in the Komi Republic and the Murmansk region. From the perspective of the nomadic Nenets, they live in the "tundras": Kanino-Timanskaya, Bolshezemelskaya, Malozemelskaya (these belong to the European part), Yamalskaya, Tazovskaya, Gydanskaya, and Taymyrskaya (of the Siberian part of Russia).

All negative and positive impacts on the way of living of the Nenets can be analyzed through the prism of an outsider (political or academic) or from the Nenets' own perspective. The discourses verbalized in these two approaches

4 *Sotsialno-demografichesky portret Rossii: Po itogam Vserossiyskoy perepisi naselenia 2010 goda* [Social-demographic portrait of Russia: Following All-Russian census of 2010] (Moscow: Statistika Rossii, 2012), 88.

5 Turaev, Vadim, Rodion Sulyandziga, Pavel Sulyandziga and Vladimir Bocharnikov, *Encyclopaedia of indigenous peoples of the North, Siberia and the Far East of the Russian federation* (Moscow, 2011), 243.

are rather different, and there is also a very wide variation in the description of the universes of the indigenous peoples by Western and by Russian academicians: the same reality and the same phenomena can be explained through the vantage points of different concepts, and different accents can be put on the subjects.[6] The Nenets people focus on things that do not always seem to be of first importance for researchers and vice versa. The "classical" threats, related to the industrial development of the north, the social transformations, environmental and climate change issues, and the dissolution of traditional lifestyle and culture, are still relevant in this approach, but the priorities change for various matters on different levels; new insights are gained and new pictures emerge that are quite different from the purely academic one. This approach does not deny expert-based evaluations but elaborates on them, as it allows the interpretation of indigenous practices of adaptation or survival to be put into the classic academic discourse of threats and challenges.

The methodology of the distinction "us–others" used by the Nenets reindeer herders and their classification and sub-categorization of the "others" can be used as foundations for the above approach. This methodology was developed by Martynova in her fieldwork during the summer of 2011 in the Tazovskiy region of Yamalo-Nenetsky okrug (YNAO).[7] In her research, based on interviews with the Nenets nomads,[8] she found that the level of "otherness" or the gradation of alienation could be different for different groups of people. Four different levels of "otherness" are distinguished: "others," or strangers; "other others," or alien strangers; "our others," or unfamiliar neighboring Nenets nomads; and "other ours" or non-nomadic Nenets (or all other Nenets but reindeer herders). Through the concept of "otherness," the social-psychological characteristics used by the nomads to describe their experience of communicating with the different "others," and through their emotional perception of such communication, the fears and threats to livelihood security are seen quite clearly. In general, research has revealed the rather high level of xenophobia among the nomads.[9] This can be explained, in turn, within the concept of livelihood

6 Forbes, Bruce C. and Florian Stammler, "Arctic climate change discourse: the contrasting politics of research agendas in the West and Russia," in vol 28 of *Polar Research*, (2009): 28–42.

7 Martynova, E.P. "'Chuzhye' v Tazovskoy tundre" ["Others" in the Tazovskaya tundra], *Vestnik Tomskogo gosudarstvennogo universiteta*, 4 (2013): 72–77.

8 The interviews taken were with representatives of the nomadic Nenets from the Tazovskiy region (5300 out of 7600 Nenets living in the area are reindeer herders, and the Nenets are a majority of the population in the region – 51.7%). Martynova, "'Chuzhye' v Tazovskoy Tundre".

9 Yu.P. Shabaev, "Narody Evropeyskogo Severa Rossii: polozhenie, specifika identichnosti" [Peoples of the Russian European North: specificity of identity], *Sotsiologicheskiye issledovaniya*, 2 (2011): 58–59.

security: the Nenets reindeer herders are afraid of the competition for lands, clash of traditions, and failure to keep their culture and lifestyle; they fear everything that could potentially cause harm to any part of their fragile universe: nature, land, reindeers, and people.

"Others" is a stigma given by the Nenets to those who work in the hydrocarbon extraction industry. These workers "are considered by the inhabitants of the tundra as strangers, temporal visitors trespassing pastures—the fundament of reindeers life, and, thus, herders' life and their families.... They often cheat, it is impossible to kick them out of the tundra, and they destroy lands and in exchange give nothing."[10] These "others" include both shift workers and managers who run or represent the companies and make negotiations with the indigenous people. The attitude that the Nenets show toward both groups is the same: the "others" are perceived as strangers, who take what they want by any means they have and do what they want without care. They cannot be trusted, since they do not follow high moral standards, and they can easily deceive you and betray your expectations.

Those who represent the hydrocarbons extraction industries are identified with the companies themselves and are seen by the Nenets as the main reason for all the troubles of the nomads. The tundra inhabitants are afraid of these people and do not trust them. They do not want to negotiate with the hydrocarbon industry representatives: due to the direct conflict of interests, one's victory brings failure to the other. Those managers are perceived as aggressive and intimidating people, who can force the Nenets to sign any documents with even slavery conditions; the people of the tundra feel timid in the face of the "big bosses."

The land issue is the key problem in the hierarchy of contemporary threats that the Nenets people face today.[11] Industrial development of the north means that the lands used by the Nenets as pastures will be (and they have already been) expropriated for the needs of the growing industries: for drill sites, pipelines, and roads. The possibility to move freely on the lands, migrating with the herds, is crucial for nomadic livelihood security and cultural resilience,[12]

10 Martynova, "'Chuzhye' v Tazovskoy tundre", 74 (author's translation).

11 Kumpula, Timo, Ana Pajunen, Elina Kaarlejarvi, Bruce C. Forbes and Florian Stammler, "Land use and land cover change in Arctic Russia: Ecological and social implications of industrial development," in vol 21 of *Global Environmental Change* (2011): 550–562, doi:10.1016/j.gloenvcha.2010.12.010.

12 Forbes, Bruce C., "Cultural resilience of social-ecological systems in the Nenets and Yamal-Nenets Autonomous Okrugs, Russia: a focus on reindeer nomads of the tundra," in *Ecology and Society*, 18(4): 36. doi:10.5751/ES-05791-180436.

and it is perceived by the Nenets people as a cornerstone question to be solved by the state, since negotiations with private companies will not help to keep the lands. Reaching a consensus in the land disputes would see the nomadic Nenets financially compensated[13] and losing everything they have—pastures, reindeers, work, sources of living, lifestyle, and identity.[14] The reindeer herders do not believe in the possibility of peaceful coexistence and sharing their lands with the hydrocarbon extraction companies or anyone else for that matter.[15] The Nenets fear that they will "not be Nenets anymore," if they are not able to freely migrate. A similar idea was conceived as far back as the nineteenth century by the Russian ethnographer Yakobiy,[16] who linked the degradation of the Samoyedic tribes with sedentarization and their dissolution into the Russian population, caused by the shrinking of the lands used as pastures.

The places where drilling rigs are erected or pipelines and roads are constructed cannot be used for the needs of reindeer herding for a long time. Moreover, routes to other pastures are also cut. The decrease in quantity and quality of pastures diminishes the variety of migration opportunities for the herds and their stewards (which is crucial during the seasonal change of the pastures). Abandoned drilling rigs, metal scrap, construction debris, and waste left by the workers multiply the negative effect of the presence of the hydrocarbon companies in the tundra and should be avoided by the reindeer herders to prevent the harm they can cause to the animals.[17]

The lands, not directly affected by the hydrocarbon extraction, suffer from the consequences of industrial development anyway: spills of drilling mud, air pollution, acid rains, and chemicals, including heavy metals, cause damage to the flora and fauna of the tundra, lakes, and rivers.[18] Some chemicals with a

---

13 Economic compensation policies are at place in the regions, and even though the company-representatives of the hydrocarbon industries (such as "Luckoil" or "Gasprom") try to improve the system of financial distribution, this system has never been assessed for fairness and they need to be further developed to guarantee just and more addressed compensational mechanisms.

14 Yu.N. Kvashnin, *Nenetskoe olenevodstvo v XX-nachale XXI veka* [The Nenets reindeer husbandry in the XX-beginning of the XXI cc.], (Salekhard-Tyumen: Koleso, 2009), 121; A.V. Golovnev, S.V. Lezova, I.V. Abramov, S.Yu. Belorussova, and N.A. Babenkova, *Entoekspertiza na Yamale: nenetskiye kochev'a i gazovye mestorozhdeniya* [Erhno-expertise on Yamal: Nenets routes and gas fields], (Ekaterinburg: ABM Press, 2014), 102–103.

15 Forbes, "Cultural resilience"; Golovnev, *Entoekspertiza na Yamale*, 93.

16 A.I. Yakobiy, *Ugasanie inorodcheskih plemyon Tobolskogo Severa* [Decline of indigenous tribes of the Tobolsk North] (Saint-Petersburg: Tip. P.P. Soykina, 1900).

17 M.A. Zen'ko, *Sovremenny Yamal: etnoecologicheskie i etnosotsialnye problemy* [Contemporary Yamal: Ethnoecological and ethnosociological problems], (Moscow, 2001), 40.

18 *O sostoyanii sanitarno-epidemiologicheskogo blagopoluchiya naseleniya v Rossiyskoy Federatsii v 2013g.: Gosudarstvenny doklad* [On conditions of sanitary-epidemiological safety

salty taste attract reindeers, which lick them.[19] Sand accumulation is a consequence of road construction[20] and improper soil reclamation.[21] Reindeers eat lichen covered with sand, which causes teeth and stomach problems; sand also destroys the vegetation in pastures, especially the fragile reindeer moss. As a result, the loss of cattle increases. For the seismologic exploration of the lands, heavy caterpillar vehicles are used, and these destroy the moss cover of the tundra, leading to permafrost disturbance, which often ends with a thermokarst effect.[22]

The bottom line, as the Nenets see it, is that industrial development leads to the disappearance of wild reindeers and to a sharp reduction in the number of fish and birds. Even the wolves are frightened of the noise coming from the drilling, which would be a positive effect, if the shift workers did not bring dogs to the tundra. The dogs, after being abandoned, group into packs and become a serious danger for both the nomadic families and the reindeer herds.[23] In some sense, they are even more dangerous than the wolves, as they are not afraid of human beings.

Even though the managers of hydrocarbon extraction companies are seen as the "others" bringing a major threat to tundra inhabitants, in real life, the Nenets people mostly see the other subgroup of "others"—the shift workers. They are seen as strangers who come to work in the tundra on fly-in, fly-out basis. Reindeer herders illegally sell them or exchange with them some food and goods because it is more profitable than working with legal official partners. Meeting the shift workers personally does not lead to the establishment of personal contacts—the workers remain as anonymous, unpleasant strangers who are in the tundra only temporarily; they cause serious damage and do not care about the land or future generations. They are not identified by the Nenets individually. They do not pique any personal interest and are seen just as representatives of a specific group. These drilling people are accused of poaching and stealing: the Nenets used to leave some of their belongings and

in Russian Federation in 2013: the State report], (Moscow, 2014), 14; Kvashnin, *Nenetskoe olenevodstvo*, 124–126, Golovnev, *Etnoekspertiza na Yamale*, 80–83.

19 Martynova, "'Chuzhye' v Tazovskoy tundre", 28.

20 D.V. Arzyutov, "Nentsy Tambreyskoy tundry: zametki iz polevogo dnevnika ob olenevodstve i sobakovodstve (2013 g.)" [The Nenets of Tambreyskaja tundra: Notes from a field-journal on reindeer husbandry and dog breeding (2013)], in *Materialy polevih issledovaniy MAE RAN*, edited by E.G. Fedorova, Vyp. 14, (Saint-Petersburg: MAE RAN, 2014), 81–82.

21 Martynova, "'Chuzhye' v Tazovskoy tundre", 28.

22 Kumpula et al., "Land use", 558; Martynova, "'Chuzhye' v Tazovskoy tundre", 73; Forbes, "Cultural resilience".

23 Arzyutov, "Nentsy Tambreyskoy tundry", 12–13; Kumpula et al., "Land use", 557; Zen'ko M.A. *Sovremenny Yamal*, 12–13.

winter clothing well packed in the tundra so that they do not carry everything while migrating with the herds, but then they would find their clothes and belongings either missing or totally destroyed and scattered around the places where they were originally left. And not least, the shift workers cause damage to the tundra by producing tons of waste and never caring about what they leave behind when they are gone. Some Nenets develop similar attitudes and stop being as environmentally friendly as they used to be,[24] though this type of behavior is considered as a deviation and condemned.[25]

"Other others" marks the people belonging to the ethnic groups who have recently appeared in the circumpolar region. Mostly, these are migrants from former USSR republics of the Caucasus and Middle Asia. They live in villages and rural settlements and usually are involved in certain forms of activities. The Caucasians are mostly sellers or shop owners, and the Middle Asians are workers in housing and construction; they also act as street cleaners. The "other others" are perceived as

> strangers, whose number has been growing; they have been spreading everywhere, there is a chance for them to come into the tundra, it is impossible to weed them out, they can cheat, they cannot be trusted, they are not eager to leave for their native lands, but they want to settle in the North.[26]

The nomadic Nenets see them quite rarely and occasionally and nevertheless they demonstrate a feeling of strong antipathy toward these particular groups[27] for several reasons: from the Nenets viewpoint, the "other others" follow barbarian traditions, and they belong to particular cultures that allow them to cheat and be aggressive—their families grow fast. In other words, these ethnic newcomers are stigmatized by every feature they have as aliens and are a source of constant fear and misunderstanding. Thus, they are expected to leave. These negative feelings toward unwelcome newcomers seem to be rather common nowadays for the ethnicities inhabiting the Russian north. The fear of aliens—the more different they are, the more dangerous they are considered—demonstrates that migrants are perceived by the Nenets as a major threat, possibly the most difficult threat to cope with, as the Nenets have never experienced the issue before, and it is seen as a totally new challenge for their well-being and culture.

24 Forbes, "Cultural resilience".

25 Golovnev, *Entoekspertiza na Yamale*, 81.

26 Martynova, "'Chuzhye' v Tazovskoy tundre", 75 (author's translation).

27 Golovnev, *Entoekspertiza na Yamale*, 85–86.

"Our others" marks the Nenets nomads from the neighboring areas, who come with their herds in search of pastures. The idea of a division of territories used for reindeer herding, with the land divided into segments, with rural settlements as centers, was introduced during the Soviet era. Since then, virtual borders have existed from the viewpoint of the Nenets, splitting the tundra into separate pieces or zones of influence. From the point of view of the Nenets, those coming from the neighboring tundra "trespass the pastures, cannot be expelled from the territory, destroy the pastures—the main treasure of the reindeer herders—steal, grow in number."[28] What seems to be most frightening in this category of the "others" is their competition for the lands (which are perceived as not belonging to them) and their consumer attitude toward the tundra, leading to the total destruction of the lichen cover, especially in the spring breeding pastures. These alien nomads are accused of the absence of care and responsible usage of the lands.

Similar cases with reindeer herders are mentioned by other researchers.[29] Some trespass into neighboring lands to find better conditions for the herds, and others move toward settlements of drill workers, with the intention of selling meat and buying some goods more cheaply than they could in their own places. All these invasions lead to overexploitation, impoverishment, and exhaustion of the pastures.

The neighboring Nenets provoke a feeling of envy, since they are perceived as having better life conditions: less industrial intrusion, richer pastures, larger territories, absence of mosquitoes, and so forth. To complete the image of the "our others," they are seen as having quite a different lifestyle and organization of livelihood, which can be defined as less civilized, and they have larger families with more children, which can cause major problems in the future by the increased competition for territorial resources.

For the nomadic Nenets, it is easier to understand and justify the reasoning and tactics of people sharing the same way of living and the same values, rather than those sharing the same place. Research shows that such sharing of the way of living and values is significantly important for the perception of the world in general: "The perception of road is more similar among herders of both regions (Bovanenkovo, YNAO and Toravei, NAO), than between a herder, a sedentary fisherman, and an indigenous villager within the same region."[30] They can be dissatisfied and can complain about behavior of the neighboring reindeer herders, but they can explain why these herders behave that way.

28 Martynova, "'Chuzhye' v Tazovskoy tundre", 76 (author's translation).

29 Kvashnin, *Nenetskoe olenevodstvo*, 123; Golovnev, *Entoekspertiza na Yamale*, 73.

30 Kumpula et al., "Land use", 559.

Another group that can be marked as "our others" includes people with other ethnic roots but who share the same type of livelihood: they live on the same lands as the Nenets, have traditional lifestyles (reindeer herders or fishermen), but they are not the subject of the affirmative action policy, since they are not officially recognized as small-numbered indigenous peoples.[31] In this case, the Nenets nomads get priority to use the lands, since other herders have to pay "land" taxes and to use the lands under general conditions. Only the Nenets fishermen get quotas in some areas, and they can sell these quotas to the representatives of other ethnic groups (Pomory, for example, in the Arkhangelsk region). These sorts of policies have led to conflicts and confrontation between the peoples sharing the same space and can form a feeling of ethnic superiority in some sense (when some nomads are "more nomadic" than others, only they exercise "genuine" traditional practices).

In addition to the relations between "our" and "other" nomads, it is necessary to admit that there is an inner source of conflict within the Nenets reindeer herders: part of them work in collective herds, and some manage herds individually.[32] The latter type of livelihood is mostly illegal (the herders are usually not registered officially as individual entrepreneurs, and they do not pay any fees and taxes); it is more risky, but nevertheless more profitable.

"Other ours" is the group of Nenets who are not involved in reindeer husbandry: they either live in the rural settlements and have totally dropped the traditional way of living or they are fishermen. As the "other ours" do not share the characteristics of the "others," "other others," and "our others," they are not seen as aliens, since they do not invade the lands and the sources and do not cheat.

As for the fishermen, they stay Nenets culturally and spiritually, and they do not live a sedentary life either. But from the reindeer herders' point of view, the life of fishermen is easier, since they only move from place to place a couple of times a year, and their relocations are organized by the fishing factories, so they do not need to migrate together with the herds. Nonetheless, their human nature is perceived as weaker —since living without reindeer herds means fewer responsibilities.

Those who inhabit the villages do not provoke fear or envy, but pity and shame instead, since they have lost their nomadic identity, together with the language and traditional skills, moral values, spiritual beliefs, and cultural practices. They have become "like Russians": they have lost their roots and

31 Shabaev, "Narody Evropeyskogo Severa", 59.

32 Forbes, "Cultural resilience".

their universe, and they have stopped talking in their native language,[33] which has made them weak in the face of bad habits and therefore open to cultural degradation. They can find nothing in life worth caring about. They are marginals, but marginals are the people living on the edge of the world, which is "ours." They are not alienated.

At the same time, the nomadic Nenets express the same desire to have apartments[34] as those who live in the settlements, even though there is no chance that they would use these apartments on a constant basis—and the very idea of settling down in villages is not at all attractive to the nomads. They are afraid of losing their sources of living and that their livelihood could be destroyed. Another dichotomy stems from the desire of the nomads to educate their children. Since the only type of education implemented in the modern life of nomads is the boarding school (taken from the Soviet system), youngsters spend a significant part of the year in the settlements, rather than in the tundra, and can hardly develop the necessary skills and attitude to become successful stewards of the herds. Staying away from their parents, herds, and the tundra does not give children enough time during the summer months to adapt to the nomadic way of life, and with time, they develop estrangement toward the tundra and the nomadic lifestyle. In the minds of the children, the worldview of the Nenets clashes with the official rational scientific outlook developed in school education. As a result, either the children lose the desire to come back to the tundra to continue the lifestyle of their parents or their parents stop them from going to school.[35] However, in recent years, boarding schools have made attempts to enrich the curriculum with classes on the traditional practices by teaching both boys and girls how to live on the tundra, but that still does not seem enough to encourage them to become real reindeer herders. As noticed by one reindeer herder, "If you do not live on the tundra when you are a child, you will not love the tundra as you should. A boy who comes for the tundra for the first time when he is sixteen sees the tundra as a harsh

33 A.A. Dregalo, and V.I. Ulyanovsky. "Evropeyskie nentsy (Arkhangel'skaya oblast', Nenetskiy Avtonomny Okrug): adaptatsionny potentsial i evolutsionnaya plastichnost'" [European Nenets (Arkhangelsk region, Nenetsky Autonomous Okrug): potential for adaptation and evolutionary flexibility], in *Korennye narody Yamala v sovremennom mire: stsenarii i kontseptsii razvitiya*. Vyp.1. 218–230 (Novosibirsk: Nonparel'. 2007), 9. Golovnev, *Entoekspertiza na Yamale*, 77; Yu.P. Shabaev, "'Buntujushaya etnichnost' na yevropeyskom severe Rossii" [Rebellious ethnicity on the European North of Russia], *Obshchestvennye nauki i sovremennost'*, 3(2006): 98.

34 Martynova, "'Chuzhye' v Tazovskoy tundre", 77.

35 Ibid.

environment and not as a home (sic)."[36] Some researchers add that children will come back to the tundra only if women come back: the Soviet project of sedentarization appears to be rather "successful" toward women, who nowadays do not see themselves in the tundra due to both the constrained conditions of living (shared dwellings) and the lack of skills needed for traditional nomadic livelihood.[37] Historically, the traditional culture of the Nenets is based on the idea of division of labor among all family members; traditional types of work for the nomads are split between the genders, but it is hard to keep these traditional functions due to the gender misbalance among the tundra inhabitants.

The number of settled Nenets differs from region to region due to the different level of impact the Soviet policies of sedentarization have had. For instance, the Nenets of NAO have suffered from the Soviet political "experiments" more than the ones living in YNAO.[38] There are more sedentary Nenets living in the first region than in the second one. Additionally, the NAO Nenets have interacted more and adopted behavioral patterns from the neighboring cultures.

To be fair, the sedentary Nenets—both from rural and urban settlements—are rather different: they can belong either to the lumpenized group or to another group that managed to integrate into the society, get an education, find work, and keep the Nenets identity.[39] The latter group is far less numerous though. As for the first one, its representatives have rather negative statistical ratings: high rates for mortality, social deviance, alcoholic syndromes, neuroses, depression, and suicides. However, the Nenets living on the tundra have not fully managed to avoid the same threats (despite their specific lifestyle of stewardship, which is hard and takes a lot of time and effort by its nature). A worrying feature common for both groups is the consumption of junk food.

The mortality rates of the Nenets population are high, and the main reasons for death are alcoholism, accidents, and suicides.[40] The Nenets people,

36 Forbes, "Cultural resilience".

37 Forbes, "Cultural resilience"; Golovnev, *Entoekspertiza na Yamale*, 78.

38 Forbes, "Cultural resilience".

39 Dregalo and Ulyanovsky, "Evropeyskie nentsy".

40 *O sostoyanii sanitarno-epidemiologicheskogo blagopoluchiya*; A.V. Artyukhov, and N.G. Khayrullina, "Tendentsii etnokulturnoy situatsii v Severnom regione" [Tendencies of ethnocultural situation in the Northern region], *Znanie. Ponimanie. Umenie.* 3 (2012): 108; K.V. Istomin, "'Atributivny stil' i problema pyanstva i samoubiystv sredi malochislennyh narodov Severa i Sibiri" ["Attributive style" and the problem of alcohol addiction and suicide among numerically small peoples of the North and Siberia], *Etnograficheskoe obozrenie*, 2 (2011): 90; B.S. Polozhiy, "Reformirovanie systemy suitsidologicheskoy pomoshi – neobhodimoe uslovie sovershenstvovaniya ohrany obshchestvennogo psikhicheskogo

together with some other northern indigenous groups, develop alcoholic dependence two to three times faster than, for instance, the Russians.[41] Alcohol addiction can become overwhelming quite quickly and can take the form of binge drinking.[42] A series of hypotheses explaining the roots of alcoholism among the indigenous people have been developed: change of lifestyle (sedentarization), feeling of social doom and disadaptation caused by poverty, economic insecurity, inaccessibility to medical help, genetic predisposition, ethnic-cultural reasons (absence of restrictive drinking traditions),[43] neurophysiological and neuropsychological peculiarities (sinistral personality with dextrocerebral domination),[44] ethnic-psychological peculiarities (a specific style of causal attribution)[45] and high levels of sensitivity, introversion, impressiveness, and autoaggressiveness.[46] All of the above could be applied as

zdorovya" [System of suicidal aid reformation is the necessary condition of developing social psychiatric health protection], *Rossiyskiy psikhiatricheskiy zhurnal*, 6 (2011): 12–13.

The first state document shows, that both NAO and YNAO are among the regions leading in the ratings of mortality, obesity, diabetes, alcoholism (both in adults and teenagers). Artyukhov claims that in the Hanty-Mansiysky region the number of alcoholic dependents among the indigenous people of the North became 13.4 times more during the years of 1993–2011, they die from murders and suicides 3–4 times more often than average. Istomin points that between 1998 and 2002 life expectancy of the indigenous peoples was 41.1 for men and 60.5 for women, which was 10years less than the average for Russia, suicidal rating 101 per 100,000, murders – 70 per 100,000. Polozhy estimates the suicidal frequency among the regions, and NAO takes the second place in that sad rating with 75,5% (per 100,000).

41 Chuhrova, M.G., I.O. Badyrgy, T.L. Udartseva. Ch.K. Mongush and V.V. Gafarov, "Osnovnye napravleniya profilaktiki alkogolisma sredi korennogo naseleniya s uchyotom kulturalnyh i psyhologichedkih osobennostey," [Main directions of alcoholism prevention among indigenous people on the basis of cultural and psychological peculiarities], in *Mir nauki, kultury, obrazovanija*. 7 (2009): 225–228.

42 Muratova, I.D., P.I. Sidorov, T.N. Ivanova, A.V. Parnyakov, L.M. Fyodorova and E.N. Belaya, "Kliniko-sotsialnye osobennosti psikhicheskogo zdorovya nentsev," [Clinic-social peculiarities of mental health of the Nenets], in *Sotsiologicheskiye issledovaniya*, 7 (1994): 66.

43 Chuhrova et al., "Osnovnye napravleniya profilaktiki."

44 Ibid.

45 Istomin, "'Atributivny stil'", 94. Istomin states that "the style of causal attribution (attributive style) of some Northern Indigenous people is that the impact of the negative outer factors will be deeper for them than for others and leads to manifestations of depression (feeling of helplessness, low self-esteem, lack of motivation) more often, which can be followed by alcohol dependence and higher risk of suicides" (author's translation).

46 B.S. Polozhiy, *Suitsidalnoe povedenie (kliniko-epidemiologicheskie i etnokulturalnie aspekty)* [Suicidal behavior (clinic-epidemiological and ethno-cultural aspects)], (Moscow: Serbsky FGU GNC SSP), 2010.

hypotheses explaining neuroses, depression, and the high level of susceptibility to suicide.

Among the Nenets population, cases of alcoholism, latent neuroses, and depression, are often not diagnosed. The lack of appropriate medical help can be partly explained by the remoteness of the Nenets settlements and especially by the moving camps of the nomads. Even with prompt specialized medical examinations, discovering the existing psychological and psychiatric problems is not immediate due to the specific behavioral patterns common to the Nenets people: health issues are hardly ever verbalized, and nobody seeks medical help for psychological or psychiatric problems. As a result, people acquire anaesthetic depersonalization and depression. Anxiety and grief arising because of a sedentary life and being far away from the tundra can be mentioned among the significant reasons for such conditions.[47]

Unfortunately, alcohol, as well as junk food of late, is easily accessible due to the expansion of civilization further into the tundra. Reindeer herders have started using snowmobiles instead of reindeers for moving between the settlements and camps, and they cover larger distances. Junk food strikes another blow to the health of the indigenous people. The Nenets living in the settlements and even the nomadic part of the population change their classic protein-lipidic type of diet (rich with meat, fish, and game) into the carbohydrate one, which consists of quick-cooking noodles, cheap biscuits, and candies. They make some economy of time by totally avoiding cooking, but eventually they destroy the cardiovascular and metabolic systems of their organisms, eventually getting a plethora of serious diseases,[48] including hypertension, ischemia, diabetes, and possibly scorbutus.

In brief, the nomadic Nenets see their sedentarized relatives as a lost part of the indigenous world with low standards of cultural and moral well-being, with a lack of motivation and life expectations, and with the total absence of knowledge and skills needed in life. The perception is that the weak nature of the settled Nenets makes them good for nothing and drives them through alcoholism and psychiatric problems toward the abyss of death, and there is no way to help them. At the same time, the reindeer herders, despite the firm

---

47 Muratova et al., "Kliniko-sotsialnye osobennosti", 67.

48 Kozlov, A.I., "Izmenenie genofonda severnyh populyatsiy: 'zakat etnosov' ili formirovanie novoy adaptivnoy gruppy?" [Northern populations genetic pool change: "decline of ethnoses" or formation of new adaptive group?], in *Vestnik arheologii, antropologii i etnographii*, 3 (2014): 99–107; A.I. Kozlov, "Vam skolko kusochkov saharu, ili pochemu nentsy ne edyat gribov" [How much sugar, or why the Nenets do not eat mushrooms], in *Rossiyskaya nauka: mechta svetla* (Moscow: Oktopus, 2006), 363–369.

pillars of their nomadic universe—stewardship and the harsh conditions of living—cannot keep their world pristine and cannot resist the diseases of civilization, as extensive contacts with the outer world are inevitable.

For the Nenets, almost all threats that make their livelihood security highly vulnerable come through people and with people. Climate challenges are not perceived as high-risk situations, but accepted as normal sporadic fluctuations of weather, which is hardly predictable and exists beyond anyone's control—therefore, the nomads are not concerned about them, or at least not as concerned as they are about industrialization.[49] Climate and environmental deviations have caused some harm to the well-being of reindeer herders, but the nomads have historically developed various adaptive strategies to avoid or to soften the damage to their livelihood. The level of livelihood vulnerability rapidly grows, and the negative effects are multiplied by the combination of many different factors: industrial development, shifts in society, environmental fluctuations, climate change, and the loss of traditional culture. Synthesis of some of these factors brings a significant change in the traditional lifestyle and day-to-day practices, sometimes making life in the tundra practically unbearable. As suggested by some authors,[50] the approach to be applied for analyzing the contemporary life of the nomads in the tundra should be holistic, as it seems to be the only way to create a full and adequate picture of the livelihood security challenges that the Nenets people face today.

In summary, reindeer herding, fishing, hunting, and foraging are very important for keeping the Nenets traditional lifestyle, but the preservation of these livelihoods is not sufficient for economic, social, cultural, and environmental sustainability. The Nenets today are not seen as vanishing: their population is growing, and their families have more members than the average family in Russia, but nevertheless they need more focused and more effective aid from the state and society. The Nenets nomads are afraid to lose their fragile world in the polar tundra and their nomadic tradition; they are afraid to be forced to sedentarize and be locked within the small settlements. All these fears make the nomads rather cautious and quite suspicious toward any kind of new activities or new people in the tundra. The Nenets perceive them as the main reason for the destructive processes that have affected or impeded every side of their livelihoods. That is why all types of newcomers get stigmatized as "others" and why they are usually not welcomed in the tundra. Among the "others" are the hydrocarbon extraction companies and their shift workers and migrants from other regions, especially from the countries of so-called near abroad. Even the

49 Forbes, "Cultural resilience".
50 Kumpula et al., "Land use", 558.

nomadic Nenets from the neighboring tundras compete for pastures and are seen as a threat.

It is idealistic and impossible to expect that hydrocarbon extraction would leave the tundra untouched. On the contrary, the pressure from those industries will be growing. Additionally, contacts with neighboring and "newly arrived" cultures, and civilization in general, will be increasing. There is no way to isolate the nomads from the "big world." To preserve the lifestyle of the indigenous people in these circumstances, it is feasible to develop a legal fundament (making more efficient environmental laws and laws on preservation of the traditional lifestyles) for their economic and social development. Another step needed is to introduce more effective measures, both economic and administrative, as well as strategies of control to make public institutions, industrial companies, and all other groups of influence involved in or affecting the indigenous livelihood follow the laws. What is also needed is an increase of the political initiatives and representation of the Nenets, and of the indigenous people in general, and support for their cultural life to make their indigenous identity stronger. These measures can decrease their current vulnerability and dependence on the outer world, increase their level of communal and ethnic consciousness and participation, and provide support for their natural cultural resilience. Finally, to be practicable, the measures intended to sustain indigenous people should be target focused. Together with this, it seems to be rational not to focus only on the preservation of the traditional lifestyle (which by any means should be preserved and strongly supported) but to introduce various inclusive policies toward the indigenous people so that they could make their own choices and steps to defend themselves and their world from the outer and inner threats or to develop new life strategies.

CHAPTER 8

The Security of the Sámi People

*Michael Sheehan**

Abstract

The Sámi people face a variety of challenges in terms of maintaining their identity, protecting their supportive natural environment, securing access to appropriate employment and broader economic goals and extending the competence of their devolved political institutions throughout Sapmi. These goals often conflict with each other, for example pursuit of economic goals impacting negatively on the environment or the protection of Sámi identity. In the past twenty years the concept of security has been given a much broader meaning, to allow it to embrace not just military issues, but also environmental, societal, political and economic issues, while the 'human security' concept has embraced economic and development issues. 'Security' thus lends itself as an umbrella concept within which to capture and relate the wide range of problems facing the Sámi. At the same time, there are dangers involved in 'securitizing' issue areas that have not been previously thought of in this way, and in Scandinavia specifically, the 'societal security' concept has been compromised by the way that Nordic governments have interpreted it. This chapter assesses these issues to determine whether 'security' is an appropriate framework for the Sámi, or whether alternative concepts such as 'resilience' might be preferable.

> We have coped in the past, and we are going to cope in the future.
>
> GUNN-BRITT RETTER[1]

1 Introduction

In looking at the relationship between the Sámi people and security and listening to the voice of the Sámi people on these crucial issues, neither the meaning of 'security', nor the meaning of 'the Sámi people' can simply be taken for

* Michael Sheehan, Professor of International Relations, and Director of the Callaghan Centre for the Study of Conflict, at Swansea University.

1 Gunn-Britt Retter, Arctic and Environmental Unit, Sámi Council, "Beyond the Impact of Climate Change – How to Cope: A Sámi Perspective on the Climate Change Discussion", in *Conference Report 2008: Forum for Development Cooperation with Indigenous Peoples*, (Tromsø: University of Tromsø/Centre for Sámi Studies, 2008).

 | DOI 10.1163/9789004314399_010

granted. Nor is it realistic to look for a single Sámi voice in this context. When security is looked at from the perspective of the problems facing the Sámi, the existing definitions of security immediately begin to be problematic, too narrowly defined and limiting to be easily or appropriately applied to the Sámi case. Once security begins to be broken down to make it more appropriate, and the variations in the experience and perspectives of different Sámi groups are brought into the equation, then it becomes clear that the effort to truly hear the voice of the Sámi on security must be detailed and wide –ranging if it is to be revealing and helpful.

'Understanding Security' is not a straightforward exercise. 'Security' has no meaning in and of itself. It is a socially-constructed concept. It has a specific meaning only within a particular social context. What a particular society understands by the term 'security' is not fixed. It can change over time to embrace different perceptions of what is valued and also to involve changing perceptions of what constitute threats to those valued dimensions of existence. In Europe, understandings of security began to evolve significantly towards the end of the Cold War, and these changes are highly significant in terms of exploring the 'security' of indigenous peoples in the European Arctic.

These changes occurred in two dimensions. The first was a so-called 'broadening' of security to embrace new sectors. For most of the Cold War security had been understood in a very narrow way. It related to external military threats to sovereign states and was addressed through possession of effective military forces for the state, possibly supplemented by membership of a military alliance. In the late Cold War this narrow definition was challenged. It was argued that security was a term that could be applied to a wider range of threats to human well-being that were distinct from military threats. These included threats to the global or regional environment, to the economic well-being of individuals and communities, and to the ability of societies to preserve their existence as distinctive cultures. One particularly influential set of definitions emerged from the so-called Copenhagen School of international relations studies which suggested a five-sector understanding of security, defined as follows:

> Military security concerns the two-level interplay of the armed offensive and defensive capabilities of states and states perceptions of each other's intentions'; political security concerns the organizational stability of states, systems of governments and the ideologies that give them legitimacy'; 'economic security concerns access to the resources, finance and markets necessary to sustain acceptable levels of welfare and state power'; societal security concerns the sustainability, within acceptable

> conditions for evolution, of traditional patterns of language, culture and religious and national identity and custom'; environmental security concerns the maintenance of the local and the planetary biosphere as the essential support system on which all other human enterprises depend.[2]

The changes in security thinking also involved an element of 'deepening'. This involved looking beyond the state as the 'referent object 'of security, that is, the thing that needed to be secured, to embrace the individual below the state, and the concept of 'society' as an alternative basis for understanding and achieving security.

These definitions were developed to fit the security challenges facing state actors, rather than a complex exceptional case like the Sámi. However they became extremely influential after the end of the Cold War, being adopted by organizations such as the UN and NATO, and it is clear that their underlying logic does not allow them to be transferred to the Sámi case in a straightforward manner. Examples of this will be explored below.

It can be argued that this broader approach to security is at least clearly a way of investigating challenges to the Sámi people in a holistic manner that the limited military definition could not achieve. However, it also reveals that the Sámi pose particular challenges when it comes to using security theory to analyze their situation. Many of these are the result not just of the definition(s) of security, but of the complexity of the idea of the Sámi as a people.

The Sámi people are the only officially recognized indigenous people living within the continental European territories of the European Union.[3] They do not possess their own nation-state and constitute minority populations in four European countries, Norway, Sweden, Finland and Russia. Estimates of the total Sámi population differ, since counting methods vary and not all Sámi participate in such exercises, but standard estimates place it at around 100,000 people, more than half of whom live in Norway. A further 25,000 live in Sweden, around 9,000 in Finland and 2,000 in Russia.[4]

2 Barry Buzan, *People, States and Fear*, 2nd ed. (Boulder: Lynne Rienner, 1991), 19–20.

3 The Sámi are not the only indigenous peoples in the European Union, since French Guiana is a French Department and part of the Eurozone, and indigenous peoples such as the Arawak, Kalina and Palikur live there. But they are the only recognised indigenous people living in the continental European territories of the EU and were recognised as such in the draft EU Treaty.

4 Veli-Pekka Lehtola, *The Sàmi People: Traditions in Transition* (Fairbanks: University of Alaska Press, 2004), 10.

As well as inhabiting different countries the Sámi speak a number of related but distinct languages. The majority speak North Sámi, but there are nine other Sámi languages, some of which are spoken by a very small number of people. Those that do not speak Sámi are divided between speakers of Norwegian, Swedish, Finnish and Russian. Within the main Sámi area, *Sapmi,* there are clear economic, political and cultural differences between Sámi populations who pursue different primary occupations, such as fishing or reindeer herding.

These distinctions are important because a fundamental element of the broader definition of security is the idea of the 'referent object'. These are 'things that are seen to be existentially threatened and that have a legitimate claim to survival'.[5] While in terms of issues like health security it would be possible to define the referent object as individuals, and therefore of individual Sámi within particular countries, when it comes to 'societal' or 'cultural' security, the situation is more complex. What 'Sámi culture' is the referent object of societal security, if there are clearly significant cultural differences between Sámi populations between and within countries? While there is clearly meaning to the idea of the Sámi people as a whole, the differences within the overall cultural unity are significant and have to be recognized when using the language of security to analyze the challenges facing them. In this respect while it is critical to hear the Sámi 'voice' on these issues, the reality is that they will be Sámi voices, rather than a single institutional or societal voice.

Using the broad language of security is potentially helpful because it allows challenges facing the Sámi to be looked at as a whole and in relation to one another. While there is a large literature on such challenges, they tend to be addressed in terms of particular security sectors, such as health[6] or human rights,[7] and usually in terms of the situation facing Sámi in a particular

5 Barry Buzan, Ole Wæver and Jaap de Wilde, *Security: A New Framework for Analysis* (Boulder: Lynne Rienner, 1998), 36.

6 For example Anne Silviken, "Prevalence of Suicidal Behaviour Among Indigenous Sámi in Northern Norway," *International Journal of Circumpolar Health* 68 (2009), 204–211;

Anna R. Spein, Harold Sexton and Siv E. Kvernmo, "Longitudinal drinking patterns in indigenous Sámi and non-indigenous youth in northern Norway," *Journal of Ethnic Substance Abuse* 5 (2006), 103–117; Magritt Brustad, Torunn Petterson, Marita Melhus and Eiliv Lund, "Mortality patterns in geographical areas with a high vs low Sámi population density in Arctic Norway," *Scandinavian Journal of Public Health* 37 (2009), 475–480.

7 Discrimination Ombudsman, (Sweden), "Discrimination of the Sámi – the rights of the Sámi from a discrimination perspective," *DO's rapporsterie, 2008:1,* (Stockholm, 2008); Ulf Morkenstam, "Indigenous Peoples and the Right to Self-Determination: The Case of the Swedish Sámi People," *The Canadian Journal of Native Studies* 25 (2005), 433–461.

country.[8] However, in order to illuminate the complexities of the Sámi-security relationship, and the need for embracing nuance and complexity in relation to both, the relationship will be analyzed in three of the security sectors proposed by the Copenhagen School, societal, economic and environmental security. These are chosen because of the five sectors, these are the three that at first glance seem the best fit.

2 Societal Security and the Sámi

The core of Sámi security concerns are oriented around questions of identity and issues related to 'societal' security. In the original broader concept of security, societal security was defined as being concerned with 'the sustainability, within acceptable conditions for evolution, of traditional patterns of language, culture and religious national identity and custom'.[9] The phrase 'within acceptable conditions for evolution', is an important one. The idea that the culture itself must be dynamic as well as a bearer of tradition is one that was emphasized by the Sámi artist and politician, Nils-Aslak Valkeapaa, who insisted that

> a culture's vitality does not consist of remaining enclosed in its own patterns of thinking – it depends on how skillful and adaptable one is at forming and transforming foreign elements, so that they suit one's own needs, and can serve one's own pattern of thought. In our days especially, Sámi culture must be capable of digesting influences from the outside with as great a self-assertion as possible – make them its own, without letting go of the connection with the old Sámi cultural background.[10]

There is evidence that Sámi leaders have been pursuing just such a strategy. Wang argues that in order to access a wider range of economic livelihoods, Sámi leaders in Sweden have begun to promote an image of Sámi culture that stresses flexibility and an ability to adapt to modernity, rather than a rigid adherence to historical stereotypes. A textual analysis of Sámi public documents in Sweden is used to argue that a dialectical image is being projected which 'on

8 Though there are exceptions for example, Dave Lewis, *Indigenous Rights Claims in Welfare Capitalist Society: Recognition and Implication* (Rovaniemi: Arctic Centre, University of Lapland, 1998).

9 Buzan, *People, States and Fear*, 20.

10 Nils-Aslak Valkeapää, "Art is For Remembering People...." In Charta 79, *The Sámi People and Human Rights* (London, 1982), 28.

the one hand speaks of an age-old people, with a retained distinctiveness of culture', but 'on the other hand (it) presents the Sámi culture as one that has been forced to change and which has become creatively active in the modern world'.[11] The Sámi Council embraces this approach, declaring that 'we have developed a rich, living and constantly evolving culture, distinct to the Sámi people'.[12]

The societal security concept has the potential to act as the master-narrative in addressing issues of Sámi security, because to a large extent all the other security issues derive from it. This has been recognized by Sámi activists themselves, who have used the language of cultural resilience to promote Sámi economic and legal objectives.[13] Societal insecurity exists 'when communities of whatever kind define a development or potentiality as a threat to their survival as a community'.[14] The danger posed by the economic, environmental or health security sectors for example is not simply that they threaten to force the Sámi population to move from the *Sapmi* region in order to escape the effects of environmental change, or find employment or secure better health care. By doing so the unity and integrity of the Sámi people is undermined, the survival of the Sámi languages put in doubt and the Sámi identity of individuals threatened by assimilation into the large populations to the south. A great deal of the literature on Sámi security focuses on these kinds of cultural security issues.[15] However, the complexity of the issue is problematic for the governments attempting to address it. The Swedish parliament in passing the Sámi Parliament Act saw the purpose of the Sámi parliament as being 'to monitor issues that

11 Elaine Wang, *Diversifying Identity, Diversifying Strategy: Revisiting the Sámi of Sweden* (University of Vermont, 2007), 5–6.

12 *The Kuellnegk Neark Declaration*, 20th Sámi Conference, (Murmansk, May 2–4, 2013), 2.

13 Christian Hicks and Ánde Somby, "Sámi responses to poverty in the Nordic countries," in Robyn Eversole, John-Andrew McNeish and Alberto D. Cimadamore, (eds.), *Indigenous Peoples and Poverty* (London: Zed Books, 2005), 275–289.

14 Buzan, Wæver and de Wilde, *Security: A New Framework for Analysis*, 119.

15 For example, Maria Sofia Aikio, "Tourism in the North and Sámi Culture," in Frank Horn, (ed.), *Economic, Social and Cultural Rights of the Sámi, International and National Aspects* (Rovaniemi: Northern Institute for Environmental and Minority Law, University of Lapland, 1998); Ole Henrik Magga, "Cultural Rights of the Saami People in Norway, Past and Present," in Takashi Irimoto and Takako Yamada, (eds.), *Circumpolar Ethnicity and Identity: Senri Ethnological Studies, No 66*, (Osaka: National Museum of Ethnology, 2004); Yelena Sergeyeva, "The Folksong Tradition of the Kola Saamis as a Display of Saami Identity," in Irja Seurujarvi-Kari and Ulla-Maija Kulonen, (eds.), *Essays in Indigenous Identity and Rights*, (Helsinki: Helsinki University Press, 1996).

relate to Sámi culture in Sweden',[16] but its own institutional framework placed responsibility for Sámi affairs with the Ministry of Agriculture, Food and Consumer Affairs, rather than with the Ministry of Culture.[17]

However, while the concept of societal security appears to lend itself as a highly appropriate prism through which to view challenges facing the Sámi, the concept itself is problematic in some ways and has been criticized by some scholars for promising more precision than is actually possible. The critics argue that the concept is problematic because it assumes more homogeneity within a society than actually exists. Is identity an object, 'something solid and constant' that can be defended, or is it a something that is variable and always evolving?[18] Much of Sámi history has been characterized by a two-fold flexibility, adapting to changing environmental conditions in order to successfully pursue lives intimately linked to the natural world, and adapting to external cultures to maintain identity without resorting to defensive violence.

It has also been claimed that society is not monolithic or holistic and that therefore 'the identity of a society does not exist prior to the identification of threats, and rather the identification of threats in fact serves to create the basic elements of societal identity'.[19] While the Sámi cultural awakening was already underway in the 1960's, it could be argued that the bitter dispute over the Alta/Kautokeino dam project was an example of this triggering a much stronger sense of Sámi identity, particularly in terms of transnational Sámi identity, than had previously existed. The need to defend this identity is seen as primary, even if perceived threat and discrimination is not as high as that facing many other indigenous populations. As Ole Henrik Magga, the Norwegian Sámi who chaired the UN Forum on Indigenous issues from 2002–4 put it, 'We do not risk being murdered, no, but the same mechanisms affect us too, irrespective of our standard of living…it's like saying that our (Scandinavian)

16 Sámitinget, 2006.

17 Although other Ministries address Sámi issues as well, for example the Ministry of Integration and Gender Equality has submitted reports on Sámi language administration. See Government Offices of Sweden, http://www.sweden.gov.se/sb/d/2188/a/19444. Cited in Elaine Wang, *Diversifying Identity, Diversifying Strategy: Revisiting the Sámi of Sweden* (University of Vermont, 2007), 4.

18 Paul Roe, "Societal Security" in A Collins, (ed.), *Contemporary Security Studies* (Oxford: Oxford University Press, 2007), 183.

19 Alem Saleh, "Broadening the Concept of Security: Identity and Societal Security," *Geopolitics Quarterly*, 6 (2010), 237.

unions should not fight for better wages because workers in Central America only earn 1% of what we earn'.[20]

At the same time, Sámi society clearly is not monolithic. While governments have tended to reify a particular conception of Sámi identity and culture based on reindeer herding, the reality is that the largest single group of Sámi in vocational terms are the Sámi fishing communities, who have expressed resentment at the way that 'Sáminess' has come to be associated with the reindeer herding Sámi.[21] There is a tension between emphasizing reindeer-herding rights because of its cultural symbolism, and the reality of the need to protect and enhance the rights of the majority non-herding Sámi population. In Sweden, a political party, the Hunting and Fishing Sámi was established and elected to the Sámi parliament demanding the same rights that and cultural profile that the reindeer herding profile had.[22] They grew quickly to become the largest party in the Sámitinget. During the crisis over the Alta-Kautokeino dispute, one of the Sámi spokesmen, Rune Stormo, noted that reindeer domestication did not become a significant means of livelihood for the Sámi until the 1600's and that 'though it has rich cultural associations, reindeer husbandry provides the main source of livelihood for less than 10% of the Sámis'.[23]

Protection of the rights of the reindeer herders is thus crucial to their security and to the maintenance of their contribution to Sámi identity, but it is by no means the only dimension of that identity or of the Sámi social-economy. Significantly, the Sámi Council insist that the Sámi, rather than the larger state communities, should be responsible for defining who is, or is not, Sámi, and see this as a vital part of Sámi self-determination.[24]

The survival of the Sámi languages is central to Sámi societal security. It is possible for peoples to have a strong and distinctive identity without a unique language, as examples like Scotland and Switzerland demonstrate, but for indigenous peoples, the language is a critical bearer of culture. It is also important in relation to access to other dimensions of security. Norway's White Paper on Sámi policy noted that 'The Government wishes a focus to be placed

20 Samediggi/Swedish Ministry of Agriculture, *The Sámi: An Indigenous People in Sweden* (Stockholm, 2005), p. 7.

21 Gro B. Ween and Marianne Lien, "Decolonisation in the Arctic? Nature Practices and Land Rights in the Norwegian High North," *Journal of Rural and Community Development* 7 (2012), 97.

22 Samediggi/Swedish Ministry of Agriculture, *The Sámi: An Indigenous People in Sweden* (Stockholm, 2005), 37.

23 Rune Stormo, "The Sámis and Sámiland: A Historical Summary," in Charta 79, *The Sámi People and Human Rights* (London, 1982), 7.

24 *The Kuellnegk Neark Declaration*, 20th Sámi Conference, (Murmansk, May 2–4, 2013), 2.

on Sámi users' encounters with the public authorities. This is important because it concerns the welfare and security under the law of individual Sámi. Investigations show that public bodies have an inadequate knowledge of the Sámi language'.[25]

Historically, the four national states where the Sámi reside have all included the Sámi within the national education systems and until comparatively recently pursued policies designed to integrate the Sámi with the majority population through enforced cultural assimilation. Sámi activists in each country have therefore had to struggle to promote the cause of access to services and education in their own languages. The UNESCO report on Sámi education in the Nordic countries noted that the majority of the Sámi people cannot speak or write Sámi, that on average Sámi have a poorer education than members of the majority population, and that 'until recently, there has been very little formal education in Sámi related subjects and industries'.[26] Recent intervention to sustain the South Sámi language demonstrates that language decline is reversible. The revitalization project in Sweden since 2001 has seen a dramatic rise in the number of elementary school children being taught in the South Sámi language.[27] The Sámi language dialects are so distinctive that they are effectively separate languages, but there are significant differences between them in terms of the number of speakers and the likely long-term viability of the languages. Of the nine distinct dialects, North Sámi has by far the largest number of speakers, perhaps as many as 80–90 percent of Sámi speakers use the North Sámi dialect throughout Norway, Sweden and Finland. Smaller numbers speak Lule Sámi, (in Norway and Sweden), South Sámi, (Sweden and Norway), Enare Sámi, (Finland), East Sámi, (Finland) and Kildin Sámi, (Russia). The other four dialects, Ume, Pite, Ter and Akkala Sámi have very small numbers of speakers and are thought to be in danger of disappearing.[28]

For some Sámi leaders, the loss of the languages is more than a historical inevitability for which no blame can be attached, but rather that 'language is one of the institutions built by human beings, that the death of a language is a chain of violent acts'.[29] In this perspective, the disappearance of a Sámi language is

25 Norwegian Ministry of Labour and Social Inclusion, *Summary of Sámi Policy: White Paper No 28* (Oslo, 2007–2008), 4.

26 Svein Lund, *Adult Education and Indigenous Peoples in Norway* (New York: UNESCO Institute for Education/Nordic Sámi Institute, 2000), 12.

27 Inuit Circumpolar Council, "*Assessing, Monitoring and Promoting the Vitality of Arctic Indigenous Languages*" (Arctic Council Sustainable Development Working Group, 2015).

28 Svein Lund, *Adult Education and Indigenous Peoples in Norway*, 4.

29 Ole Henrik Magga, "Norwegian Sámi Council," in *Proceedings of the Arctic Indigenous Languages Symposium*, (Tromsø, 2008), 36.

not the inevitable result of a shrinking population or of the pressures of globalization, but is rather the ultimate legacy of the policies of colonialism and enforced assimilation pursued by national states in previous centuries. With language survival central to Sámi identity, this makes the maintenance and growth of the existing Sámi languages an existential security threat.

Language survival is also seen as critical for addressing other threats facing the Sámi, notably the problems posed by rapid environmental change. For Gunn-Britt Retter of the Sámi Council's Arctic and Environmental Unit, 'Our knowledge has developed over thousands of years and our language is an instrument to bring the knowledge forward from generation to generation. This knowledge is especially important today with rapid changes, including climate change'.[30] Language is also specific, Sámi reindeer herder Inger Marie Gaup Eira argues that it is crucial in the structuring and sharing of knowledge, such that some part of traditional knowledge are difficult to convey accurately in translation.[31]

Societal security is thus central to Sámi concerns, and is under a number of clear pressures. Many of those pressures are the result of problems evident in other security sectors, such as economic and environmental security.

3 Economic Security

Like societal security, to be of value in analyzing Sámi issues, the definition of 'economic security' needs to be detached from its original state-centric focus, where it is defined as 'the level of access the state has to the resources, finance and markets necessary to sustain acceptable levels of welfare and state power'.[32]

This state-centric definition is of little relevance in the Sámi context, but the economic dimension of security is crucial to the survival of the Sámi as a people. The first part of the definition is clearly state-centric and oriented toward a traditional military understanding of security. However, the focus on levels of welfare in the second part of the definition can provide a basis for an understanding of economic security that relates to Sámi concerns. The idea of economic security in the modified sense of 'access to the resources necessary to sustain acceptable levels of welfare and well-being for the Sámi, individually,

30 Retter, "Beyond the Impact of Climate Change – How to Cope".

31 Inger Marie Gaup Eira, in *Proceedings of the Arctic Indigenous Languages Symposium*, (Tromsø, 2008), 14.

32 Buzan, Wæver and de Wilde, *Security: A New Framework for Analysis*, 20.

as communities and as a people' would be a valid one and is certainly reflected in the literature on the Sámi.[33] For the Sámi Council, a key objective is not only for the Sámi people to be empowered so that they have an effective voice in shaping economic development within *Sapmi*, it also wants to ensure that, where such development takes place, the Sámi people and parliaments should be the direct beneficiaries of an appropriate proportion of the wealth thus generated, so as to be able to fund developments reflecting their own priorities.

Economic security is often analyzed in relation to the poverty impacting upon populations in the less developed countries. However, 'poverty' is also a socially-constructed concept and there are a number of different ways of thinking about economic security in this sense, only some of which are fully relevant for the Sámi case. Caroline Thomas has argued that most governments and international organizations operate with an orthodox conception of poverty, which focuses on whether or not people have the money necessary to purchase adequate supplies of food and other necessities. Globalization has led to this understanding of poverty becoming universalized. However, the monetary income level that indicates such poverty is measured differently in different countries. In addition, a narrow focus on an absolute level of monetary poverty does not place the issue within broader dimensions of the quality of life that an individual or a community aspire to.

One way of assessing the economic security of the Sámi might be to use an alternative proposed measure of poverty, relative poverty. In this approach, the poverty of individual Sámi or of Sámi communities would be defined in relation to the economic circumstances of other members of the national society. Thus the situation of Sámi in Finnmark would be assessed in relation to the relative economic situation of the Norwegian population as a whole.

However, dissatisfaction with the limitations of this conception has led the United Nations Organization to make a distinction between 'income poverty' and 'human poverty', with the former relating to monetary measures of poverty and the latter to the tangible elements needed for an adequate quality of existence. A basic needs perspective would include also the provision of the basic social services necessary to prevent individuals from falling into poverty. Even this approach needs to be widened beyond questions such as housing or health care provision, to include for example, a cultural dimension.

33 Robert Paine, "Changes in the Ecological and Economic Bases in a Coastal Lappish District," *South-Western Journal of Anthropology* 14 (1958); Thomas Hahn, Property Rights, Ethics and Conflict Resolution, Foundations of the Sámi Economy in Sweden, *Acta Universitatis Agriculturae Sueciae Agraria* (Uppsala, 2000); Elina Helander, "Sámi Subsistence Activities-Spatial Aspects and Structuration," *Acta Borealia* 2, (1999).

Poverty for the UN therefore is not a concept that can be seen purely in monetary terms and located within the economic security dimension. It covers a range of factors, which spill over into other dimensions of security, and include social, political and cultural dimensions, and for the Sámi, the latter embraces the environmental security dimension. The UN Social Transformation Program therefore suggested that 'Poverty is not just economic, it is social, political and cultural. It undermines human rights – economic (the right to work and have an adequate income), social (access to health care and education), political (freedom of thought, expression and association) and cultural (the right to maintain one's cultural identity and be involved in a community's cultural life)'.[34] It is in this wider sense that poverty and economic security become relevant to Sámi security. But as with societal security, the concept of economic security can only be used in the Sámi case by accepting the complexity of the Sámi experience in this sector, and the critical interrelationships with other security sectors such as the societal and environmental ones.

In a general sense economic development in the Sámi region is clearly necessary to sustain levels of employment which can sustain the Sámi population in the region. However, there are divisions of interest between the Sámi and other national citizens and commercial entities because of conflict between the impact of certain forms of economic activity such as mining and tourism, and the desire to protect the local environment and the related Sámi cultural identity. For many Sámi these are existential security issues and evidence of a continuing colonialist mentality by national governments. Swedish Sámi activist May-Britt Ohman describes it as 'ongoing and reinforced aggressive state supported colonization of our territories',[35] while the Sámi Council asserts that 'colonization of *Sapmi* is not a practice of the past, but rather a continuing process today first and foremost enshrined in the accelerating industrialization of the Sámi land and sea territories absent our consent'.[36]

There is also the previously noted conflict between groups of Sámi engaged in different forms of employment such as fishing and reindeer herding, when it comes to the debate about ownership of Sámi cultural identity signifiers. In the early 1980's it was the Sámi fishing communities in Norway that had the highest unemployment rates, the highest uptake of welfare benefits and whose areas had the highest rates of depopulation, but they were not seen by outsiders as the archetypical Sámi. For Sámi fishing communities the ability to sustain traditional fishing patterns is as culturally significant as is reindeer herding for

34 Pierre Sane, UNESCO, Assistant Director-General, *MOST Newsletter*, No 10 (UN, 2001), 1.

35 Professor May-Britt Ohman, Personal Communication, 28 April 2015.

36 *The Kuellnegk Neark Declaration*, 20th Sámi Conference, (Murmansk, May 2–4, 2013), 3.

other communities. For example the Skolt Sámi argue that the significance of the Atlantic salmon fishery to their traditional culture has never been properly recognized by the national fishery agencies, and as a result they have had little or no influence on issues where they feel that the fishery is being endangered, as with pollution of the Naatamo river from the Norwegian Sydvaranger mine or disease spread by farmed salmon escaping from Norwegian fish farms.[37]

The interdependence of security issues facing the Sámi is such that even well-meaning external efforts to improve their situation can be problematic. For example the Norwegian governments 'big push' policies after 1976 were designed to help Sámi communities escape poverty though initiatives such as payments to herders, investments in housing, infrastructure and education, and herd management to increase production and therefore income. However, a detailed study of the impact on herding communities argued that they had been counterproductive in many ways because the larger herds had resulted in damaged lichen pastures and made the herds less resilient to consequences of climatic change and more vulnerable to predators and harsh weather conditions. This had produced an economic security trap where 'the maladaptive policies may trap people in a system that becomes increasingly more susceptible to environmental fluctuations thereby compromising the economic viability over time'.[38]

4 Environmental Security

Another element of the broader security definition, the concept of 'environmental security', remains useful even in its original formulation as 'the maintenance of the local and planetary biosphere as the essential support system upon which all other human enterprises depend'. In this regard, an environmental security literature on the Sámi can also be identified.[39] However, as

37 Gleb Raygorodetsky, "The Skolt Sámi's Path to Climate Change Resilience," *Development and Society* (United Nations University, 2013). http://ourworld.unu.edu/en/the-skolt-Sámi-path-to-climate-change resilience.

38 Vera H. Hausner, Per Fauchald, Torkild Tveraa, Elisabeth Pedersen, Johnny-Leo Jernsletten, Birgitte Ulvevadet, Rolf A. Ims, Nigel G. Yocoz and Kari Anne Brathen, "The Ghost of Development Past: The Impact of Economic Security Policies on Saami Pastoral Ecosystems," *Economy and Society*, 16 (3) Available at http://www.ecologyandsociety.org/vol16/iss3/art4/main.html.

39 Lydlia Heikkilä, "Sámi reindeer herding confronted with modern environmental management," in Lars Magne Andreassen, (ed.), *Sámiske landskapsstudier, Rapport fra et arbeidsseminar*, Diedut No 5, (Nordic Sámi Institute, 2004); Jukka Nyyssönen, "Establishing

with all the security sectors, in the case of the Sámi, there are both specific dimensions to how it operates in *Sapmi*, and difficulties in isolating its effects from the other security sectors.

Climate change is posing a wide range of challenges for the Sámi. The Mean winter temperatures in the Sámi Kautokeino region are predicted to increase from −16.0C. to −5.2.0C, and spring temperatures from −5.2 to + 1.50C by the end of the century, with precipitation increasing by 10%.[40] The 20th Sámi Conference of the Sámi Council, held in Murmansk in May 2013, noted that the Sámi people were being impacted not only by the effects of environmental changes on their livelihoods, but also by adaption and mitigation strategies put in place by the national states.[41] The latter point was echoed by Sámi reindeer-herder Olav Mathias-Eira, who lobbied the UK government on the issue in 2008, arguing that, 'We are paying a double price because we suffer all the climate change and also we are going to suffer all the actions Western states take to tackle it'.[42]

This issue encapsulates the complexity of the security sectors for the Sámi. Global warming is impacting Arctic indigenous populations more rapidly than is the case for most other human populations, but the strategies that states are pursuing in order to address this are often themselves highly problematic for the Sámi. Renewable energy developments such as construction of dams for hydro-electricity production take land away from the Sámi, while wind-farms disturb reindeer migration patterns. The latter dimension is seen in the reaction of some reindeer herders to different forms of development. Sámi Johan Mathis Turi, founding President of the Association of World Reindeer Herders for example argues that

Territorial Sovereignty in Finland –the environmental consequences of the property rights regime in Inari," in Stanley Engerman and Jacob Metzer, (eds.), *Land Rights, Ethno-Nationality and Sovereignty in History* (London: Routledge, 2004);

Helena Ruotsala, "The reindeer herder's environment," in Ludger Miller-Wille, (ed.), *Human Environmental Interactions: Issues and Concerns in Upper Lapland, Finland*, Arctic Centre Report, No 26, (Rovaniemi, Arctic Centre, University of Lapland, 1999); Elina Helander, "Sustainability in the Sámi Area: The X Factor," in Elina Helander, (ed.), *Awakened Voice: The Return of Sámi Knowledge*, Diedut No 4 (Nordic Sámi Institute, 1996).

40 Anders Oskal, Johan Mathis Turi, Svein D. Mathiesen and Philip Burgess (eds.), *Ealat – Reindeer Herders Voice: Reindeer herding, traditional knowledge and adaption to climate change and loss of grazing land* (Arctic Council, 2008), 12.

41 *The Kuellnegk Neark Declaration*, 20th Sámi Conference, (Murmansk, May 2–4, 2013), 6.

42 Emily Dugan, "Climate change plea from tribe of herders who face extinction," *Independent*, May 10, 2008. The language used in the title of this newspaper article is indicative of the lack of knowledge about the Sámi in the British media.

> 'Even though it can severely disrupt the livelihood of reindeer herders, oil and gas development may not be the worst thing that can happen to reindeer husbandry: in contrast to alternative sources for energy that affect our animals such as windmills and hydro-electric power plants, oil and gas development can prove to be profitable. Such development can provide a financial foundation for the positive development of reindeer herding societies'.[43] Nevertheless, infrastructural build-ups associated with these kinds of developments can have a major impact on land use, resulting in considerable loss of pasture land.

Rising temperatures associated with climate change impact upon Sámi communities in a variety of ways. For the Skolt Sámi north of Lake Inari for example one concern is that the region will become increasingly infested with the autumnal moth which can defoliate birch forests, but which cannot tolerate extremely low temperatures. In an outbreak in 1966, trees in colder micro-climates survived while those on warmer south facing slopes were devastated. Norway has seen two outbreaks of autumnal moth since 2005.[44]

In addition, as Norwegian Sámi President Egil Oli has stressed, rising temperatures mean that as the Arctic icecap melts, fossil fuel resources become more accessible and trans-Arctic shipping lanes open up, producing greater state interest in the region and threatening developments that will impact the Sámi, with the risk that the Sámi voice will not be listened to sufficiently.[45]

The rapidly changing environment produces mixed reactions in terms of the ability of the Sámi to use traditional knowledge as part of their environmental security strategy. In the wider environmental context there is a confidence that traditional knowledge will prove critical, that 'traditional knowledge is alive and well, and is just as relevant today as it was generations ago'[46] and that 'traditional ecological knowledge must form the basis for regulations, laws and policies and decision-making on the environment and natural resources management'.[47] Yet at the individual level there is doubt in the face of the

43 Johan Mathis Turi, quoted in Oskal, Turi, Mathiesen and Burgess, 11.

44 Gleb Raygorodetsky, "The Skolt Sámi's Path to Climate Change Resilience."

45 Egil Oli, "Accelerated development of non-renewable resources, rights and climate change in Sámi areas." In *Conference Report 2008: Forum for Development Cooperation with Indigenous Peoples* (Tromsø: University of Tromsø/Centre for Sámi Studies, 2008).

46 Egil Oli, "Accellerated development of non-renewable resources, rights and climate change in Sámi areas."

47 Retter, "Beyond the Impact of Climate Change – How to Cope".

changes. For Olav Mathias-Eira, 'traditional knowledge is no good any more, you just can't trust the ice'.[48]

Nevertheless, there is increasing recognition in the wider scientific community that the traditional knowledge of populations such as the Sámi reindeer herders has become crucial in understanding the effects of Arctic climate change and in suggesting adaptation strategies to cope with it.[49]

The inter-relationship between environmental security and other security sectors for the Sámi operates in both directions. The loss of the smaller Sámi languages is not simply a setback for cultural diversity or Sámi societal continuity, it also impacts upon efforts to cope with the effects of climate change. Gunn-Britt Retter argues that 'the extinction of each language results in the irrecoverable loss of unique cultural, historical and ecological knowledge' and the dominant national language often lacks the vocabulary for this specialist knowledge.[50]

5 Conclusions

This overview has attempted to make clear the complexity of the interrelated security challenges facing the Sámi by highlighting certain dimensions and Sámi perspectives on them, in order to demonstrate the need for holistic approaches to the problems if the varied needs and perspectives of the many stakeholders in these issues are to be effectively addressed.

It is worth recognizing that the idea of 'security' itself is somewhat alien to Sámi thinking and practice. The Latin roots of this word have connotations of stability and permanence. However, the Sámi concept of security is in many ways a distinctive one. It emphasizes evolution and adaptability to changing circumstances, rather than a focus on stability. Johan Mathis Turi argues that 'We have some knowledge about how to live in a changing environment. The term *stability* is a foreign word in our language. Our search for adaptation strategies is therefore not connected to *stability* in any form, but is instead focused on constant adaption to changing conditions'.[51]

---

48 Emily Dugan, "Climate change plea from tribe of herders who face extinction," *Independent*, May 10, 2008.

49 Oskal, Turi, Mathiesen and Burgess, *Ealat – Reindeer Herders Voice*, 10.

50 Gunn-Britt Retter, Norwegian Sámi Council and Member of the Sámi Parliament. In *Proceedings of the Arctic Indigenous Languages Symposium* (Tromsø, 2008), 26.

51 Turi, quoted in Oskal, Turi, Mathiesen and Burgess, 25–26.

CHAPTER 9

Securing Sámi Livelihoods – Does Mining Undermine Traditional Ways of Living?

Anna Petrétei[*]

Abstract

The needs of indigenous peoples in general relate to land, water, and other natural resources in order to sustain their traditional livelihoods. However, these needs typically compete with other societal interests, thus creating tension between the indigenous and non-indigenous groups. Due to sensitive environmental conditions, the problem is even more challenging in the Arctic. The growing need for natural resources has resulted in the significant expansion of extractive industries across the entire region. Despite their positive effect on local economies, the actions of these industries negatively impact not only the environment but also indigenous livelihoods. It is suggested that natural resource extraction and other major development projects in or near indigenous territories are one of the most significant sources of abuse of the rights of indigenous peoples worldwide as they threaten the environmental integrity of the lands on which these peoples live. Environmental challenges are one of the most significant and relevant aspects of human security threats against indigenous peoples. The problem is clearly visible within Sámi territories in the North, where mines and other development projects have recently been established, endangering traditional Sámi livelihoods and thus the Sámi culture. This paper addresses the particular concerns regarding Sámi livelihood practices.

1 Introduction

The needs of indigenous peoples in general relate to land, water, and other natural resources in order to sustain their traditional livelihoods. However, these needs typically compete with other societal interests.[1] Arctic indigenous

---

* Anna Petrétei, Researcher, Northern Institute for Environmental and Minority Law, Arctic Centre, University of Lapland.

1 Allard, Christina, *Two Sides of the Coin: Rights and Duties – The Interface Between Environmental Law and Saami Law Based on a Comparison with Aoteoaroa/New Zealand and Canada.* (Luleå 2006), 15.

 | DOI 10.1163/9789004314399_011

peoples face specific challenges due to environmental problems, such as pollution and climate change, which seriously affect their rights to their traditional territories and to the natural resources of those territories.[2]

On the other hand, the growing global need for minerals, oil and gas has resulted in the significant expansion of extractive industries in recent decades. Territories inhabited by indigenous peoples are generally rich in resources. According to estimations made in 2012, 50% of the gold produced between 1995 and 2015 and up to 70% of the copper produced by 2020 will be extracted from the territories of indigenous peoples.[3]

Although extractive industries often boost local economies, they also have negative impacts on the environment and local livelihoods.[4] According to S. James Anaya, former UN Special Rapporteur on the rights of indigenous peoples, natural resource extraction and other major development projects in or near indigenous territories are one of the most significant sources of abuse of the rights of indigenous peoples worldwide.[5]

Most indigenous peoples have developed highly specialized livelihood strategies and occupations that include, among others, reindeer herding, hunting, fishing, trapping, shifting cultivation or gathering food and forest products, and, in some cases, handicrafts.[6] They are therefore dependent on the rights to natural resources and the management of natural resources for their subsistence. Because of indigenous peoples' dependence on natural resources, the interest in preserving these resources in the long term is significant.[7] The

2 Heinämäki, Leena, "Environmental Rights Protecting the Way of Life of Arctic Indigenous Peoples: ILO Convention No. 169 and the UN Draft Declaration on Indigenous Peoples," in: *Arctic Governance, Juridica Lapponica* 29, ed. Timo Koivurova, Tanja Joona and Reija Shrono, (Rovaniemi, Oy Sevenprint Ltd, 2004): 231–233.

3 International Work Group for Indigenous Affairs, "Indigenous peoples, transnational corporations and other business enterprises", briefing note (January 2012), 1. Available at: www.iwgia.org/iwgia_files_publications_files/0566_BRIEFING_2.pdf.

4 Heikkinen, Hannu I., Élise Lépy, Simo Sarkki and Teresa Komu, "Challenges in acquiring a social licence to mine in the globalising Arctic," in *Polar Record* (Cambridge University Press, 2013). Available at: http://journals.cambridge.org/download.php?file=%2FPOL%2FS0032247413000843a.pdf&code=a0124c34e876009e7005a5003ed21b36.

5 "Report on extractive industries operating within or near indigenous territories" (2011). A/HRC/18/35, para 82.

6 Etot Tamayo, ed., *Traditional livelihoods and indigenous peoples*; (Asia Indigenous Peoples Pact. Chiang Mai, 2010): preface.

7 Skogvang, Susann Funderud, "Legal Questions Regarding Mineral Exploration and Exploitation in Indigenous Areas," in *Michigan State University College of Law Journal of International Law* 22 (2013). Available at SSRN: http://ssrn.com/abstract=2313741 or http://dx.doi.org/10.2139/ssrn.2313741.

extractive industries in the North are posing a real danger to the livelihoods of the indigenous peoples there. These livelihoods are not only a source of food for indigenous peoples, but are also a part of their heritage and culture.

The main issue studied in this paper[8] is the legal framework protecting indigenous rights and livelihoods against the effects of activities related to extractive industries. Following an overview on the relevant security concerns, the applicable international framework is described, with special regard to the pertinent legal instruments. National legislations are also examined. The particular focus is on how national mining codes take indigenous rights into account. Finally, an assessment of the right of the Sámi people to their traditional livelihoods is provided.

2 Security Concerns

As mentioned, extractive industries generally have a positive impact on local economies. The revenues from natural resource extraction contribute substantially to the gross domestic product and therefore boost state economies as well. Thus, most companies in the extractive sector are rather influential. The way the revenues generated by these companies are spent has a significant impact on economic growth, the environment, domestic security, and social well-being.[9] Mineral wealth can increase vulnerability, which results in the weakening of states' ability to effectively govern and maintain security.[10]

Because the lands inhabited by indigenous groups often cover rich mineral deposits and because traditional indigenous livelihoods are highly dependent on land and other natural resources, indigenous people are particularly threatened by the impacts of the mining industry. As some livelihoods are

8 One of the core research areas of the HuSArctic project (Human Security as a promotional tool for societal security in the Arctic: Addressing Multiple Vulnerability to its Population with Specific Reference to the Barents Region) is the importance of security to maintain traditional subsistence and livelihoods, particularly in the case of indigenous peoples. Author considers the present work as a significant contribution to the HuSArctic project.

9 Global Investigative Journalism Network – Covering the Extractive Industries. Available at: http://gijn.org/resources/covering-the-extractive-industries/.

10 US Agency for International Development, Office of Conflict Management and Mitigation: Minerals & Conflict – A Toolkit for Intervention, 3. Available at: http://www.iisd.org/sites/default/files/pdf/2004/envsec_minerals_conflict.pdf.

indicative of "indigenousness",[11] any major impact on them is a direct threat to indigenous societal security as well. Mining activities may induce a change in the criteria upon which a certain societal group is formed. For instance, reindeer herding is a significant indicator of "Sáminess" for many Sámi. In cases where mining impedes reindeer herding activities, it simultaneously threatens the unity, current status, and established structure of Sámi society. One could argue that in this respect mining can be regarded as a means of modernization and therefore that such activities should be encouraged. Although maintaining traditional livelihoods is essential for the survival of indigenous culture, indigenous peoples naturally have to adapt (at least to some extent) to the changing world around them. This has also been stated by the Human Rights Committee in a case concerning Finnish Sámi; the Committee clarified that traditional livelihoods need not be done as they were done in the past but can be adapted to changing circumstances and developing technologies.[12] Extractive industrial activities obviously modernize the lives of local and indigenous communities. However, they also adversely impact the environment and inevitably destroy nature, the most important basis of traditional indigenous livelihoods.

Some initiatives have been established with the aim of ensuring security and human rights in mining and other extractive industries. The US–UK Voluntary Principles on Security and Human Rights,[13] a multi-stakeholder initiative involving governments, companies, and nongovernmental organizations, seeks to improve security by ensuring human rights in the oil, gas, and mining industries through regular consultation with host governments, local communities, civil society, and companies.[14] Specifically, the Principles guide companies in conducting a comprehensive human rights risk assessment to ensure that human rights are respected. Of the countries with Sámi populations, Norway is the only one to participate in this initiative.

3 International Law Framework

When describing the general international law framework of the protection of Sámi rights, interests, and livelihoods against the adverse impacts of mining,

11 For instance, reindeer herding in Sweden and Norway can only be practiced by the Sámi people.

12 See para. 9.3. *Länsman et al. v. Finland*, Communication No. 511/1992, U.N. Doc. CCPR/C/52/D/511/1992 (1994).

13 The principles were established in 2000.

14 For more information see also: http://www.state.gov/documents/organization/196344.pdf.

several international legal instruments are applicable. Indigenous peoples' rights under international law have evolved from existing international law, including human rights treaties, to address the specific circumstances and priorities of those peoples, such as rights to their lands, territories and resources, and self-determination. The implementation of indigenous rights has yet to be improved. Some of the most difficult human rights challenges for indigenous peoples stem from pressures on their lands, territories, and resources as a result of activities associated with development and the extraction of resources.[15]

One of the most relevant human rights instruments is certainly the International Covenant on Civil and Political Rights (ICCPR). The holistic protection of indigenous peoples' rights is based on article 27 of the ICCPR. This article provides protection of the right to the enjoyment of culture by a member of a minority group in community with other members of the same group by setting up an absolute barrier for denying indigenous peoples and individuals the right to exercise their culture.[16,17]

Concerning the rights of indigenous peoples, the most important instrument to date is the 2007 United Nations Declaration on the Rights of Indigenous Peoples (UNDRIP).[18] The Declaration implies that culture not only indicates an emotional bond among the community members but also provides the basis for the group's collective physical survival. Although UNDRIP is a non-binding document, it should be noted that it is endorsed by most countries in the world.[19] Even if this Declaration is not legally binding in international law as such, it does exert legal and political influence in various ways.[20]

15 Indigenous Peoples and the United Nations Human Rights System. Fact Sheet No. 9/Rev.2. United Nations, New York and Geneva, 2013. Available at: http://www.ohchr.org/Documents/Publications/fs9Rev.2.pdf.

16 Skogvang, "Legal Questions Regarding Mineral Exploration and Exploitation in Indigenous Areas," 334.

17 The monitoring body of the treaty, the Human Rights Committee (HRC) provided a broad interpretation of 'culture' in its general comment: "With regard to the exercise of the cultural rights protected under article 27, the Committee observes that culture manifests itself in many forms, including a particular way of life associated with the use of land resources, especially in the case of indigenous peoples. That right may include such traditional activities as fishing or hunting and the right to live in reserves protected by law." (General Comment 23, para. 7.).

18 The text of the Declaration is available online in English at: http://www.un.org/esa/socdev/unpfii/documents/DRIPS_en.pdf.

19 Wiessner, Siegrfried, "The Report on the Rights of Indigenous Peoples" (International Law Association, 2010), 43.

20 Although the Declaration as a whole cannot be considered a rightful expression of customary international law, the International Law Association (ILA) holds that some of its key provisions can reasonably be regarded as corresponding to established principles of

The Declaration is the most comprehensive instrument detailing the rights of indigenous peoples in international law. It contains minimum standards for the recognition, protection, and promotion of indigenous rights. Although not uniformly or consistently implemented, the Declaration regularly guides states and indigenous peoples in developing laws and policies that have an impact on indigenous peoples, including the means to best address the claims made by indigenous peoples.[21]

The only legally binding instrument is the International Labour Organization Convention Concerning Indigenous and Tribal Peoples in Independent Countries (ILO 169).[22] The Convention is recognized as the key instrument aimed at protecting indigenous peoples and their cultures and languages with special state actions. The Convention grants collective entitlement of indigenous peoples concerning the rights of ownership and possession over the lands they traditionally occupy and their right to continue to use resources on lands that they may not occupy but only use traditionally for their subsistence and livelihoods.[23] Traditional activities, such as hunting, fishing, and trapping are recognized as important factors in the maintenance of their cultures and in their economic self-reliance and development. Therefore, governments shall ensure that these activities are strengthened and promoted.[24] Norway is the only country with a Sámi population that has ratified ILO Convention 169. The result of the ratification was the adoption of the Finnmark Act.[25] The purpose of the Act is to facilitate the management of land and natural resources in the county of Finnmark in a balanced and ecologically sustainable manner for the benefit of the residents of the county and particularly as a basis for Sámi

general international law. Former UN Special Rapporteur, S. James Anaya has also noted ("Report on the situation of human rights and fundamental freedoms of indigenous people", 2008, UN Doc. A/HRC/9/9) that some of the basic rights embodied in the Declaration are considered to be representational of customary international law. Additionally, the legally binding Convention on Biodiversity (CBD) has acknowledged that the Declaration sets a legal standard for indigenous peoples' rights. Mainly for these reasons, the Declaration has been used as a guiding legal document when interpreting indigenous peoples' rights.

21 Indigenous Peoples and the United Nations Human Rights System. Fact Sheet No. 9/Rev.2. United Nations, New York and Geneva, 2013. Available at: http://www.ohchr.org/Documents/Publications/fs9Rev.2.pdf.

22 Convention Concerning Indigenous and Tribal Peoples in Independent Countries (1989). Available in English at: http://www.ilo.org/dyn/normlex/en/f?p=NORMLEXPUB:12100:0::NO::P12100_ILO_CODE:C169.

23 Article 14.

24 Article 23.

25 The text of the Finnmark Act is available online in English at: http://www.wipo.int/wipolex/en/text.jsp?file_id=244972.

culture, reindeer husbandry, and the use of non-cultivated areas, commercial activity, and social life.[26] Although the Finnmark Act enhances Sámi rights in Finnmark, it has also been widely criticized.[27] The Sámi Parliament rejected it, claiming that the Act violated Norwegian legal precedent and national and international laws on the rights of indigenous peoples.[28] Other criticism states that all rights are non-discriminatory between Norwegians, Kvens, and Sámi in the region. Moreover, Sámi people outside the Finnmark region cannot participate in the decision-making process to the same extent as the Sámi in Finnmark. Therefore, Sámi have no clear ownership rights over the land for the purposes of practicing their traditional livelihoods, not even in the case of Finnmark.

The relatively new international legal concept of "free, prior, and informed consent (FPIC)" is also applicable to cases where mining is to be conducted on indigenous lands. This concept is rooted in the right to self-determination and is protected by shared Article 1 of the International Covenants on Civil and Political Rights and on Economic, Social and Cultural Rights. According to the Human Rights Committee and the Committee on Economic, Social and Cultural Rights, whenever a state unilaterally extinguishes indigenous peoples' rights to lands and resources, it is in contravention of the right to self-determination.[29] Therefore, the committees acknowledged that indigenous peoples hold this right under international law.[30] UNDRIP restates this right to self-determination and highlights specific instances in which this right must be respected. These include, among others, the approval of any project impacting the lands or resources of indigenous peoples.[31]

The legal treatment of Sámi in the four countries[32] where they live has followed the evolution of international law as regards indigenous peoples. Although Sámi are now officially recognized as an indigenous people, these

26 Chapter 1, Section 1 of the Finnmark Act.

27 Skogvang, "Legal Questions Regarding Mineral Exploration and Exploitation in Indigenous Areas," 339–340. Available at: http://digitalcommons.law.msu.edu/ilr/vol22/iss1/9.

28 Joona, Tanja, "The Political Recognition and Ratification of ILO Convention No. 169 in Finaland, with Some Comparison to Sweden and Norway," in *Juridica Lapponica* 37 (University of Lapland, Rovaniemi). 184.

29 Gilbert, Jeremie, Helen Tugendhat, Velérie Couillard, and Cathal Doyle, "Business, Human Rights and Indigenous Peoples: The Right to Free, Prior and Informed Consent," Forest Peoples Programme (2009). Available at SSRN: http://ssrn.com/abstract=1403985 or http://dx.doi.org/10.2139/ssrn.1403985.

30 Therefore, indigenous peoples are nowadays referred to as "rightholders" instead of "stakeholders".

31 Article 32 of the UNDRIP.

32 Norway, Sweden, Finland and Russia.

four countries have committed themselves to very different international legal obligations vis-à-vis the Sámi. All are party to the above-mentioned ICCPR, of which Article 27 provides strong protection for indigenous peoples and their traditional livelihoods.[33] The Framework Convention for the Protection of National Minorities,[34] the Council of Europe's main minority treaty, is also applicable in all four countries. The three Nordic states are bound by the European Charter for Regional or Minority Languages[35] and by UNDRIP.[36] ILO 169, the only legally binding indigenous-specific convention, has so far been ratified by Norway only. However, there are differences as to the role these international standards play in the domestic legal systems of these four countries. In practice, international legal dimensions and domestic laws overlap. One should always implement national laws in light of the relevant and applicable international legal instruments. The combination of the two will provide actual regulation.

4 National Legal Protection of Sámi Rights against the Adverse Impacts of Mining

The special status of the Sámi as an indigenous people is guaranteed at the highest legal levels in the constitutions of Norway,[37] Finland,[38] Sweden,[39] and

33 "In those States in which ethnic, religious or linguistic minorities exist, persons belonging to such minorities shall not be denied the right, in community with the other members of their group, to enjoy their own culture, to profess and practice their own religion, or to use their own language."

34 CETS No.: 157, available online in English at: http://conventions.coe.int/Treaty/en/Treaties/Html/157.htm.

35 CETS No.: 148, available online in English at: http://conventions.coe.int/treaty/en/treaties/html/148.htm.

36 The Russian Federation abstained from voting.

37 Article 108 of the Norwegian Constitution: "It is the responsibility of the authorities of the state to create conditions enabling the Sámi people, as an indigenous people, to preserve and develop its language, culture and way of life". The article on the Sámi in the Norwegian Constitution was amended in May 2014. The amended text is available at: https://www.stortinget.no/Global/pdf/Constitutionenglish.pdf?epslanguage=no.

38 Section 17 (3) of the Finnish Constitution "The Sámi, as an indigenous people, as well as the Roma and other groups, have the right to maintain and develop their own language and culture. Provisions on the right of the Sámi to use the Sámi language before the authorities are laid down by an Act." The Constitution of Finland is available in English at: https://www.finlex.fi/fi/laki/kaannokset/1999/en19990731.pdf.

39 Chapter 1, Article 2, Paragraph 6, Instrument of Government. "The opportunities of the Sámi people and ethnic, linguistic and religious minorities to preserve and develop a cultural and social life of their own, shall be promoted." The Instrument of Government

Russia.[40] In addition to recognizing their status as an indigenous people, these national legal systems also provide protection for Sámi rights and interests, particularly against the adverse impacts of mining activities. Generally, reindeer herding is the means of livelihood most affected by extractive industries. Therefore, the right to reindeer herding enjoys special protection in most countries. Each of the countries in question has a wide range of legal instruments regulating mining and related activities. However, in all the countries there is one main legal act that governs mining.

The main legal act governing mining activities in Norway is the Minerals Act.[41] The Act contains several provisions dealing with the Sámi people, with special regard to the Finnmark area where Sámi interests are particularly taken into account.[42] It is important to note that in Norway, reindeer herding can only be conducted by people of Sámi origin. Only those who have the right to a reindeer earmark can conduct reindeer husbandry in the Sámi reindeer herding areas.[43] The right to a reindeer tag requires that the person be a Sámi and that they themselves, their parents, or their grandparents rely or previously relied on reindeer herding as their main occupation.[44]

The Swedish Minerals Act[45] also contains special provisions to protect Sámi rights and interests. In Sweden, similarly to Norway, reindeer herding is a right

---

is available in English at: http://www.riksdagen.se/en/Documents-and-laws/Laws/The-Constitution/.

40 Article 69 of the Russian Constitution, "The Russian Federation shall guarantee the rights of the indigenous small peoples according to the universally recognized principles and norms of international law and international treaties and agreements of the Russian Federation". The Constitution of the Russian Federation is available in English at: http://archive.kremlin.ru/eng/articles/ConstIntro01.shtml.

On the regional level, the status of the Sámi as an indigenous people is confirmed by Article 21 of the Charter of the Murmansk region: "Government authorities of the Murmansk region contribute to indigenous people of the Kola Peninsula – Sámi – in the realization of their rights to maintain and develop their native language, national culture, traditions and customs". Approved by Murmansk Regional Duma, November 26, 1996. The text of the Charter is available in Russian at: http://www.duma-murman.ru/info/legal/framework/ustav.pdf.

41 Act of 19 June 2009 No. 101 relating to the acquisition and extraction of mineral resources (the Minerals Act). Available in English at: http://www.regjeringen.no/upload/NHD/Vedlegg/lover/mineralsact_translation_may2010.pdf.

42 As already mentioned, the Minerals Act was widely criticized, also by the Sámi themselves. Therefore, the Sámi Parliament worked out their own Mineral Guidelines in 2011.

43 Article 9 of the Reindeer Husbandry Act. The Act is available online in Norwegian at: https://lovdata.no/dokument/NL/lov/2007-06-15-40.

44 Article 32 of the Reindeer Husbandry Act.

45 Minerals Act, 1991:45.

exclusively reserved for Sámi people. According to the Reindeer Herding Act,[46] persons of Sámi origin have the right to use land and water resources to take care of themselves and their reindeer. For the reindeer herding rights to apply, the person must be a member of a Sámi village.[47] According to the Swedish Supreme Court, the Sámi right to herd reindeer in winter pasture areas is based on customary law.[48] The reindeer herding area in Sweden represents over 50% of the state's territory. The vast majority of the herding area is located in the Norrbotten and Västerbotten regions, regions where most of the Swedish mineral deposits are also found. On the other hand, mining interests are also strongly protected in Sweden; not surprisingly, Swedish policy and jurisdiction is currently the most attractive for mining investments worldwide.[49] The land use conflict is therefore obvious and inevitable.

In Sweden and Norway, only Sámi can practice reindeer herding, but in Finland it is not an exclusive Sámi livelihood. This is also the reason why in Finland much emphasis is put on who is on the electoral roll of the Sámi Parliament, as this is the only criterion upon which Sámi can be recognized.[50]

In Finland, the main legal act applicable to mining is the Mining Act.[51] Unlike the previous Mining Act from 1965, the current Finnish Mining Act[52] provides relatively strong protection for the Sámi.[53] The Act states that the

46 1971:437, the text of the Act is available in Swedish at: http://www.notisum.se/Pub/Doc.aspx?url=/rnp/sls/lag/19710437.htm.

47 Section 1 of the Reindeer Herding Act.

48 Nordmaling case. For more information see Allard, Christina, "The Swedish Nordmaling case," in *Arctic Review on Law and Politics* 2 (2011): 225–228.

49 For more information see the report of Fraser Institute, published in 2014: http://www.fraserinstitute.org/research-news/news/display.aspx?id=20902.

50 According to Chapter 1 Section 3 of the Finnish Sámi Parliament Act (974/1995), "Sámi means a person who considers himself Sámi, provided: (1) That he himself or at least one of his parents or grandparents has learnt Sámi as his first language; (2) That he is a descendent of a person who has been entered in a land, taxation or population register as a mountain, forest or fishing Lapp; or (3) That at least one of his parents has or could have been registered as an elector for an election to the Sámi Delegation or the Sámi Parliament." The text of the Act is available in English at: http://www.finlex.fi/fi/laki/kaannokset/1995/en19950974.pdf.

51 Mining Act, 627/2011. The text of the Act is available in English at: http://www.finlex.fi/en/laki/kaannokset/2011/en20110621.pdf.

52 The new Mining Act entered into force on 1 July 2011.

53 For more information on the drafting of the new Mining Act see also: Koivurova, Timo and Anna Petrétei, "Enacting a New Mining Act in Finland – How were Sámi Rights and Interests Taken into Account?" in vol 1 of *Nordisk Miljörättslig Tidskrift/Nordic Environmental Law Journal*, ed. Gabriel Michanek (2014): 119–133.

activities referred to in the Act shall be adapted in the Sámi Homeland in order to secure the rights of the Sámi as an indigenous people.[54] The Act contains several provisions that are to be applied specifically within the Sámi Homeland area.

The main Russian legal instrument regulating mining activities is the Russian Federation Law on Subsoil.[55] Although according to the Russian Constitution and federal laws, the rights of indigenous minority peoples to traditional natural resources is part of the human right to a favourable environment and an essential part of the human right to life,[56] the Sámi people are not specifically protected by the Law on Subsoil. The act contains only one reference to numerically small indigenous peoples:[57] the protection of their interests in the process of using mineral resources is the responsibility of regional authorities.[58] In practice, this means that priority is given to commercial interests and not to indigenous peoples.[59] In Russia, reindeer herding is declared to be a traditional Sámi livelihood; it is included in the "Integrated List of Types of Traditional Economic Activities of the Numerically Small Indigenous Peoples of the Russian Federation".[60] Russian mining legislation does not protect these activities; the protection is provided by the relevant legislation on agriculture.[61]

In general, Russian legal instruments aim at improving the living conditions of indigenous minority peoples. However, in many cases their rights and freedoms are not realized because of the lack of appropriate material, financial maintenance, and strong control from the state.[62]

54 Chapter 1, Section 1 of the Mining Act. See also Koivurova and Petrétei, "Enacting a New Mining Act in Finland – How were Sámi Rights and Interests Taken into Account?"

55 The Law of the Russian Federation "On Subsoil" – № 2395–1 (1992).

56 Garipov, Ruslan, "Extractive Industries and Indigenous Minority Peoples' Rights in Russia" in vol 1 of *Nordisk Miljörättslig Tidskrift/Nordic Environmental Law Journal*, Gabriel Michanek (2014): 72.

57 Sámi people in Russia are recognized as "numerically small indigenous peoples".

58 Article 4 (10) of the Law on Subsoil.

59 Garipov, "Extractive Industries and Indigenous Minority Peoples' Rights in Russia," 73.

60 Ratified by Government RF Decree of May 8, 2009 N 631-r.

61 For more information on the history of mining on Sámi lands in Russia, see also: Koivurova, Timo and Vladimir Masloboev, Kamrul Hossain, Vigdis Nygaard, Anna Petrétei, Svetlana Vinogradova, "Legal Protection of Sámi Traditional Livelihoods from the Adverse Impacts of Mining: A Comparison of the Level of Protection Enjoyed by Sámi In Their Four Home States," in vol6 of *Arctic Review on Law and Politics*, (2015): 11–51.

62 Garipov, "Extractive Industries and Indigenous Minority Peoples' Rights in Russia," 73.

The Sámi-specific provisions of relevant legal instruments may be subdivided into three categories: obligations, obstacles, and special rights of the Sámi Parliament.

a *Obligations of Applicants to Perform a Certain Action or Initiate a Certain Procedure in Order to Safeguard Sámi Interests*

According to the Norwegian Minerals Act, the administration and use of mineral resources pursuant to the Act ensures that the foundations of Sámi culture, commercial activity, and social life are safeguarded.[63] The rules of international law relating to indigenous peoples and minorities have to be taken into consideration when applying the Act.[64] When searching for mineral resources in Finnmark, the searching party shall give written notice to the Sámi Parliament, the Finnmarkseiendommen,[65] the landowner, and the relevant area and district boards for reindeer management. Traditional herding societies, the siidas, shall be given oral notice when possible.[66] In the case of an exploration permit application in Finnmark, the mining authority[67] shall inform the landowner, the Sámi Parliament, the relevant area and district boards for reindeer management, and the municipality of the permit.[68] An exploring party shall give written notice of exploration to the Sámi Parliament and the relevant area and district boards for reindeer management. Whenever practically possible, the siidas shall be given oral notice.[69]

A specific section[70] of the minerals Act is dedicated to applications for exploration in Finnmark. Within the Finnmark area, a special permit granted by the Directorate of Mining is needed in addition to the exploration permit in order to undertake exploration or pilot extraction. Exploring parties are obliged to obtain information about directly affected Sámi interests in the area that is to be explored. According to this Section, special consideration shall be given to the interests of Sámi culture, reindeer management, commercial activity,

63 Section 2 of the Minerals Act.

64 Section 6 of the Minerals Act. However, it is debated whether ILO Convention 169 is fully implemented by this section. For more information on the discussion see also Ravna, Øyvind, "The Fulfilment of Norway's International Legal Obligations to the Sámi – Assessed by the Protection of Rights to Lands, Waters and natural Resources," in *International journal on Minority and Group Rights* 21 (2014): 325–327.

65 Finnmark Estate, the agency managing the lands in Finnmark.

66 Section 10 of the Minerals Act.

67 The Directorate of Mining.

68 Chapter 4, Section 13 of the Minerals Act.

69 Section 18 of the Minerals Act.

70 Section 17 of the Minerals Act.

and social life. If the application is granted, conditions may be imposed to safeguard these interests.

According to the Swedish mining legislation, the Sámi bear the same status and rights as other landowners. In addition to that, the Sámi are holders of special rights and thus their interests have to be taken into consideration. According to the Minerals Act, holders of special rights, including affected Sámi villages, shall be involved during certain stages of the granting of exploration permits and exploitation concessions. For instance, they shall be notified at the stage of exploitation and the drafting of the work plan.[71,72] During the concession stage, Sámi villages take part in the environmental impact assessment (EIA) procedure.[73]

Sámi rights were strengthened in 2014, thanks to relevant changes to the Swedish Minerals Act and Ordinance. Sámi can now require the work plan to be translated into Sámi language. The amendment also ensures that the affected parties receive the information they need to safeguard their rights against the permit holder.[74]

In Finland, the holder of an ore prospecting permit must submit a notification of all work on the terrain that could cause any damage or harm and of the erection of any temporary structures. Within the Sámi Homeland,[75] the notification must also be submitted to the Sámi Parliament, the appropriate local reindeer owners' associations within the special reindeer herding areas,[76] and

71 Chapter 3, Section 5 of the Minerals Act.

72 This means involvement from an early stage, as the work plan has to be prepared before the exploration work begins.

73 See also: Koivurova et al., "Legal Protection of Sámi Traditional Livelihoods from the Adverse Impacts of Mining: A Comparison of the Level of Protection Enjoyed by Sámi in Their Four Home States," 11–51.

74 Information by the Mining Inspectorate in English can be found at: http://www.svemin.se/MediaBinaryLoader.axd?MediaArchive_FileID=39fa14b0-3c5c-4f50-a7d7-85191d12d80e&FileName=140807-information I Mining I Inspectorate- pdf. The amended text is available in Swedish at: fhttp://www.riksdagen.se/sv/Dokument-Lagar/Forslag/Propositioner-och-skrivelser/Battre-information-och-tydliga.

75 According to Section 4 of the Act on the Sámi Parliament, the Sámi homeland means the areas of the municipalities of Enontekiö, Inari and Utsjoki, as well as the area of the reindeer owners' association of Lapland in Sodankylä. The Act is available online in English at: http://www.finlex.fi/fi/laki/kaannokset/1995/en19950974.pdf.

76 An area specifically intended for reindeer herding as stipulated in the Reindeer Husbandry Act.

to a village meeting of the Skolt people in the Skolt area.[77,78] Special notification rules are applicable during after-care measures in exploration areas in the Sámi Homeland.[79] Goldwashers in the Sámi Homeland must provide advance written notification.[80] Within the Sámi Homeland, the mining authority[81] shall provide information about the final inspection of a gold panning area.[82]

According to the Mining Act, special procedural provisions are applicable in the Sámi Homeland, Skolt area, and special reindeer herding areas. The permit authority shall establish the effects caused by the activity on the rights of the Sámi as an indigenous people to maintain and develop their own language and culture. It shall also consider measures in order to decrease and prevent damage. Several factors are to be taken into account: any corresponding permits valid in the vicinity of the area; which areas key to the rights of the Sámi as an indigenous people the application pertains to; and other forms of usage of areas that interfere with the rights of the Sámi as an indigenous people.[83] In order to strengthen the protection of Sámi interests, the special provisions are also applicable to projects that are implemented outside the Sámi Homeland but have considerable significance as regards the rights of the Sámi as an indigenous people.

If clarification is necessary, the permit authority may arrange an event to which the following parties are to be invited for consultation: representatives of the Sámi Parliament; the Skolt village meeting; the Skolt Council; the local reindeer owners' associations concerned; the applicant; the authority or institution responsible for the management of the area; and representatives of the local fishing area and forests in joint ownership.[84] Special provisions are also to be found in permits that are already granted. All permits shall include the necessary provisions for ensuring that the permitted activity will not endanger the status of the Sámi as an indigenous people in the Sámi Homeland or the rights of the Skolts in the Skolt area in accordance with the Skolt Act.[85]

77 Area referred to in the Skolt Act: Kolttalaki 253/1995.

78 Chapter 2, Section 12 of the Mining Act.

79 Chapter 2, Section 15 of the Mining Act.

80 Section 27 of the Mining Act.

81 The mining authority in Finland is the Finnish Safety and Chemicals Agency (Turvallisuus- ja kemikaalivirasto).

82 Section 30 of the Mining Act.

83 Section 38 of the Mining Act.

84 Section 38 of the Mining Act.

85 Sections 51, 52 and 54 of the Mining Act.

The Sámi Parliament shall be informed about permit decisions involving the Sámi Homeland.[86] In the case of final inspection, the mining authority shall inform the Sámi Parliament in the Sámi Homeland, the Skolt village meeting in the Skolt area, and the local reindeer owners' associations in special reindeer herding areas.[87]

b *Obstacles to Granting a Permit in the Sámi Homeland*

Mining legislation does not only obligate applicants to perform a certain action or initiate a certain procedure in order to safeguard Sámi interests, but it also ensures the protection of Sámi rights by posing impediments in certain cases.

Pursuant to the Norwegian Minerals Act, the special permit required in addition to the exploration permit in the Finnmark area may be refused if granting the application would be contrary to Sámi interests. In Norway, the adoption of a new Planning and Building Act in 2010 strengthened the role of the municipality as the planning authority to safeguard the foundations of Sámi culture, business, and society when it comes to changes in land use within its territory.[88] This practically means that the municipality can impede mineral projects in case they endanger Sámi interests. Moreover, according to the Act, the Sámi Parliament is given authority to raise an objection.[89]

In Finland, a specific section in the Mining Act is dedicated to the obstacles. According to Section 50, a mining permit must not be granted if the planned activities would substantially undermine the preconditions for engaging in traditional Sámi sources of livelihood or maintaining and developing the Sámi culture; would substantially impair the living conditions of Skolts and the possibilities for pursuing a livelihood in the Skolt area; or would cause considerable harm to reindeer herding in the special reindeer herding areas. Nonetheless, a permit may be granted if it is possible to remove the impediment through permit regulations.[90]

c *Special Rights of the Sámi Parliament*

To further ensure the status of the Sámi, the Sámi Parliament might be granted special rights under mining legislation. In Norway, the Sámi Parliament,

86 A copy of the decision shall be submitted to the Sámi Parliament, the Skolt village meeting, or to the local reindeer owners' associations. Section 58 of the Mining Act.

87 Section 145 of the Mining Act.

88 Planning and Building Act Article 3–1.

89 Planning and Building Act Article 5–4.

90 Section 50 of the Mining Act.

together with the landowner, the municipality, and the relevant area and district boards for reindeer management, has to be given the opportunity to comment on the permit applications. If the Sámi Parliament or the landowner opposes the granting of an application, the Ministry makes the decision. If the Ministry grants an application, the Sámi Parliament or the landowner may appeal to the King. In such cases, the appeal has a suspensive effect.[91]

In Finland, the Sámi Parliament has the right to initiate proceedings against activities having a detrimental impact in the Sámi Homeland.[92] Furthermore, a special right of appeal is guaranteed on the grounds that the permitted activity undermines the rights of the Sámi as an indigenous people to maintain and develop their own language and culture.[93]

5 Assessment of the Sámi Right to Traditional Livelihoods

Mining is a controversial activity, regardless of whether the actual mining site is located on indigenous lands or not. It is difficult to tell whether mining activities really undermine the right of Sámi people to their traditional livelihoods. The impact of mining development on indigenous peoples may be positive, negative, or both, depending on various factors such as geographical location, community characteristics, past experiences with mining, the nature of the mining activities, and the way companies approach managing the impact of these factors. These impacts tend to generate complicated socio-economic interactions and unexpected secondary impacts, which can be negative in nature. The scale and nature of the impacts also varies over the different life phases of the mining projects.[94]

The notion of FPIC has emerged as an influential theme in contemporary debates about mining and development. The concept relates to many individual and collective rights that are relevant in the context of mineral extraction, particularly indigenous land rights, the recognition of and respect for culture, the right to economic participation, the right to a livelihood, and the right to a clean environment.[95] S. James Anaya, former UN Special Rapporteur on the

91 Section 17 of the Minerals Act.

92 Section 159 of the Mining Act.

93 Section 165 of the Mining Act.

94 International Council on Mining and Metals: Good Practice Guide – Indigenous Peoples and Mining, 2010–3, 9. Available at: https://www.icmm.com/document/1221.

95 John R. Owen, Deanna Kemp: 'Free prior and informed consent', social complexity and the mining industry: Establishing a knowledge base. In: *Resources Policy* 41 (2014) pp. 91–92.

rights of indigenous peoples, has stated that in its prevailing form, the model for advancing natural resource extraction within the territories of indigenous peoples appears to run counter to the self-determination of these peoples in the political, social, and economic spheres.[96]

Constructive relationships between mining companies and indigenous peoples should be based on mutual respect, meaningful engagement, trust, and mutual benefit. It is essential to recognize the potential vulnerability of indigenous peoples and to respect their rights, interests, and special connections to the land they traditionally owned or customarily used when mining projects are being established. It is of great importance to adopt and apply engagement and consultation processes that ensure the meaningful participation of indigenous communities in decision making through means that are consistent with their traditional decision-making methods and that are based on good faith negotiations.[97]

6 Conclusion

The tension between the Sámi people and actors in the mining industry is obvious. Mining activities often spark conflicts between indigenous communities, companies, and governments. In 2013, Sámi activists very strongly opposed the mining plans of a British mining company in the region of Jokkmokk in Sweden because the proposed activity encroached on their grazing lands and put pressure on their traditional livelihoods.[98] The situation is even more urgent in Finland, where the law has not yet provided firm guidance in cases of mining on Sámi lands, as the relatively new Mining Act only came into force in 2011.[99] The issue became even more topical when an Irish company declared its plans to conduct open pit diamond mining within the Sámi Homeland in northern Finland.[100] It is interesting to know that even the Human Rights Committee

96 S. James Anaya, "Report of the Special Rapporteur on the Rights of Indigenous Peoples: Extractive Industries Operating Within or Near Indigenous Territories," (2011), 82. Human Rights Council, Eighteenth Session, Agenda Item 3,A/HRC/18/35.

97 International Council of Mining & Metals: Indigenous Peoples and Mining. Position Statement, May 2013, 2. Available at: https://www.icmm.com/document/5433.

98 Bush, Daniel, "Mine dispute intensifies in Arctic Sweden," *Barents Observer*, 30 September, 2013.

99 More information: Koivurova and Petrétei, "Enacting a New Mining Act in Finland – How were Sámi Rights and Interests Taken into Account?"

100 More information: http://barentsobserver.com/en/business/2014/06/lapland-diamond-plans-cause-cross-border-pollution-concern-13-06 (13 June 2014).

noted the concern of the Sámi reindeer breeders that the quality of slaughtered reindeer could be adversely affected by a disturbed environment.[101]

Unfortunately, the presence of valuable minerals on their lands creates the potential for disruption to the peace and security of indigenous peoples. In many cases, business supersedes security concerns, posing a real threat to the survival of indigenous societies. Considering the adverse impacts resulting from extraction of natural resources on the livelihoods of indigenous peoples, there is an urgent need to recognize, protect, and enforce their rights both at the international and national levels.

---

101 Human Rights Committee states in Communication No. 511/1992. U.N. Doc. CPR/C/52/D/511/1992 (8 November 1994), para 9.3.

CHAPTER 10

ILO 169 and Securing of Sámi Rights to Lands, Nature-based Livelihood, and Natural Resources

*Øyvind Ravna**

Abstract

Since the end of the 1980s, Norway has undertaken several commitments pursuant with international law that protects Sámi lands, culture, language, and way of life. The most prominent commitment, which put Norway in a key position in securing indigenous Sámi rights to land, nature-based livelihood, and natural resources in Nordic countries, is the International Labour Organization (ILO) Convention No. 169 concerning Indigenous and Tribal Peoples in Independent Countries. This chapter discusses the commitment undertaken under this Convention; more specifically, it analyzes the legislation adopted by Norway in accordance with its obligations under Article 14 and 15 of the ILO Convention No. 169. This includes the 2005 Finnmark Act, which ensures Sámi rights to land and natural resources by transferring state land to a regional ownership body and prescribing the legal identification and clarification process of lands. Importantly, the Act states that "[t]hrough prolonged use of land and water areas, the Sámi have collectively and individually acquired rights to land in Finnmark." The author concludes that despite this clear statement of the Finnmark Act, the obligation to identify and secure Sámi lands, have hardly been met. By emphasizing the former state colonial dispositions, is the law is not applied in such a way that it protects the Sámi right to traditional lands and natural resources, as intended by the legislators.

1 Introduction

As expressed by H.M. King Harald while commencing the third Sámi Parliament in 1997, the Kingdom of Norway is established on the territory of two peoples, the Sámi and Norwegians.[1] In addition to being a national minority, the Sámi are regarded as indigenous people; they are descents of the population that solely inhabited the northernmost parts of present-day Norway at

* Professor at the Faculty of Law, University of Tromsø, The Arctic University of Norway and Adjunct Professor at the Faculty of Law, University of Lapland, Finland.

1 St.meld. nr. 55 (2000–2001) Om samepolitikken, 17.

 | DOI 10.1163/9789004314399_012

the time of colonization by the Norse population. This indicates Norway commitment to securing the civil, political, and human rights of the Sámi minority population. Among these is the right to land and natural resources, which enjoys protection as the substantial bases for both culture and property.

Acknowledging that the Sámi are an indigenous people, in 1990, Norway ratified the ILO Convention No. 169 concerning Indigenous and Tribal Peoples in Independent Countries (ILO 169). Norway also adopted an amendment to the Constitution (Article 110 (a); now Article 108), which obligates Norway to safeguard the Sámi language, culture, and way of life. Then, in 1999, Norway passed the Human Rights Act, which incorporated the International Convent on Civil and Political Rights (ICCPR), which had precedence over other legislations. Article 1 (self-determination) and 27 (rights to enjoyment of cultures and use own language for minorities) are the most important provisions for the Sámi people. The ILO 169, the Constitution Article 108, and the ICCPR Article 27 form the basis for the protection of Sámi culture, language, and livelihood in Norway, and thus, the legal basis for the Norwegian Sámi policy. Norway also signed the 2007 UN Declaration on the Rights of Indigenous Peoples and actively promoted it.

Although the Sámi's homelands are spread across four countries—Finland, Norway, Sweden, and the Russian Federation, all of which have constitutional provisions protecting the Sámi or indigenous minorities—Norway is the only country to have ratified the ILO 169. In addition, Norway implemented the Convention through internal legislation. This chapter is, therefore, limited to the situation in Norway, which by the implementation of the ILO 169, hails as an example for other Nordic countries.[2] Other Nordic countries such as Finland are in the process of ratifying ILO 169 which further supports the need for a discussion of the present topic.[3]

This study aims to review the commitments undertaken by Norway to secure rights to lands, nature-based livelihood, and natural resources of the Sámi and analyzes whether the internal implementation of the concerned obligations comply with international law. Thus, it primarily focuses on ILO 169 and internal legislation adopted for its implementation. It also briefly examines

2 Anaya, James, *The situation of the Sámi people in the Sápmi region of Norway, Sweden and Finland*, para 44. http://unsr.jamesanaya.org/docs/countries/2011-report-sapmi-a-hrc-18-35-add2_en.pdf, accessed on March 10, 2015.

3 However, in March 2015, the Finnish government officially put the ratification into hold, http://www.nrk.no/sapmi/ilo-169-saken-utsatt-til-neste-regjeringsperiode-i-finland-1.12258902, accessed on May 25, 2015.

other obligations such as the Constitutional amendment, including the ICCPR Article 27, as they contribute to the strengthening of these obligations.

2 Legal Commitments to the Sámi Undertaken by Norway

a *ILO Convention 169 Concerning Indigenous and Tribal Peoples in Independent Countries*

ILO 169, which Norway was the first to ratify worldwide, is of key significance to the Sámi rights to lands, nature-based livelihood, and natural resources. Of particular importance is the introductory provisions of Article 1 and 2, which define the concept of indigenous people and establish the general purposes of the Convention; Article 6, which ensures the rights to be consulted; Article 7, which ensures the right to decide one's priorities and participate in "the formulation, implementation and evaluation of plans and programmes for national and regional development which may affect them directly"; and Article 8, which protects indigenous customs and customary law and obligates the governments to respect them.

However, the most significant aspect of the Convention in securing indigenous land rights is Chapter II entitled "Land." The chapter covers Articles 13–20 of the Convention, of which Article 14 is the provision most familiar to lawyers, indigenous representatives, and activists. It is considered the most crucial in securing indigenous traditional lands and livelihood.[4] It is not without reason that Article 14 is the most referred among the seven articles forming the Land chapter. Article 14 (1) reads:

> The rights of ownership and possession of the peoples concerned over the lands which they traditionally occupy shall be recognised. In addition, measures shall be taken in appropriate cases to safeguard the right of the peoples concerned to use lands not exclusively occupied by them, but to which they have traditionally had access for their subsistence and traditional activities. Particular attention shall be paid to the situation of nomadic peoples and shifting cultivators in this respect.

In addition, the second and third paragraphs of the article contain key provisions and state that

4 NOU 1993: 34 Rett og forvaltning av land og vann i Finnmark, 70.

> Governments shall take steps as necessary to identify the lands which the peoples concerned traditionally occupy, and to guarantee effective protection of their rights of ownership and possession.
>
> Adequate procedures shall be established within the national legal system to resolve land claims by the peoples concerned.

Despite its unambiguous wording, earlier discussions have raised questions on whether Article 14 requires states to recognize the ownership rights of indigenous people to traditional lands or it strong use rights are sufficient.[5] Today, the prevailing opinion is that the wording is to be followed, that is, that indigenous communities have the right to collectively own their traditional lands.[6] Thus, it has great significance because it provides a basis for both identifying ownership rights of the Sámi and defining areas where the Sámi have use rights.

Although Article 15 has not received the same attention as Article 14, it is no less important in safeguarding Sámi rights to natural resources, particularly when planning and establishing extractive industries within indigenous traditional lands. The provision poses four obligations on state authorities: a general obligation to involve the indigenous people in decision-making processes and three specific and extended obligations in cases where the state retains the ownership of mineral or sub-surface resources or rights to other resources pertaining to lands. In this regard, the provision includes the obligations to consult the people before undertaking or permitting the exploration or exploitation of such resources as well as provide benefits and ensure fair compensation for any damage they may sustain as a result of such activities.

More specifically, Article 15 (1) reads:

> The rights of the peoples concerned to the natural resources pertaining to their lands shall be specially safeguarded. These rights include the right of these peoples to participate in the use, management and conservation of these resources.

5 Ulfstein, Geir, "Indigenous Peoples Right to Land," in *Max Planck* UNYB 8 (2004): 21–23. See also the discussion in NOU 1993: 34 Rett og forvaltning av land og vann i Finnmark, 70–72 and NOU 1997: 5 Urfolks landrettigheter etter folkerett og utenlands rett, 33–37; the latter is more consistent with the current view that indigenous peoples are entitled to ownership.

6 Anaya, James, *Indigenous Peoples in International Law* (Oxford University Press, 2nd ed., 2004), 143. See also Åhren, Jon Matthias, "International Human Rights Law Relevant to Natural Resource Extraction in Indigenous Territories – an Overview," in *Nordisk miljörättslig tidskrift* (2014): 21–38.

The *participation obligation* ensures and concretizes the terms of such rights outlined under Article 7 by clearly stating that indigenous people have the right to participate in the use, management, and conservation of resources in their traditional areas.[7] According to *Hans Petter Graver* and *Geir Ulfstein*[8] the provision implies that the indigenous people shall be represented in bodies that make decisions and are responsible for natural resource management in indigenous areas. However, they argue that since the provision uses the word "participate," the management does not have to be left to the indigenous people or that they should be given conclusive influence in matters concerning resources in their areas. Nevertheless, this means that decisions made on the basis of, for example, the 2009 Mineral Act and 2008 Planning and Building Act[9] cannot be settled without Sámi representation in bodies that make decisions or exercise the management of resources.

Further, Article 15 (2) reads:

> In cases in which the State retains the ownership of mineral or sub-surface resources or rights to other resources pertaining to lands, governments shall establish or maintain procedures through which they shall consult these peoples, with a view to ascertaining whether and to what degree their interests would be prejudiced, before undertaking or permitting any programmes for the exploration or exploitation of such resources pertaining to their lands. The peoples concerned shall wherever possible participate in the benefits of such activities, and shall receive fair compensation for any damages which they may sustain as a result of such activities.

The *consultation obligation* expressed in Article 15 (2) (first sentence) is posed on the government when the state retains the ownership of mineral resources that will be extracted, which is the case in Norway.[10] It can be referenced if the provision requires the government to establish special consultation

7 NOU 2007: 13 Den nye sameretten, 850.

8 Graver, Hans Petter and Geir Ulfstein, *Folkerettslig vurdering av forslaget til ny Finnmarkslov*, see http://www.regjeringen.no/nb/dep/jd/dok/rapporter_planer/rapporter/2004/folkerettslig-vurdering-av-forslaget-til/3.html?id=278380, accessed on March 10, 2015. The Sámi Rights Committee will not extend the provision so far, see NOU 2007: 13 Den nye sameretten, 1044.

9 Lov [Act] June 19, 2009, no. 101 om erverv og utvinning av mineralressurser (mineralloven) [The Mineral Act] and Lov [Act] June 27, 2008 no. 71 om planlegging og byggesaksbehandling (plan- og bygningsloven) [The Planning and Buliding Act], respectively.

10 The Mineral Act, *supra* note 9, Section 7, para 1.

arrangements in the case of such mineral resource exploitation. However, the case law of the ILO organs in complaints does not draw a distinct separation between the obligations derived from Article 6 and Article 15 (2).[11] The fact that there is a special provision for consultations in Article 15 (2) next to the general rule in Article 6, suggests that it is particularly important that the governments implement real consultations prior to the exploitation of natural resources, of which states have retained ownership in the indigenous traditional territories.[12] Article 15 (2) is also more specifically designed than Article 6, since it poses a particular obligation of consultation on plans to allow the exploitation of natural resources to which the state claims ownership. In this regard, it strengthens the obligations for consultations settled in Article 6 (1).

Article 15 (2) (second sentence) ensures *a benefit-sharing commitment*, stating that the indigenous people "shall wherever possible participate in the benefits of such activities". This obligation extends beyond the commitment to economically compensate for damages to the lands, which is ensured in the following statement "[the people concerned] shall receive fair compensation for any damages which they may sustain as a result of such activities."[13] The benefit-sharing commitment establishes that indigenous people should not only be economically compensated for damages and losses but also partake in the benefits of the industry's profits.

In sum, by ratifying the ILO 169 in 1990, Norway acknowledged the rights of the ownership and possession by the Sámi over the lands they traditionally occupied. Furthermore, Norway acknowledged the obligation to include the Sámi in decision-making processes related to the lands and extended the obligations in cases of mineral resource extraction and benefit sharing. It further moved to fulfill these obligations by adopting the 2005 Finnmark Act, which "shall apply with the limitations that follow from ILO Convention No. 169 Concerning Indigenous and Tribal Peoples in Independent Countries."[14]

---

11 Graver and Ulfstein, *Folkerettslig vurdering av forslaget til ny Finnmarkslov*; and the Sámi Law Committee in NOU 2007: 13 Den nye sameretten, 1044.

12 Sámi Law Committee in NOU 2007: 13 Den nye sameretten, 1044.

13 As for the compensation for damages, loss, and inconvenience as a result of intervention, the Sámi, as others, are secured by Constitution § 105, Expropriation Act (October 23, 1959, no. 3) and other laws, including the European Convention on Human Rights, Protocol 1, Article 1, to receive full compensation for interference. We do not further discuss this in this paper.

14 Lov [Act] June 17, 2005, No. 85, relating to legal relations and management of land and natural resources in Finnmark (The Finnmark Act) [Lov 17. juni 2005 nr. 85 om rettsforhold og forvaltning av grunn og naturressurser i Finnmark fylke (finnmarksloven)], Section 3. An English translation of the Act can be found at www.ub.uio.no/ujur/ulovdata/lov-20050617-085-eng.pdf, accessed on March 10, 2015.

b *International Covenant on Civil and Political Rights and Its Relation to the Norwegian Constitution*

Before discussing the implementation of ILO 169, it is useful to cite certain commitments mentioned in the introduction. Although the ICCPR came into effect on March 23, 1976, the obligation was significantly strengthened in 1999 as Norway adopted the Human Rights Act.[15] The Act incorporates the ICCPR into Norwegian law. Article 27, which protects the rights of minorities' culture, is of particular interest given the topic of this chapter:

> In those States in which ethnic, religious or linguistic minorities exist, persons belonging to such minorities shall not be denied the right, in community with the other members of their group, to enjoy their own culture, to profess and practise their own religion, or to use their own language.

The jurisprudence from the *UN Human Rights Committee* (the Covenant's monitoring body) shows that Article 27 not only sets up a ban on denying minorities the enjoyment of their culture but also mandates the states to take positive measures "to protect the identity of a minority and the rights of its members to enjoy and develop their culture and language."[16]

What makes Article 27 particularly interesting in relation to securing the lands and resources of indigenous people is its interpretation of the protection of the substantial basis for a minority culture in a manner that includes a particular way of life associated with the use of land and resources. The Human Rights Committee's quotation states:

> The Committee observes that culture manifests itself in many forms, including a particular way of life associated with the use of land resources, especially in the case of indigenous peoples. That right may include such traditional activities as fishing or hunting.[17]

In addition to confirming that the provision protects the use of land resources related to minorities, the statement particularly applies to indigenous people. In the context of the Sámi, this means that lands, pastures, waters, and other

15 Lov [Act] May 21, 1999 no. 30 om styrking av menneskerettighetenes stilling i norsk rett (menneskerettsloven) [The Human Rights Act].

16 Report of the Human Rights Committee, vol. 1, General Assembly Official Records, 49th Session, Supplement No. 40 (A/49/40). General Comment No. 23, adopted on 50th Session, 08.04.1994, para. 6.2.

17 Ibid., para. 7.

natural resources of importance for traditional livelihoods all enjoy legal protection. In this way, the provision establishes a threshold for interference in lands and natural resources that could threaten Sámi culture and livelihood, both for individuals and communities. Extending this threshold is considered a violation of Article 27.

In Report no. 28 (2007–2008) to the Norwegian Parliament, the government acknowledges this while endorsing the statement of the Ministry of Labour and Social Inclusion:

> In relation to the Sámi as an indigenous people, it is a common interpretation that the provision [Article 27] includes the substantive bases for the Sámi total cultural practices, also referred to as a natural basis for Sámi culture.[18]

The case law from the Human Rights Committee also clarifies that the modern ways of exercising traditional culture-related industries, such as coastal fishing with modern gear and reindeer herding with motor vehicles, enjoy protection under Article 27.[19] As the former chief justice of the Norwegian Supreme Court and head of the Coastal Fishing Committee, *Carsten Smith*, ironically said in response to the attorney general's submission of the draft of the Coastal Fishing Committee;[20] the Sámi cannot be expected to continue using oars and sails to enjoy the legal protection of their coastal fishing.

ICCPR Article 27 constitutes a significant legal obligation in securing the natural resources and lands used by the Sámi as it sets a threshold for such interventions. The Human Rights Committee's statement above also applies to the legal clarification process, particularly when the law or those enforcing the law do not pay attention to Sámi-property or use rights. This helps strengthen the legal obligations of ILO 169 in relation to the application of the law in legal clarification processes.

Article 108 of the Norwegian Constitution protects Sámi language, culture, and livelihood, and reads as follows:

18 St. meld. nr. 28 (2007–2008) *Samepolitikken* (Recommendation to the Parliament from the Ministry of Labour and Social Inclusion on the Governmental Sámi Policy), 33. Translated by the author.

19 Apirana Mahuika v. New Zealand, Comm. 547/1993, U.N. Doc. CCPR/C/70/D/547/1993, views adopted 27 October 2000 (HRC 2000), para. 9.4.

20 Smith, Carsten, "Retten til fiske i havet utenfor Finnmark," in *Arctic Review on Law and Politics* 1 (2010): 4–27 at 22. The bill of the Coastal Fishing committee; NOU 2008: 5 *Retten til fiske i havet utenfor Finnmark* included a proposal to codify rights for coastal fisheries based on historical use.

> The authorities of the State shall create conditions enabling the Sámi people to preserve and develop its language, culture and way of life. Translation from https://www.stortinget.no/globalassets/pdf/english/constitutionenglish.pdf, accessed on May 25, 2016

The article was adopted by the Norwegian Parliament on April 21, 1988, and included as Article 110 (a) by an amendment in May of the same year. In the 2014 revision of the Constitution, the wording was amended and the article renumbered to 108, without changes in the content. The article is based on a recommendation by the Sámi Rights Committee that dates back to 1984, when one of the objectives of the Committee was to overturn past assimilation policies. More precisely, the Committee aimed at putting in place a legal obligation to safeguard Sámi language, culture, and way of life and its further development, such that

> State authorities will therefore have no legal right to pursue a policy in conflict with this principle. The provision sets the requirements for both legislation and other government actions.[21]

It is of particular interest that Article 108 is modeled after ICCPR Article 27.[22] The link between these two provisions helps strengthen the mutual obligations, in which Article 108 must be interpreted in accordance with the "requirements of international law committed to the Norwegian authorities."[23] This means that Article 108 not only creates a legal obligation for the Norwegian authorities in the implementation of the country's Sámi policy but also significantly contributes to protecting lands and natural resources as a basis for Sámi culture.

There is little case law relating to Article 108. However, Norwegian Sámi policy shows that the article had repercussions beyond its political and moral significance. For instance, it substantially contributed to the 2004 establishment of the Sis-Finnmárkku Diggigoddi (Inner Finnmark District Court), which is a district court for central Sámi areas comprising Sámi-speaking judges skilled in Sámi culture and customary law and with a special responsibility of safeguarding Sámi customary law.[24]

In addition, Article 108, together with the Human Rights Act of 1999 which incorporates ICCPR 27, also contributes to the strengthening of the obligations

21 NOU 1984: 18 Om samenes rettsstilling, 433.

22 Ibid., 441.

23 Sámi Rights Committee II in NOU 2007:13 Den nye sameretten, 191.

24 NOU 1999: 22 Domstolene i første instans, 72.

under ILO 169, Article 14 and 15, where failure of implementation can result in the violation of Sámi rights to exercise culture and livelihood.

3 Implementation of Provisions Aimed at Securing Sámi Rights to Lands and Natural Resources[25]

a *The Finnmark Act and Its Legislative History*

By ratifying ILO 169, Norway committed to safeguarding the rights of ownership and possession of the Sámi to lands they traditionally occupied as well as the right to use lands not exclusively occupied by them, but to which they traditionally had accessed.

Norway has taken an active approach to these commitments by adopting the *2005 Finnmark Act* to implement them into national legislation.[26] Before discussing these commitments, I briefly explore the background and legislative history of the Act, which is a land law aimed at securing rights to lands and renewable natural resources.

Irrespective of the developments in the 1980s acknowledging the Sámi as an indigenous people entitled to the ownership of their traditional lands, the topic of Sámi rights to lands and waters remained highly controversial. This was clearly observed in the implementation of ILO 169. In the 2003 government bill of the Finnmark Act, it was assumed that the ILO obligations could be met by transferring state-held lands to a regional body, where the Sámi Parliament appointed three of the six board members.[27] The Sámi were, thus, entitled to enjoy substantial participation in the governance of all former state lands, including the presumptively Norwegian coastal sector. Consequently, the government did not see the need to identify particular lands to which the Sámi community could claim ownership, as Article 14 of ILO 169 prescribes.

The government bill was met with broad opposition, particularly from the Sámi Parliament, which argued that the bill was contrary to international law.[28] This led to a situation considered unique in the Norwegian history of

---

25 This section is partly elaborated upon in Ravna, Øyvind, "The Fulfilment of Norway's International Legal Obligations to the Sámi – Assessed by the Protection of Rights to Lands, Waters and Natural Resources," in *International Journal on Minority and Group Rights* 21 (2014): 297–329.

26 See *supra* note 14.

27 Ot.prp. nr. 53 (2002–2003) Om lov om rettsforhold og forvaltning av grunn og naturressurser i Finnmark fylke (Finnmarksloven) [The Finnmark Act], 90–91.

28 Innst. O. nr. 80 (2004–2005), 17.

legislation; the bill was subject to an examination by two independent law experts, Hans Petter Graver and Geir Ulfstein. They found that the draft was not in accordance with international law obligations to the Sámi.[29]

Graver and Ulfstein's critique and report led to consultations between the Parliamentary Standing Committee of Justice, the Sámi Parliament, and the Finnmark County Council. During these consultations, the legislature acknowledged that Norway needed to identify the rights to specific lands and waters in Finnmark to meet the ILO obligations under Article 14.[30] Accordingly, legal clarification had to be included as a key element in the Finnmark Act. Rather than addressing the legal clarification process to the ordinary courts, it was suggested that the rights to lands and waters in Finnmark be identified by a "surveying commission and a jurisdictional tribunal."[31] Consequently, the Finnmark Commission "to establish the scope and content of the rights held by Sámi and other people on the basis of prescription or immemorial usage" and the Uncultivated Land Tribunal for Finnmark "to settle disputes concerning such rights" were established to fulfill commitments in line with ILO 169, particularly Article 14 (2) and (3). The two bodies, thus, stand as the most important institutions established to meet the legal commitments Norway undertook by signing ILO 169.

b *How Does the Finnmark Act Meet the Obligations under ILO 169?*

The Finnmark Act was established as a result of the Sámi rights development that occurred during the turn of the century. In addition to securing Sámi land rights, the purpose of the Act is to govern land and renewable nature resources in Finnmark. The preamble, Section 1 of the Act pronounces that its objective is to "facilitate the management of land and natural resources on the previously State-held lands of Finnmark, for the benefit of the residents of the county" and "particularly as a basis for Sámi culture, reindeer husbandry, use of non-cultivated areas, commercial activity and social life."

In addition, and as already mentioned, the Finnmark Act was adopted to meet ILO 169's obligations of identifying traditional Sámi lands. Before detailing related substantive obligations, it is important to refer to Section 3:

> The Act shall apply with the limitations that follow from ILO Convention No. 169 concerning Indigenous and Tribal Peoples in Independent

29 Graver and Ulfstein, see *supra* note 8.

30 Innst. O. nr. 80 (2004–2005), 17.

31 Ibid., 17 and 28.

> Countries. The Act shall be applied in compliance with the provisions of international law concerning indigenous peoples and minorities and with the provisions of agreements with foreign states concerning fishing in transboundary watercourses.

This is a direct incorporation of ILO 169 into the area of the Finnmark Act, ensuring that the Act cannot be applied in contradiction to the ILO Convention.

The obligations to the Sámi are clearly pronounced in Section 5, paragraph 1:

> Through prolonged use of land and water areas, the Sámi have collectively and individually acquired rights to land in Finnmark.

The Section reflects the commitment of ILO 169, Article 14 (1), to ensuring the rights of ownership and possession of the Sámi over the lands they traditionally occupy (see Section 2.1 of this paper).

Furthermore, Section 7 is of importance: it regulates the composition of the Finnmark Estate board by ensuring that, of the six board members, the Finnmark County Council and the Sámi Parliament elect three members each with personal deputies. The provision is another follow up of ILO 169's Article 14 (1) and the only way suggested by the government as a follow up to these obligations in the 2003 governmental bill. The provision must also be seen as a follow up of Article 15 (1), which stipulates that "the natural resources pertaining to their lands [of the peoples concerned] shall be specially safeguarded. These rights include the right of these peoples to participate in the use, management and conservation of these resources." However, it is yet to be formally established whether the local people, both Sámi and non-Sámi, which through immemorial usage have acquired historical rights to the resources in nearby outlying fields, can participate in the governance, management, and benefits of these resources.

Sections 29 and 36 authorize the Finnmark Commission and Uncultivated Land Tribunal for Finnmark. As mentioned, the establishment of these bodies is a direct result of the implementation of Article 14 (2) and (3) of ILO 169. To this effect, it is important to interpret Chapter 5 of the Finnmark Act in accordance with these provisions while bearing in mind that it appeared during consultations between the Sámi Parliament and Parliamentary Standing Committee of Justice.

In addition, Section 29 poses a particular duty on the Finnmark Commission as per the current national law to "investigate rights of use and ownership to the land to be taken over by Finnmarkseiendommen pursuant to Section 49."

According to the preparatory works, the "current national law" indicates that the Sámi customary law must be included as a source.[32]

Although the review above is not exhaustive, it shows that the Finnmark Act has a broad range of provisions intended to meet the obligations of ILO 169. Given Chapter 5 of the Finnmark Act on the identification process, the lack of effort in identifying the categories of lands as enlisted in ILO 169, Article 14, can be questioned.

c *Implementation of the Finnmark Act in Relation to the Identification and Protection of Sámi Lands and Collective Use Rights*

The legal identification and clarification process, aimed at defining the ownership and use rights ensured in the Finnmark Act, Section 5, para 1 (see above), was initiated in March 2008, when the Finnmark Commission was established. This investigation is not only of regional or national interest but also of interest outside of Norway. Norway, by fulfilling its commitments toward the Sámi, can serve as an example for other Nordic countries.[33] In addition, the four Finnmark Commission reports published by the end of 2014 are the first specific documents on Sámi rights to particular land areas, whose emergence can be attributed to more than 30 years of Sámi rights discussions.[34]

The first report concerns the islands of *Stjernøya* and *Seiland* in the Alta Fjord in West Finnmark.[35] The area covered in the report is inhabited by both Sámi and non-Sámi coastal population. It is also used as summer pastures for nomadic Sámi reindeer herders. In addition, the mining company *Sibelco Nordic* produces a valuable mineral, nepheline syenite, on the island of Stjernøya.

While taking a stand on substantive questions concerning the local Sámi, non-Sámi population, and nomadic Sámi reindeer herders' usage and ownership rights on the two islands, the Finnmark Commission finds that none of the land users in the investigation fields have acquired collective property rights. However, the Commission finds that there are established use rights with an independent legal basis. Yet, this finding does not imply that the local

32 Inst. O. nr. 80 (2004–2005), 19

33 As shown in the introduction, the UN Rapporteur of Rights of Indigenous Peoples. James Anaya, *The situation of the Sámi people in the Sápmi region of Norway, Sweden and Finland* (2011), see *supra* note 2, hailed the Finnmark Act as an example for other Nordic countries.

34 Finnmarkskommisjonen, *Rapport felt 1 Stjernøya/Seiland*, March 20, 2012 (Report 1), *Rapport felt 2, Nesseby*, February 13, 2013 (Report 2), *Rapport felt 3 Sørøya*, October 16, 2013 (Report 3), and Rapport felt 5, Varangerhalvøya Øst, 24 June, 2014 (Report 5), http://www.domstol.no/no/Enkelt-domstol/Finnmarkskommisjonen/Dokumenter/Rapporter/, accessed on March 10, 2015. Report felt 4, Karasjok, which was opened in 2011, is still under investigation.

35 Ibid., Report 1.

population has the rights to use natural resources without permission from the Finnmark Estate or participate in the management and conservation of these rights, as prescribed by ILO 169 Article 15 (1). In fact, neither the locals nor the reindeer herders acknowledge any rights that go beyond what the groups already enjoy in relation to the 2007 Reindeer Husbandry Act and Sections 22 and 23 of the Finnmark Act.[36]

Remarkably, the Commission refuses to take a position on the claim of royalty from reindeer herders, given the Sibelco's mining activities on their pastoral lands. This is because the question must be solely answered on the basis of international law, that is, ILO 169, which according to the Commission cannot be done because the Commission itself is not mandated to interpret international law.[37]

In the second report published in February 2013, which covers the Sámi municipality of Nesseby in the eastern parts of Finnmark, the conclusions reached in relation to the collective rights are substantially the same as those in the first report, although the landscape, location, and evidence of use significantly vary.[38] Reports 3 and 5, published in October 2013 and June 2014, confirm the "case law" established in the previous two reports in terms of collective rights.[39]

It is noteworthy that the legislature in the preparatory works of the Finnmark Act indicates that the case law in the two precedent Supreme Court cases of Selbu and Svartskog[40] should be followed as source of law:

> It is opinion of the majority [of the Parliamentary Standing Committee of Justice] that the assessment of evidence in recent case law has been satisfactory. Resent Norwegian case law, especially the Selbu and Svartskog cases, have given instructions on how traditional Sámi use shall be considered as the basis for the acquisition. It will be important sources of law for the commission and the court.[41]

The Finnmark Commission found that the local people's use of lands in all the four fields investigated is identical is the same extensive, flexible, and

36 For more details, see Ravna, Øyvind, "The First Investigation Report of the Norwegian Finnmark Commission," in *International Journal on Minority and Group Rights* 20 (2013), 443–457.

37 *Supra* note 34, Report 1, 50.

38 *Supra* note 34, Report 2.

39 *Supra* note 34, Reports 3 and 5.

40 Published in Norsk Retstidende (NRt.) (2001), 769 ff., and 1229 ff.

41 Inst. O. nr. 80 (2004–2005), 36. (translated by the author).

long-lasting as to that of locals in Manndalen, who won the title to the land in the Supreme Court case of Svartskog.[42] However, it does not conclude in accordance with the Supreme Court case. Instead, it argues that the state's dispositions and administrative deeds have been so extensive in all the four fields that it has extinguished both the property rights of the local people, including the reindeer herders, and the rights to participate in the governance of lands and natural resources. As a result, these rights were acquired by the state and transferred to the Finnmark Estate when the Finnmark Act came into force in 2006.

Rather than emphasizing Sámi's use of lands or Sámi customary law, the Finnmark Commission has identified governmental dispositions, lack of local, and informal management of natural resources to be of law-making significance. Thus, it is not the failure in meeting the requirements of the rules of immemorial usage—i.e., the continuous and intensive use of land and natural resources in good faith of the lawfulness of the use—that create problems for the recognition of the rights of the local people, but the heavy emphasis on the former state colonial regime's legal transactions and allocations.

Accordingly, the previous state ownership, which the Finnmark Act aims to abolish, prevents the upholding of obligations to the Sámi in the same Act (Section 5), which is stating that "the Sámi have collectively and individually acquired rights to land in Finnmark."

In Report 5, the local informal management of natural resources is recognized to a greater extent than in previous reports. However, this does not imply any legal consequences as the Commission emphasizes that the population mainly were of Norwegian or *Kven* (Finnish) origin, and thus, had greater knowledge of property law. Consequently, they did not, as the Sámi in Manndalen, intend for collective ownership rights, provided they addressed it as usage rights.[43]

The application of the law shown above supports the need to inquire whether Norway follows up with its legal obligations to the Sámi when identifying and recognizing Sámi rights to lands and waters.

4 Summary

Although the process of identification of land could be better realized according to the categories in ILO 169, the above review shows that the provisions in

42 *Supra* note 34, Report 1, 64; Report 2, 65; and Report 3, 51.

43 *Supra* note 34, Report 5, 58.

the Finnmark Act were implemented by the legislature in such a way that the law is able to meet the obligations in ILO 169. However, the application of the law, conducted by the Finnmark Commission, has not had the same focus in terms of ensuring these obligations.

By placing heavy emphasis on governmental dispositions, the Finnmark Commission has not been able to acknowledge any rights beyond the provisions already embodied in the Finnmark Act for the local inhabitants, Sámi, and non-Sámi in the four fields investigated thus far. In addition, the Commission argues that the Sámi and others have not exercised a local, informal governance and management of lands. The governmental dispositions can, thus, be categorized as an argument against both exclusive and extensive local use, and the good faith of the local population. The cumulative character of the requirement rules of immemorial usage implies that the absence of good faith cannot be outweighed by embracing the continuous and intensive use of land and natural resources during historical times, or vice versa.

In addition, when accounting for the special guidelines for the legal clarification process embedded in the preparatory work, including the reference to the Selbu and Svartskog cases of the Supreme Court, it becomes highly relevant to ask whether government dispositions and the absence of local control is too heavily emphasized, both methodologically and practically.

The weight of state dispositions and absence of local control can also be a more undefined argument to achieve honorable legal and factual considerations. That public ownership and the management of previous state lands contribute in easy access to outdoor recreational resources, which are desirable in today's society, may be one such policy consideration.

Importantly, both methodologically and in relation to the question initially raised, heavy weight on state dispositions and the so-called "lack of local governance" or "honorable" policy considerations imply that the objectives of the Finnmark Act have hardly been met. Thus, it does not help that the ILO obligations are well implemented in the law itself. Here, the objective of a "significant historic shift to local control"[44] and the two fundamental acknowledgments in Finnmark Act, Section 5, is noteworthy: "[t]hrough prolonged use of land and water areas, the Sámi have collectively and individually acquired rights to land in Finnmark" and that "[t]his Act does not interfere with collective and individual rights acquired by Sámi and other people through prescription or immemorial usage."

Consequently, the law is not applied in such a way that it actually protects the rights of the ownership and possession of traditionally occupied Sámi

44 Ot.prp. nr. 53 (2002–2003), 7.

lands. In addition, the application does not contribute to strengthening the rights of the Sámi to participate in the use, management, and conservation of natural resources pertaining to their lands, as originally intended by the legislators.

Nevertheless, the methodological and practical challenges faced by the Finnmark Commission should also be acknowledged. To assess the significance of governmental dispositions in relation to the good faith of parties and their legitimate use in an environment of varying factual circumstances, where the state has indisputably exercised broad public governance, while the Finnmark Act signals a shift in the ownership and a duty to safeguard obligations to the Sámi, is not easy. By a general proprietary law approach, the landowner dispositions must certainly be heavily emphasized in relation to the claimant's good faith. The situation in Finnmark, however, is different. The landowner position of the government in the Sámi areas has long been both unclear and disputed[45] and the state has acknowledged that it is "difficult to conclude for sure that state ownership can be fully maintained."[46] The state, or legislature, has also acknowledged responsibilities to both the Sámi and non-Sámi population in Finnmark by assuming that "there is a need for a clear recognition of the independent rights on ordinary property law basis, not because the legal situation has to be altered or modified, but to make it clear that the former position of the State as landowner, has not been an obstacle to obtaining such rights."[47]

Accordingly, the law cannot be applied in a manner that the former position of the state, as per a colonial doctrine, prevents Norway from identifying Sámi collective rights to lands and waters, complying with international legal obligations to the Sámi, and thereby, not ensuring Sámi rights to lands and a traditional nature-based livelihood. Recently, the ILO Committee of Experts on the Application of Conventions and Recommendations (CEACR) requested the Norwegian government to provide information on the progress made regarding the survey and recognition of the existing rights of indigenous peoples in Finnmark County, including how the rights and interests of the Sámi have been accounted for in the process.[48] It will be interesting to see how the Norwegian government responds to this inquiry.

45 See Nrt. (1979), 492 (Varfjell-Stifjell), where Sámi reindeer herders were not affected by the statute of limitations as a result of uncertainty about the ownership of unregistered land in Finnmark.

46 Ot.prp. nr. 53 (2002–2003), 43.

47 Ibid., 96.

48 Observation (CEACR), adopted in 2014, published 104th ILC session (2015), Indigenous and Tribal Peoples Convention, 1989 (No. 169), Norway, http://www.ilo.org/dyn/normlex/en/f?p=1000:13100:0::NO:13100:P13100_COMMENT_ID:3175673, accessed on May 20, 2015.

CHAPTER 11

Russian Sámi in Context of Indigenous Security

*Svetlana Vinogradova**

Abstract

The Russian Sámi are an example of an indigenous community in the North that from the perspective of the problem under consideration is in an extreme situation. Along with global challenges, such as climate change and the impact of markets, the population is influenced by national (All-Russia) and regional factors. In general, the current situation of indigenous peoples in Russia can be characterized as "overcoming of the Soviet legacy." In practice, this requires laborious and lengthy work on the formation of a new policy to support this population. The Kola Peninsula, the area traditionally inhabited by Russian Sámi, was subjected to intensive industrial development during the Soviet period. The indigenous population suffered collectivization, sedentarization, and resettlement. As a result, the Sami's traditional economy and lifestyle were seriously transformed. Currently, the Sámi are a small minority of the population of the Murmansk region (about 0.2 percent). Preservation of identity, language, and cultural traditions in such situation becomes problematic. A traditional Sámi economic activity, which is based on reindeer herding, does not play an important role in the regional economy. Murmansk Oblast is one of the most industrialized areas of the northern world; the regional economy is focused on extraction of resources. The development of gas and mining projects is also promising in the region. The situation requires the development of methods and instruments for Sámi security at different levels: state (including regional) governance, society, and the indigenous community. Unfortunately, these processes are being slowly promoted in the region.

Introduction

The Sámi are indigenous people of the Euro-Arctic region, including northern parts of Finland, Norway, and Sweden, as well as the Kola Peninsula of Russia.

* Svetlana Vinogradova, Researcher, Kola Science Centre of the Russian Academy of Sciences, Russia.

 | DOI 10.1163/9789004314399_013

This territory is regarded as the Sámi homeland, where their history dates back thousands of years.[1] The Sámi way of life and their culture formed over the centuries based on the use of natural resources that ensure the survival of people in the extreme conditions of the Far North.

The progress of industrial civilization in the Northern and Arctic regions has created serious security threats to the indigenous peoples living in these territories. Reduction of traditional territories as a result of industrial development, environmental impact, and changes in the social and cultural landscape negatively affects the livelihoods of indigenous peoples.

The Russian Sámi are an example of an indigenous community of the North who are in an extreme situation. Along with global challenges, such as climate change or the impact of markets, these people are affected by national (Russian) and regional factors.

In general, the current situation of indigenous peoples in Russia can be characterized as one of "overcoming the Soviet legacy." Since the beginning of *perestroika* in Russia, it is recognized by the wide range of specialists that indigenous peoples have their own style of development based on traditional economic forms, lifestyles, and culture.[2] However, the transformations that took place in Russia in the previous century do not allow the majority of indigenous peoples to return to traditional lifestyles and systems of settlement.

In addition, the Kola Peninsula is one of the most industrialized and urbanized regions of the circumpolar North. In this context, the search for mechanisms of indigenous security becomes particularly important because they form survival strategies for small ethnic communities that are facing strong challenges. In practice, this requires laborious and lengthy work to protect these population groups at different levels: state government (including regional authorities), society, and the indigenous community.

This article gives a picture of the Russian Sámi in the current conditions and shows the most serious risks to Sámi security today. Additionally, existing and developing Russian instruments for protecting Sámi are analyzed.

---

1 Eriksson, Johan, "Partition and Redemption. A Machiavellian analysis of Sámi and Basque Patriotism," (Umea University, 1997).

2 Pika, Alexander, "Neotraditionalism in the Russian North," in *Indigenous Peoples and the Legacy of Perestroika*, ed. Grant, Bruce (Seattle and London, University of Washington Press, 1999).

1 Modern Risks to Sámi Security

At the present time, indigenous peoples of the North and Arctic all over the world are facing common challenges, such as climate change and competition for natural resources. However, the Kola Sámi situation is complicated by the "Soviet legacy" from one side and the presence of rich mineral resources on the other.

1.1 *Sámi as an Ethnic and Cultural Minority of the Population of Murmansk Oblast*

On the modern ethnic map of the Kola Peninsula, the Sámi constitute an insignificant minority among an alien multiethnic majority: They number only about 0.2 percent of the total population of the region,[3] mainly formed during the twentieth century as a result of intensive industrial development and growth in the strategic importance of the Northern and Arctic regions.

According to Russian regulations, citizens' ethnic affiliations are determined based on their self-identity. This explains much of the changes in the number of the Sámi population (Table 11.1). For instance, during the 1990s the total number of Sámi increased by approximately 18 percent. This increase is explained by the growing ethnic identity of the indigenous peoples in Russia during the Soviet period.[4]

TABLE 11.1 *Dynamics of the Kola Sámi population*[5]

Source, year	Number (persons)
Census, 1926	1,708
Census, 1989	1,615
Census, 2002	1,769
Census, 2010	1,599

3 *Korennue malochislennue narodu Severa na territorii Murmanskoy oblasti. Rezultatu Vserossiyskoy perepisy naseleniy 2010 goda.* [*Indigenous small-numbered peoples of the North in the Murmansk oblast. Results of all-Russian census 2010*], Murmansk, Murmanskstat, 2013. (Available in Russian.)

4 Gutsol, Natalia and Larissa Riabova, "Kola Sámi and regional development," in *Conflict and cooperation in the North*, ed. Kaepi, Kristiina and Johan Eriksson (Umea, 2002): 313–343.

5 Kiseleva, T.A. "K voprosu o mestah prozhivaniya Kol'skih Saamov 1917–1967 gg [About places of Kola Sámi inhabitants]," in *Priroda i hozyaistvo Severa.* [*Nature and economics*

A number of negative demographic trends have led to the low birth rate among the Sámi. As shown by the 2010 Census, the average modern Sámi family consists of three to four people. In the eighteen to forty-five years age group, 65 percent of Sámi women and fewer than 50 percent of Sámi men are married. The percentage of never-married men and women among the Sámi is more than twice the indicators for Russians residing in the region. Only 18 percent of Sámi women have three or more children.[6] This situation can be explained by destruction of the integrity of the traditional Sámi family during the collectivization years and by the difficulty finding partners caused by residing in small communities connected by relationships.

Unlike the general trend of stable population outflow outside the region, for the Kola Sámi, the low migration level from places of traditional residence is typical. Only about 10 percent of all Russian Sámi live outside the Murmansk region.[7] The most mobile segments of the Sámi population are women and the youth move for work or school in more prestigious locations. Often, women do not return to their native settlements and, instead, marry men of other nationalities. As a result, marriages with representatives of other ethnic groups are very common among Sámi. Some time ago, the level of such marriages was estimated by scientists at 80 percent.[8] However, since children born in mixed families are often registered as Sámi, the ongoing assimilation processes cannot be described with sufficient accuracy.

The small number of Sámi affects preservation of traditional culture. This is primarily reflected in the language situation. During the 2010 Census, 100 percent of Sámi indicated knowledge of the Russian language, but only 17

of the North] (Murmansk, 1984): 82–85. (Available in Russian.); *Korennue malochislennue narodu Severa na territorii Murmanskoy oblasti Rezultatu Vserossiyskoy perepisy naseleniy 2002 goda.* [*Indigenous small-numbered peoples of the North in the Murmansk oblast. Results of all-Russian census 2002*] (Murmansk, Murmanskstat, 2007). (Available in Russian); *Korennue malochislennue narodu Severa na territorii Murmanskoy oblasti Rezultatu Vserossiyskoy perepisy naseleniy 2010 goda.* [*Indigenous small-numbered peoples of the North in the Murmansk oblast. Results of all-Russian census 2010*] (Murmansk, Murmanskstat, 2013). (Available in Russian).

6 *Korennue malochislennue narodu Severa na territorii Murmanskoy oblasti Rezultatu Vserossiyskoy perepisy naseleniy 2010 goda.* [*Indigenous small-numbered peoples of the North in the Murmansk oblast Results of all-Russian census 2010*] (Murmansk, Murmanskstat, 2013). (Available in Russian).

7 Ibid.

8 Gutsol and Riabova, "Kola Sámi and regional development," 313–343.

percent can use the Sámi language.[9] The situation is due to the lack of conditions for the preservation and dissemination of the language. In Russia, the educational standards for teaching the Sámi language are not developed. As a consequence, the Sámi language is taught only at Lovozero elementary school and the Northern National College.

1.2 *Socio-Economic Vulnerability of the Sámi*

Analysis of the socio-economic characteristics of the Kola Sámi shows that at present they are one of the most socially vulnerable population groups of the Murmansk region.

According to the 2010 Census, the majority of the Sámi, namely, 60 percent, are rural residents. In general, Sámi settlements are remote and difficult to access. Even now, some Sámi settlements cannot be reached by car. For instance, Krasnoshchelye, a village in the east of the Kola Peninsula, is connected to the mainland only via helicopter.

Similar to all peripheral territories, Sámi settlements have poorly developed social infrastructures. For instance, there are serious shortages of medical institutions. Consumer services are represented by rare small businesses. In these areas, the lack of qualified specialists is acute, including the health and education sectors.[10]

Unfortunately, official data on Sámi incomes and living standards are nonexistent. Relevant statistical surveys are not conducted in the region. However, studies carried out with qualitative methods, including expert interviews, showed that the most sensitive social issues for the Sámi are unemployment and poverty.[11]

Post-Soviet transformations have dramatically affected all aspects of Sámi life. However, adaptation to labor markets was the most severe. During the 1990s, the number of employed Sámi decreased by 31.2 percent.[12] Analysis of the structural

---

9 *Korennue malochislennue narodu Severa na territorii Murmanskoy oblasti Rezultatu Vserossiyskoy perepisy naseleniy 2010 goda.* [*Indigenous small-numbered peoples of the North in the Murmansk oblast. Results of all-Russian census 2010*] (Murmansk, Murmanskstat, 2013). (Available in Russian).

10 *Munitsipal'nue obrazovaniy Murmanskoy oblasti* [*Municipalities of Murmansk oblast*] (Murmansk, Murmanskstat, 2014). (Available in Russian).

11 Vinogradova, Svetlana, *Korennue malochislennue narodu Severa: social'no-economicheskye aspectu gosudarstvennoy politiki* [*Indigenous small-numbered peoples of the North: socio-economic aspects of state policy*] (Apatity, 2012). (Available in Russian).

12 *Osnovnue pokazately social'no-economicheskogo polozeniy raionov prozivaniy narodov Severa na territorii Murmanskoy oblasty* [*Basic indicators of socio-economic situation in the

changes in the employment of Kola Sámi has shown that during the transition period this population group was partly forced out of all of the sectors of the regional economy, including the traditionally important agriculture sector.[13]

According to the 2010 Census, the unemployment rate among the Sámi was 21 percent, which is three times higher than the regional level.[14] Agriculture (namely, local reindeer herding) and education remain the main employment sectors of the indigenous population. In a professional-qualification context, most employed Kola Sámi work as unskilled laborers. Women mainly work as cleaners, junior nurses, etc. Some women sew traditional clothes and shoes from reindeer fur and skins. Men work as agricultural workers in reindeer-breeding, watchmen, loaders, and occasionally as truck or tractor drivers. Skilled specialists are rare among the Sámi, especial among the rural population. The only exceptions are the education and cultural sectors of the local infrastructure.

The low adaptive capacity of the Sámi in the labor market is primarily due to problems in education. Among Sámi older than fifteen years old, only 11 percent have attained higher education (mainly cultural workers and teachers) and 21 percent have attained secondary special education.[15] Unfortunately there are no special programs aimed at improving Sámi education and skills in the Murmansk region. In the region, there is only a single special educational institution—the Northern National College, situated in Lovozero village.

1.3 *The State of the Traditional Economy*

The traditional economic activity of the Sámi was based on the complex use of natural resources and from the earliest period was built on a combination of fishing, hunting, and reindeer herding. This combination of activities depended on territorial, ecological, and cultural characteristics of place of living.[16]

areas of peoples of the North settlement on the territory of Murmansk oblast] (Murmansk, Oblstat, 1999). (Available in Russian).

13 Vinogradova, *Korennue malochislennue narodu Severa: social'no-economicheskye aspectu gosudarstvennoy politiki.* [*Indigenous small numbered peoples of the North: socio economic aspects of state policy*].

14 *Korennue malochislennue narodu Severa na territorii Murmanskoy oblasti Rezultatu Vserossiyskoy perepisy naseleniy 2010 goda* [*Indigenous small-numbered people sof the North in the Murmansk oblast. Results of all-Russian census 2010*] (Murmansk, Murmanskstat, 2013). (Available in Russian.)

15 Ibid.

16 Lukyanchenko, Tatyana, *Material'nay kultura Saamov Kol'skogo poluostrova v kontse XIX–XX vekah* [*The material culture of Sámi of the Kola Peninsula in the end of XIX–XX centuries*] (Moscow, 1971). (Available in Russian.)

In coastal districts, harvesting sea animals, as well as cod and herring, was very important, and in continental districts, hunting animals for their furs and fishing in rivers and lakes. However, the main traditional and the most profitable part of Kola Sámi economics over the centuries was salmon fishing on Kola Peninsula rivers. Salmon and fur trading stimulated the development of market relations for indigenous people. The entire traditional Sámi lifestyle was determined by salmon fishing.[17] The role of reindeer herding in the traditional Sámi economy also depended on the location, but as a whole, Sámi reindeer herding had a subsidiary transportation function. Productive reindeer herding developed intensively in eastern territories of the Kola Peninsula.[18] Nevertheless, reindeer herding was always an essential part of Sámi life. The role of reindeer herding is expressed in the level of Sámi self-identity as people with a semi-nomadic way of life and as reindeer herders.[19]

The traditional Kola Sámi economic complex in its classic sense as a combination of reindeer herding, hunting, and fishing, which requires seasonal migration, has not survived to the present. Repeatedly throughout Kola Sámi history, their traditional economic model, culture, and lifestyle have influenced the new economic and political systems. At the same time, the use of renewable and non-renewable natural resources and differences in methods for managing natural resources led to conflicts.

Before the twentieth century, from the point of impact upon Sámi economics, culture, and lifestyle, the coming and settling of Komi-izhemtsy on the Kola Peninsula and colonization of the Barents Sea coast were the main events. As a result, the Sámi communities lost their most important salmon fishing grounds because of new settlements. At the same time, reindeer herding started to play a more important role in the economic structure of Kola indigenous people under the more progressive and strong Komi-izhma reindeer-herding system.[20]

17 Gutsol, Natalia, "The Kola Sámi: modern conditions of life and protection of rights" (paper presented at the conference "Cooperation in the field of cultural monuments protection, coordinating the Norwegian-Russian Commission on Environmental Protection," Neiden, Norway, November 1997).

18 Charnoluskii, Vladimir, "Zametki o pastbe i organizatsii stada u Loparey" ["Notes on the grazing and organization of herds of Lapps"], in *Kola collection. Proceedings of anthropological and ethnographic research group of the Kola Expedition* (Leningrad, 1930): 23–69. (Available in Russian.)

19 Zolotarev, David, *Kol'skie lopari* [*The Kola Laps*] (Leningrad, 1928). (Available in Russian.)

20 Konakov, Nikolay, "Ecological adaptation of Komi resettled group," in *Arctic anthropology* 30 (1993): 92–102; Yurchenko, Aleksey "Etnicheskie aspekty kolonizacii poberezh'ya Barenceva morya v seredine XIX – nachale XX vekov" ["Ethnic aspects of the colonization

This destructive pressure on traditional Sámi culture and economy intensified during the socialist transformation, accompanied by repeated increases in population and changes in the ethnic structure of the region. In this respect, during the collectivization period, the cultures and livelihoods of all indigenous peoples of the Northern and Arctic regions in the Soviet Union changed dramatically: the process of a gradual transformation to a sedentary lifestyle started during this period.

The result of these processes was the final destruction of the Sámi traditional economic complex and system of settlement. In general, the Soviet policy of paternalism, aimed at integration of indigenous peoples in the "united nation – the Soviet people," has led to the loss of Sámi mechanisms of traditional livelihood.

Contemporarily, the main livelihood for Russian Sámi is reindeer herding. Past local livelihoods such as fishing and hunting have lost their importance and play a secondary role, as well as the handicraft industry and plant harvesting.

The Murmansk region is not part of the main reindeer-herding regions of the country. The reindeer number about seventy thousand, which is only 4 percent of the total number in Russia.[21]

At the same time, reindeer herding is an insignificant sector in the economy of the Murmansk region. The percentage of agriculture of the gross regional product does not exceed 1 percent; consequently, the percentage of reindeer breeding is even smaller (there are no specific regional statistics).[22]

In general, in the Murmansk region about 6,500 hectares of pasture are allocated for reindeer-herding activities that constitute almost half of the territory.[23]

At present, reindeer herding in the Murmansk region is represented by various legal forms. Productive trade reindeer-breeding is concentrated at the two

on Barents coast in the middle XIX – begining XX century"], in *Nauka i biznes na Murmane* [*Science and Business on the Murman*] (Murmansk, 2001). 5–12. (Available in Russian.)

21 *Itogi Vserossiyskoy sel'skohosystvennoy perepisi 2006 goda. Sel'skoe hosiystvo raionov Kraynego Severa i priravnennyh k nim mestnostey* [*Results of all-Russian agricultural census of 2006. Agriculture of the Far North and equated areas.*] (Moscow, 2008). (Available in Russian.)

22 Kalinnikov, Vladimir, ed., *Murmanskay oblast v XXI veke. tendentcii, faktoru i problemu social'no-economicheskogo razvitiy.* [*The Murmansk region in the XXI century: tendencies, factors and challenges of socio-economic development*] (Apatity, 2009).

23 *Itogi Vserossiyskoy sel'skohosystvennoy perepisi 2006 goda. Sel'skoe hosiystvo raionov Kraynego Severa i priravnennyh k nim mestnostey* [*Results of all-Russian agricultural census

enterprises Tundra and Olenevod, agricultural cooperatives in the Lovozero district. In addition, there are small reindeer-breeding enterprises and farms. However, the number is insignificant. As a rule, private reindeer are owned by herdsmen who work at reindeer enterprises or by their relatives. These reindeer graze in herds where their owners work together with cooperative reindeer on a contract basis as the private reindeer owners themselves have no direct access to land. This practice has existed since the first reindeer collective farms were started in the early 1930s.[24]

Reindeer herding is recognized as a traditional economic activity of indigenous small-numbered peoples at the legislative level.[25] However, the participation of Sámi representatives in the reindeer-herding enterprises of the Murmansk region is extremely low. Among shareholders of large cooperatives, Sámi-reindeer breeders are a minority. They are a small percentage, which makes it impossible for them to influence decision-making processes. As a rule in practice, Sámi work at reindeer-herding cooperatives as hired herdsmen or unskilled workers. By the beginning of 2012, according to information about regional administration, employees of reindeer-breeding enterprises of the region numbered 733 people; of them, 118 are Sámi (a little more than 12 percent of the total working-age Sámi population).[26]

The modern reindeer-herding trade established during the Soviet period as a specific agriculture sector and currently concentrated at the two big reindeer-herding enterprises principally differs from traditional (in the historical retrospective) Sámi reindeer herding (Table 11.2).

In general, modern reindeer herding develops not at the expense of increasing the number of reindeer but because of improvement in the production base. For instance, at the Lovozero settlement, Kola Sámi and Finnish partners opened a modern workshop for processing reindeer meat and

of 2006. Agriculture of the Far North and equated areas] (Moscow, 2008). (Available in Russian.)

24 Jernsletten, Johnny-Leo and Konstantin Klokov, *Sustainable Reindeer Husbandry* (Centre for Sámi Studies, University of Tromso, 2002).

25 Order of the Government of the RF dated 8 May 2009. №631-r Concerning approval of the List of traditional places of habitation and economic activities of indigenous small numerically peoples of the Russian Federation and the List of traditional economic activity of indigenous small numerically peoples of the Russian Federation. Legal database "Garant" – Retrieved from http://base.garant.ru/195535.

26 Vinogradova, *Korennue malochislennue narodu Severa: social'no-economicheskye aspectu gosudarstvennoy politiki* [*Indigenous small-numbered peoples of the North: socio-economic aspects of state policy*].

TABLE 11.2 *Differences between modern and traditional reindeer-herding on the Kola Peninsula*[27]

Modern Productive Reindeer Herding	Traditional Reindeer Herding of Kola Sámi
Large herds (from 1,000 to 10,000 head)	Small herds (to 1,000 head)
Production orientation (breeding stock 60–70% of herd)	Transportation orientation (breeding stock 40% of herd)
All-year-round partial guarding	Free grazing of reindeer
Herdsmen work in teams, in shifts, in considerable isolation from their families	Herdsmen with their families live near reindeer pastures
Reindeer are owned by joint stock company	Reindeer are owned by family, tribal
There is management of the reindeer-breeding enterprise (not reindeer breeders)	Decision-making rights belongs to family, tribal (reindeer breeders)

producing delicious products for the regional market and several customers in central Russia.

Other traditional economic activities have lost their economic importance for the Kola Sámi. There is no commercial hunting in the Murmansk region. River and lake fishing became almost inaccessible for the Kola Sámi due to limited access to resources, the traditional salmon fishing grounds, and the insuperability of the existing institutional barriers for indigenous residents.

In recent years in the region the additional coastal fishing quotas were granted for Sámi. However, few mechanisms for implementing this privilege have been installed at the federal level because of bureaucratic obstacles. The quotas apply only to legally registered Sámi organizations located only in the territories of traditional settlement of small numbers of indigenous peoples. The quota registration process is extremely difficult for bureaucratic reasons. As a result, the measures initially aimed at improving the socio-economic

27 Jernsletten and Klokov, *Sustainable Reindeer Husbandry*; Charnoluskii, "Zametki o pastbe i organizatsii stada u Loparey" ["Notes on the grazing and organization of herds of Lapps"]; Lukyanchenko, Material'nay kultura Saamov Kol'skogo poluostrova v kontse XIX–XX vekah [*The material culture of Sámi of the Kola Peninsula in the end of* XIX–XX *centuries*].

situation of the Sámi in practice have become a matter for debate, conflicts, and speculation.[28]

As for salmon fishing, this trade as an opportunity for profitable activity is gone for the Sámi. In general, salmon fishing has become an important income source for representatives of the non-indigenous population of the Kola Peninsula. The salmon rivers remain the subject of trading and profiteering. The development of sports fishing recently became widespread on former Sámi grounds, and takes place without considering the interests of indigenous residents. Sámi who live in the territory of the Murmansk region are allowed to fish freely in lakes and rivers but only for their own needs and within fixed limits.[29]

1.4 *Extraction of Mineral Resources on Sámi Land: New Challengers*

The Murmansk region is one of the most industrialized regions of the Russian North. The basis of regional economic development is a rich natural resource potential, with the key role of the mineral base. The Murmansk region has a strong mining complex, which consists of mining and chemical enterprises, ferrous and non-ferrous metallurgy, specializing in extracting and primarily processing raw materials. The Kola mining complex has great economic and social importance for the Murmansk region. It plays a significant role in the economy of the Northwest and Russia as a whole, and is integrated in global economic relations.[30]

All large industrial enterprises located in the Murmansk region, including the Kola mining complex, were founded in 1930–1950, when accelerated development of the region began. The resettlement of indigenous peoples and transformations in their lifestyle, carried out in that time, are associated with collectivization. However, some Sámi territories were used for industrial development. Relocation led to very serious social and cultural consequences

28 Indigenous small- numbered peoples of the North. Official website of the Government of the Murmansk region (available in Russian): http://www.gov-murman.ru/natpers/centre/; Forum of Russian Sámi: http://Sámi.forum24.ru/.

29 Gutsol, Natalia, "The Kola Sámi: modern conditions of life and protection of rights" (paper presented at the conference "Cooperation in the field of cultural monuments protection, coordinating the Norwegian-Russian Commission on Environmental Protection," Neiden, Norway, November 1997); Indigenous small-numbered peoples of the North. Official website of the Government of the Murmansk region: http://www.gov-murman.ru/natpers/centre/.

30 Kalinnikov, Vladimir, ed., *Murmanskay oblast v XXI veke: tendentcii, faktoru i problemu social'no-economicheskogo razvitiy* [*The Murmansk region in the XXI century: tendencies, factors and challenges of socio-economic development*] (Apatity, 2009).

for Sámi: Traditional ways of life were destroyed; many hunting and fishing grounds were abandoned. As a result, by the end of 1960, a new system of Sámi resettlement and management had formed in the Murmansk region.[31] It persists to the present but only partially corresponds with the traditional system.

Currently, only three municipal districts of the Murmansk region (Lovozerskiy, Kolskiy, and Terskiy) and one urban district (Kovdorsky, namely, the Jena rural area) have the status of territories of traditional resettlement and management of indigenous small-numbered peoples.[32] Most industrial enterprises of the Murmansk region are located outside these territories. Even in areas that have this status, mining enterprises are located far from the pastures and other Sámi trade areas. These factors contribute to the lack of open conflicts between the mining sector and indigenous peoples in the region.

However, there is potential for such conflicts in the future that increases the actuality of the Sámi protection in the development of extraction projects. The development of potential resources determines not only the modern profile of the regional economy but also its prospects. More than one hundred mineral deposits constitute a promising raw material base of region.[33] For instance, in the Lovozerskiy district, where 55 percent of all Sámi reside and the main pastures are located, there are a number of promising deposits, including the platinum deposits of Fedorova-Pana massif, kyanite deposits in the Keivy district, and gold and molybdenum in Kolmozero. The development of these fields may reduce the reindeer pastures and degrade the ecology of the territories of indigenous peoples. Investigations of this issue show that the indigenous population and local authorities are afraid of such developments.[34]

31 Gutsol, Natalia, Svetlana Vinogradova and Antonina Samorukova, *Pereselennye gruppy Kol'skih Saamov* [*Relocated Kola Sámi groups*] (Apapity, KSC RAS, 2007). (Available in Russian.)

32 Order of the Government of the RF dated 8 May 2009. №631-r Concerning approval of the List of traditional places of habitation and economic activities of indigenous small numbered peoples of the Russian Federation and the List of traditional economic activity of indigenous small numerically peoples of the Russian Federation. Legal database "Garant" – Retrieved from http://base.garant.ru/195535.

33 Ibid.

34 Koivurova, Timo et al. "Legal Protection of Sámi Traditional Livelihoods from the Adverse Impacts of Mining: A Comparison of the Level of Protection Enjoyed by Sámi in Their Four Home States," in *Arctic Review on Law and Politics* 1 (2015): 11–51.

2 Instruments for Development of Sámi Security

Existing challenges facing the Sámi require the development of adequate mechanisms to protect them. The mechanisms should include state support, especially special legislation frames, and Sámi self-development institutions.

2.1 *Features of Russian Legislation for the Protection of Indigenous Peoples*

In Russia, Sámi have the status of indigenous small-numbered people of Murmansk Oblast, which is defined in the federal law "On Guarantees of Rights of Indigenous Small-numbered Peoples of the Russian Federation" as follows:

> peoples who live on the territories of traditional residence of their ancestors, who maintain their traditional way of life, economies and crafts, whose numbers in the Russian Federation are less than 50 thousand and who identify themselves in independent ethnic communities.[35]

The determination of such status sets the legal basis for state protection of the appropriate population group, which, at the state level, is accepted as one of the most vulnerable in Russia.

Currently, an extensive legislative framework for the protection of indigenous small numbered peoples has been established in the Russian Federation, which, in accordance with the federal structure of Russia, includes federal and regional laws.

At present, in Russia, the regional level of regulation has become more important as here the principal basic approaches can be brought nearer to solutions of concrete problems. Especially many of the discontinuities in the legislation can be taken into account at the regional level. Unfortunately, the regional legal frames for indigenous small-numbered peoples are poorly developed in the Murmansk Oblast. The region has accepted two basic laws: On State Support of Indigenous Small-numbered Peoples of the North in the Murmansk Region Carrying Out Traditional Economic Activities and Crafts (2008) and On Reindeer Herding in Murmansk Oblast (2003).

These laws have a very perfunctory and declarative tone. This is well illustrated in terms of reindeer herding. This trade is a traditional economic

35 Federal Law adopted 30 April 1999, N82-FZ"On guarantees of rights of indigenous small-numbered peoples of the Russian Federation" Legal database "Garant" – Retrieved from http://base.garant.ru/180406.

activities of indigenous peoples of the North and a necessary condition for preservation of their lifestyle and original culture. However, according to experts, the relevant regional law is overloaded by biological and zoo-technical terms, has shifted priority to reindeer-breeding enterprises, and lacks articles ensuring the direct rights of reindeer breeders, communities of indigenous peoples, and private reindeer owners.[36] Under ineffective regional laws, the main instrument for legal protection of Sámi rights is legislation at the federal level.

In general, the main approaches to indigenous issues are contained in the Russian Constitution. Article 69 provides:

> The Russian Federation shall guarantee the rights of the indigenous small peoples according to the universally recognized principles and norms of international law and international treaties and agreements of the Russian Federation.[37]

Russia has not ratified the main international documents related to indigenous peoples, for example, International Labour Organization Convention No. 169 "On indigenous peoples and peoples having tribal life style in independent countries" (1989). As a result, the provisions of these documents are not obligatory in the Russian Federation and have only an advisory function. However, on the whole, principles and approaches that are declared in the federal legislation concerning indigenous peoples correspond to the global rules.[38]

In Part 1 of Article 72 of the Russian Federal Constitution, key problems of this population group to solve are identified—protection of the traditional habitat and lifestyle.[39]

Principles of Russian state policy are formulated in the Concept Paper on the Sustainable Development of Indigenous Peoples of the North, Siberia and the Far East of the Russian Federation (Concept Paper), thus defining the federal policy from 2009 to 2025 for improving socio-economic conditions; protecting

36 The Law of the Murmansk region N 380-01-ZMO of 14.01.2003 "On reindeer herding in the Murmansk region". Available in Russian: http://base.garant.ru/16943802/.

37 The Constitution of the Russian Federation. Available: http://www.constitution.ru/en/10003000-01.htm.

38 Anaya, James, *Report of the Special Rapporteur on the situation of human rights and fundamental freedoms of indigenous people. Situation in the Russian Federation.* Retrieved from http://ap.ohchr.org/documents/dpage_e.aspx?si=A/HRC/15/37/Add.5.

39 The Constitution of the Russian Federation, Available: http://www.constitution.ru/en/10003000-01.htm.

traditional environments, way of life, and cultural values of indigenous peoples; and specifying time frames and benchmarks for implementation.[40]

The federal legal framework for the protection and promotion of the rights of indigenous peoples consists of three laws that specifically address indigenous peoples: On Guarantees of the Rights of Small-numbered Indigenous Peoples of the Russian Federation (On Guarantees), passed in 1999; On Territories of Traditional Nature Use of the Small-numbered Indigenous Peoples of the North, Siberia and the Far East of the Russian Federation (On Territories), adopted in 2001; and On General Principles of Organization of *Obshchina* [clan or clan-type community] of Small-numbered Indigenous Peoples of the North, Siberia and the Far East of the Russian Federation (On Obshchina), adopted in 2000.

In addition to the main laws, concerning indigenous peoples directly, special articles in many legislative acts govern the basic spheres of life. The special observations on indigenous small-numbered peoples are contained in the Land, Forest, and Water Codes of the Russian Federation as well as in almost fifty other federal laws.[41]

As noted in the Report of the UN Special Reporter, the Russian Federation has taken important steps toward ensuring the realization of the human rights of small-numbered indigenous peoples. The guarantees set out in the federal legislation include group and individual rights of indigenous peoples as the main issues: free use of land and renewable natural resources in the territories they have traditionally occupied and where they engage in traditional economic activities; the rights to establish self-government bodies in places of compact settlement and to form communities and other organizations; the right to receive compensation for damage to their traditional environment due to industrial activities; the right to have courts consider customary law in as far as it does not contradict federal or regional legislation; and other entitlements.[42]

2.2 *Measures of Sámi State Support*

Since the early 2000s, the main form of state support for indigenous small-numbered peoples is the realization of federal and regional programs aimed at

40 Resolution of the Government of the Russian Federation N 132-p of 04.02.2009 "On the Concept of Sustainable Development of Indigenous Peoples of the North, Siberia and the Russian Far East". Available in Russian: http://base.garant.ru/194908/.

41 Kryazhkov, Vladimir, *Korennye malochislennye narody Severa v rossiyskom prave* [*Indigenous small-numbered peoples of the North in Russian legislation*] (Moscow, NORMA, 2010).

42 Anaya, *Report of the Special Rapporteur on the situation of human rights and fundamental freedoms of indigenous people. Situation in the Russian Federation.*

the social and economic development of this population group. Currently, the third such program, covering the 2012–16 period, is under way in the region. The program provides support for indigenous organizations in the form of subsidies and funding various activities, aimed at preserving the traditions and customs of the indigenous peoples of the North and popularization of their national culture.[43]

From 2009 to 2013, eighteen Sámi communities received financial support that has allowed them to acquire mobile wooden houses, snowmobiles, cars, boats, generators, and other equipment necessary for implementing traditional economic activities. National holidays, festivals, exhibitions, as well as "round tables," seminars, and conferences, are regularly held in the frame of program realization. Annually, literature on the Sámi language and training materials on Sámi topics are published, and television and radio thematic programs in the Sámi and Russian languages are produced.[44]

In addition, state support for industries accepted as traditional for indigenous peoples is provided in Russia. In the Murmansk region, there are benefits for reindeer-herding enterprises when renting lands for grazing, as well as additional quotas for certain fish species (cod and haddock) for enterprises run by indigenous peoples.

To coordinate the work on issues of indigenous peoples at the regional level, in 2004 the Murmansk regional government established the Murmansk Regional Center of Indigenous Peoples of the North with the status of a government regional institution.[45]

2.3 *Kola Sámi in Regional Political Context*

When *perestroika* started, serious positive changes took place in the lives of the indigenous population. Researchers note self-identity growth among Sámi during this period, and, as a result, intensive processes of formation of Sámi public organizations, active contacts with foreign Sámi, and representatives of other national minorities of Russia.

In the political context during the 1990s, the Kola Sámi moved from an almost imperceptible small ethnic group dependent on the interests of the Soviet state to an ethnically and politically (in national and international scales)

43 Indigenous small-numbered peoples of the North. Official website of the Government of the Murmansk region (available in Russian): http://www.gov-murman.ru/natpers/centre/.

44 Ibid.

45 Ibid.

significant community.[46] During this period, two important public organizations, the Non-governmental Sámi organization of the Murmansk region and the Association of the Kola Sámi, which is integrated in RAIPON,[47] began to function. At present, they actively supplement each other. In 1992, the Sámi of the Russian Federation became members of the international organization Sámi Union.

Beginning in 2008, three congresses of Kola Sámi, general meetings of representatives elected by the Sámi community, have been held in Murmansk. Among others, the question of a permanent representative Sámi body was discussed during a congress. After several attempts, the Council of Representatives of Indigenous Peoples was created as a collegial advisory body under the government of the Murmansk region. The main purpose of the council is to develop and implement a set of institutional, economic, and legal regional measures aimed at protecting the Sámi native habitat, traditional way of life, livelihood, and crafts. The council operates on a voluntary basis and in accordance with the principles of voluntariness, autonomy in decision-making within its competence, openness, and consideration of public opinion.[48]

However, the activity of Sámi political organizations is limited mainly to decision making on Sámi issues as well as their interaction with regional business and government. Integration of Sámi in common regional political processes is quite low.

2.4 *Self-organization of Kola Sámi*

Right up until the beginning of the twentieth century, Kola Sámi maintained the basic principles of their traditional socio-economic and territorial organization, whose main unit was the socio-territorial community, *pogost* (Sámi, *siida*). The territory of the *pogost* included permanent (winter) and temporary (seasonal) settlements of the community's representatives as well as migration

46 Gutsol, Natalia and Larissa Riabova, "Kola Sámi and regional development," in *Conflict and cooperation in the North*, ed. Kaepi, Kristiina and Johan Eriksson (Umea, 2002): 313–343.

47 Russian Association of Indigenous Peoples of the North, Siberia and Far East.

48 Resolution of the Government of the Murmansk region on 11 February 2009. N 57-PP "On Provisions on the Board of representatives of indigenous peoples of the North at the Murmansk Region Government". Available in Russian: http://gov-murman.ru/region/Sámi/convocation/.

routes, tribal lands, and fishing areas. This structure of Kola Sámi settlements was predetermined by the semi-nomadic life, which was typical.[49]

The concept of *pogost* in Sámi life was crucial not only as a definition of a geographic place of habitation and economic structure but also in the process of self-identification. Territorial organization, the economic model of each *pogost*, and the social (family related) structure of the community were connected as a well-coordinated mechanism, which had very strong inner logic. Being a self-sufficient unit in an economic as well as a social meaning, the *pogost* played a large role in an individual person's life.[50]

According to researchers, the number of Sámi *pogost*s on the territory of Kola Peninsula since the seventeenth century until the beginning of the twentieth century, when this system was destroyed, varied from sixteen to nineteen.[51]

Modern forms of Sámi self-organization correspond to issues of national culture preservation and the development of traditional trades. At present, in the Murmansk region, there are eleven Sámi public organizations and thirty-two family-tribal communities (*obschina*). According to information from the Murmansk Regional Center of Indigenous Peoples of the North, almost all Sámi adults are involved in an organization and public activity.[52]

The main task of Sámi public organizations is to preserve cultural traditions. Characteristically, these organizations work not only in areas traditionally inhabited by indigenous peoples but also in cities and industrial centers of the Kola Peninsula.

The process of organizing *obschina*s started after adoption of the federal law On General Principals of Organization of Obschina of Indigenous

49 Gutsol, Natalia, Svetlana Vinogradova and Antonina Samorukova, *Pereselennye gruppy Kol'skih Saamov* [*Relocated Kola Sámi groups*] (Apapity, KSC RAS, 2007). (Available in Russian.)

50 Ibid.

51 Volkov, Nikolay, "Rossiyskie Sámi: istoriko-etnographicheskiy ocherk" ["Russian Sámi: historical-ethnographical essay"] (Kaytokeyno, 1996). (Available in Russian.); Ushakov, Ivan, *Kol'skay zemly* [*The Kola land*] (Murmansk, 1997). (Available in Russian.)

52 Indigenous small-numbered peoples of the North. Official website of the Government of the Murmansk region: http://www.gov-murman.ru/natpers/centre/; Chuprova, Nina "Rol' obschin korennuh malochislennuh narodov v sohranenii I razvitii natsional'nuh traditsiy, kultuty i yasuka, narodnuh remesel I promuslov Sámi" ["Role of obschinas of indigenous small-numbered peoples in saving and development of national traditions, culture and language and Sámi handicrafts"] (paper presented at the scientific conference "Biblioteka kak social'nuy institute sohraneniy i ustoychivogo razvitiy kultur i kulturnogo samovurazenia korennuh narodov severa," 20–23 November 2012) (Murmansk, 2013). (In Russian.)

Small-numbered Peoples of the North, Siberia and Far East of RF in 2000. According to the law:

> communities of indigenous peoples – self-organization forms of persons referring to this people and united by family-tribal or territory-neighbors principles, created for defense of their traditional habitat, preservation and development of the traditional life style, economy, trades and culture.[53]

According to the law, association in the community allows for traditional economic activities but in a non-commercial way. Solutions to issues of its internal organization and interrelations between its members can be made based on the traditions and customs of indigenous peoples.

In the Murmansk region, the process of organization of the Kola Sámi communities has been developing quite actively. However, cases of giving lands for traditional activities are very few and are reduced to allotment of pastures for reindeer herding in line with other land users and based on payable long-term leases. Currently, only four communities among the thirty-two lease land plots for reindeer herding. The total area is less than 4 percent of all pastures of the Kola Peninsula.[54]

Most communities restrict Sámi activities to seasonal coastal fishing (under special quotas) and handicrafts. Some have attempted to develop ethnic tourism projects.[55] The main Sámi *obschina* problems are connected to allocation of pastures. The lack of free land suitable for reindeer herding results in a collision of interests between the communities and other land users, as a rule, big enterprises. The second set of problems is economic.[56] A lack of available funds and difficulties in receiving loans are partly compensated by subsidies

53 Law of Russian Federation on 20 July 2000, N104 FZ "On General Principles of Organization of *Obshchina* [clan or clan-type community] of Small-numbered Indigenous Peoples of the North, Siberia and the Far East of the Russian Federation," Legal database "Garant" – Retrieved from http://base.garant.ru/182356.

54 Indigenous small-numbered peoples of the North. Official website of the Government of the Murmansk region: http://www.gov-murman.ru/natpers/centre/.

55 Ibid.

56 Vinogradova, Svetlana "Rodovay obschina kak obschestvennuy institute (na primere kolskih Sámi) [Obschina as social institute (case of Kola Sámi)]," in *Gragdanskie initsiativy v sfere etnicheskoy politiky. Vosmognosty posrednichestva grazdanskih struktur v dele predupregdeniy i urególirovaniy etnicheskih konfliktov*, ed. Zorin, Vladimir and Valery Stepanov (Moscow, 2013): 106–113. (Available in Russian.)

from the Programs for the Socio-Economic Development of the Indigenous Peoples of Murmansk Oblast.

Conclusions

The Russian Sámi are an example of an indigenous community of the North that is facing extreme challenges posed by the historical background and contemporary global trends in the development of Northern and Arctic regions.

Since the end of the nineteenth century, the Kola Peninsula, an area traditionally inhabited by Sámi, has been extensively industrially developed and populated. As a result, on the modern ethnical map of the Kola Peninsula the Sámi constitute an insignificant minority among a multiethnic population, mainly formed during the twentieth century by migrants from other regions of the Soviet Union. Preservation of the Sámi identity, language, and cultural traditions in such situations becomes problematic without special measures for protection.

During the Soviet period, indigenous peoples of the North suffered from collectivization, sedentarization, and resettlements that led to considerable transformation of all aspects of Kola Sámi life and to actual exclusion from part of their traditional territories. Most dramatically, the Sámi livelihoods were transformed. The traditional Kola Sámi economy as a combination of reindeer herding, hunting, and fishing, which requires seasonal migration, has not survived. The contemporary main livelihood for Russian Sámi is reindeer herding, which does not play an important role in the regional economy.

In addition, in general, the Kola Peninsula is one of the most industrialized areas of the circumpolar North. The economy is focused on extraction of resources. The region is promising for the development of gas and mining projects. Modern systems of Kola Sámi settlements provide a lack of direct consultation between them and the mining companies. However, further development of the region may lead to a reduction in Sámi areas and thus destabilize the situation and cause conflicts.

In this way, the Sámi situation in Murmansk Oblast requires the development of methods and instruments for Sámi security at different levels: state (including regional) governance, society, and the indigenous community.

Currently, an extensive legislative framework for the protection of indigenous small numbered peoples has been established in the Russian Federation, which, in accordance with the federal structure of Russia, contains federal and regional laws. In the last decade, the mechanisms of state support of indigenous peoples of the North in the form of programs for socio-economic development and bodies of state administration to coordinate these processes were established. Thus, in Russia, gradually a new context and new conditions for the development of indigenous peoples are being formed.

Unfortunately, these processes are being promoted slowly in the region. Analysis of the socio-economic characteristics of the Kola Sámi show that they remain one of the most socially vulnerable population groups of the Murmansk region. The most sensitive social issues for the Sámi are unemployment and poverty. Most Sámi live in rural areas where they face typical issues of peripheral territories such as remoteness, difficulty of access, and low level of social infrastructure development.

To a great extent, the situation can be changed through the development of Sámi self-organization. The most effective in this regard are *obschina*s (family-tribal communities). According to legislation, the *obschina*s are created for the defense of Sámi traditional habitat, preservation, and development of the traditional lifestyle, economy, trades, and culture. At the same time, the obschina is the main object for state support, aimed at socio-economic development of indigenous peoples as well as social institutions closed to traditional forms.

Active *obschina* organization and development in the Murmansk region indicate that in terms of social security issues Sámi give preference to indigenous mechanisms that are based on ethnic identity, traditions, and culture.

CHAPTER 12

Challenges to the Human Security of Elderly Sámi in Finnish and Swedish Lapland

*Shahnaj Begum** and *Päivi Naskali***

Abstract

The indigenous Sámi people inhabit the northern parts of Finland and Sweden. They adhere to a traditional way of life and practice a distinct culture connected to their natural surroundings, forming a unique cultural identity. In this chapter, we look into how the concept of human security applies in assessing the well-being of elderly Sámi in the region. Climate change and developments such as mining and other industrial activities are causing significant socio-environmental changes that affect elderly Sámi. While both positive and negative impacts can be identified, risks pertaining to health and well-being are prevalent. We analyse these risks in light of data collected in Finnish and Swedish Lapland during the years 2012 and 2014. In particular, we examine the concerns and challenges which elderly Sámi face as regards the economy, environment, food and health. In concluding, we offer some recommendations on how the well-being of elderly Sámi can be promoted in response to the prevailing human security challenges.

1 Introduction

The article undertakes to determine the degree of human security in the lives of elderly[1] Sámi. Well-being and human security are intertwined. The concept of well-being is a broad, multidimensional one.[2] Human security is also a

* Shahnaj Begum, Researcher at the Unit for Gender Studies in the Faculty of Education of the University of Lapland.

** Päivi Naskali, Professor of Gender Studies at the University of Lapland, Dean of the Faculty of Education.

1 'Elderly' in this paper refers to 'elder persons', 'old people', 'senior persons', including 'elderly men and women'. Since in Finnish and Swedish research an elderly person is a person aged 65 and over, we also take this age as our point of reference.

2 Vaara, Elina et al., "What is wellbeing for the elderly?," in *Ageing, Wellbeing and Climate Change in the Arctic: An interdisciplinary analysis*, ed. Naskali, Päivi, Marjaana Seppänen and Shahnaj Begum (Routledge – Earthscan, Forthcoming, 2015).

 | DOI 10.1163/9789004314399_014

multifaceted construct, one whose component features span many disciplines. It combines security, rights and development. In this research, we have applied human security in its *people-centred* aspect,[3] which places the individual at the 'centre of analyses'. Well-being is socially defined based on the historical and cultural context and also on the different stages of life. As used here, the concept denotes an absence of the particular challenges that elderly Sámi people face in their communities, examples being health-related problems exacerbated by climate change, social isolation, mining activities and out-migration of the younger generation. In this chapter well-being is viewed as a component of human security.

The northern parts of Finland, Sweden, Russia and Norway are home to both non-indigenous and Sámi populations. The area known as the Sámi homeland, or Sápmi, stretches from Central Norway and Sweden through the northernmost part of Finland into the Kola Peninsula. While the Sámi inhabit a rather large area, our focus in this chapter is on Sámi living in the Finnish and Swedish parts of the homeland and, in particular, the elderly members of the Sámi communities. In Finland the Sámi homeland comprises the municipalities of Enontekiö, Inari and Utsjoki, as well as the reindeer-herding area of the municipality of Sodankylä.

Several statistics show that elderly people now live longer than earlier.[4] Longevity has increased all over the world because of developments such as urbanization, industrialization and improved standards in health care and in social services.[5] Living longer does not mean that everyone is guaranteed a healthy and happy life, however. Elderly persons are treated as an expensive

3 Tadjbakhsh, Shahrbanou and Anuradha M. Chenoy, *Human Security: Concepts and Implications* (London & New York: Routledge, 2007), 7. Accessed April 30, 2015. https://docs.unocha.org/sites/dms/HSU/Publications%20and%20Products/Human%20Security%20Tools/Human%20Security%20in%20Theory%20and%20Practice%20English.pdf (accessed 30 April, 2015).

4 Heleniak, Timothy and Dimitry Bogoyavlensky, "Arctic populations and Migration," *in Arctic Human Development Report,* ed. Einarsson, Niels, Joan Larsen and Fondahl Gail (Copenhagen: Nordisk, 2014), 54.

5 Hassler, Sven, Per Sjölander and Urban Janlert, "Northern Fennoscandia," in *Health Transitions in Arctic Populations,* ed. Young, T. Kue and Peter Bjerregaard (Toronto: University of Toronto Press, 2008), 103–116; Dimitry Bogoyavlenskiy and Andy Siggner "Arctic Demography", in *Arctic Human Development Report,* ed. Nilsson, Niels, Joan Larse N., Annika Nilsson and Oran R. Young (Akureyri: Stefansson Arctic Institute, 2004), 27–41; Sköld, Peter, Per Axelsson, Lena Karlsson and Len Smith, "Infant mortality of Sámi and settlers in Northern Sweden: the era of colonization 1750–1900," in *Glob Health Action* 4 (8441), (2011).

group.[6] However in the European Union's policy areas healthy ageing has been put forward as an important goal.[7] An individual's well-being depends on his or her socio-economic situation, standard of living, life style and co-related surroundings. As a result, the promotion of well-being, directly or indirectly, strengthens human security.

In the Arctic, the indigenous population lives primarily in rural areas.[8] It is evident from different reports that the elderly population has become a demographic challenge for the Nordic countries.[9] As members of this group, Finland and Sweden are highly developed countries, but this does not ensure that the people living in the remote areas of Lapland have a secure life; various challenges affect them and their wellbeing. According to the first Arctic Human Development Report (2004), the elderly, women and children are the most vulnerable groups.[10] The vulnerability of elderly populations is distinct in that ageing gradually reduces their physical strength and stamina; they are easily affected by viral and bacterial diseases, becoming less resistant to disease overall. Moreover, in remote areas, the availability of essential services is poor, making everyday life burdensome. This region also has a poor transport infrastructure,[11] hampering communications between villages, for example. The superior motorway networks to be found in the municipalities in northern Sweden may be seen as an advantage for that region as compared with its Finnish counterpart.

The extensive changes facing the region, ones proceeding much faster than before, also impact the lives and well-being of the elderly. To cite one example, the consequences of climate change and other human activities pose new

---

6 Keskitalo-Foley, Seija and Päivi Naskali, "Tracing gender in political ageing strategies and the press in Finnish Lapland," in *Ageing, Wellbeing and Climate Change in the Arctic: An interdisciplinary analysis*, ed. Naskali, Päivi, Marjaana Seppänen and Shahnaj Begum (Routledge – Earthscan, 2016), 30–48.

7 *Healthy Ageing: A challenge for Europe, The Swedish National Institute of Public Health* (2006). Accessed 1 May, 2015. http://www.healthyageing.eu/sites/www.healthyageing.eu/files/resources/Healthy%20Ageing%20-%20A%20Challenge%20for%20Europe.pdf.

8 Kozlo, Andrew and Dmitry Lisitsyn, "Arctic Russia," in *Health Transitions in Arctic Populations*, ed. Young, T. Kue, and Peter Bjerregaard (Toronto: University of Toronto Press, 2008), 94–95

9 *Gender and Climate Change*. Accessed October 19, 2012. http://www.equalclimate.org/filestore/Pdf/DeskstudyGenderandccreport.pdf.

10 Bogoyavlenskiy and Siggner 2004, *supra* note 5, 27–41.

11 Spiekermann, Klaus and Hallgeir Aalbu, "Nordic Peripherality in Europe," (2004), Nordregio Working Paper. Accessed 11 May, 2015. http://www.diva-portal.org/smash/get/diva2:700450/FULLTEXT01.pdf.

challenges to the environmental infrastructure. These developments entail risks in the lives of people belonging to one of the region's most vulnerable groups – the older members of the Sámi communities. One risk is the erosion of social integrity. Nuttall notes, for example, that new forms of identity develop as in- and out-migration cause threats to existing cultures and livelihoods.[12] However, these tends do not have similar effects all across the region. In the case of Lapland, in-migration is not as common as out-migration, which has been specifically cited as a problem by informants and researchers.[13] In our field work we have studied out-migration in the village of Angeli in Finland and in a village near the Kallak area in Sweden. The Sámi in Lapland traditionally maintain certain practices as part of their culture and these are connected to their identity. Although the terms *culture* and *identity* create some tension in Arctic society as a whole,[14] such as preservation of traditional culture based identity versus formation of identity based on imported cultural practices, they represent particularly important considerations for elderly Sámi. They want to keep their societal norm as intact as possible. Their mental well-being is threatened due to the increasing risk of losing incentives connected to their identity. Community identity is one of the major components of human security, while other aspects of human security, such as health, environment, the economy and food are connected in one way or another to community identity. The Commission on Human Security (CHS), established in 2001, defines human security as follows:[15]

> to protect the vital core of all human lives in ways that enhance human freedoms and human fulfilment. Human security means protecting fundamental freedoms – freedoms that are the essence of life. It means protecting people from critical (severe) and pervasive (widespread) threats and situations. It means using processes that build on people's strengths and aspirations. It means creating political, social, environmental, economic, military and cultural systems that together give people the building blocks of survival, livelihood and dignity.

12 Nuttall, Mark, *Protecting the Arctic: Indigenous Peoples and Cultural Survival* (Amsterdam: Harwood Academic Publishers, 1998).

13 Rasmussen, Rasmus Ole, "Gender and Generation: Perspectives on Ongoing Social and Environmental Changes in the Arctic," in *Journal of Women in Culture and Society* 34 (3) (2009): 525.

14 Schweitzer, Peter, Peter Sköld and Olga Ulturgasheva, "Cultures and Identities," in Arctic Human Development Report, ed. Nilsson, Niels, N. Joan Larsen and Gail, Fondahl (Copenhagen: Nordisk Ministerråd, 2014).

15 Tadjbakhsh and Chenoy 2007, *supra* note 3, 6.

Human security for the elderly, in particular the focal population in the present research, faces many critical challenges. However, this topic has largely been ignored in academic literature to date. The lack of research on elderly issues in the Arctic has also been identified in the recently published Arctic Human Development Report (AHDR, 2014).[16] The AHDR considers that more research should be done to promote the well-being of the elderly. The promotion of human security for the elderly promotes their well-being.

Our research in this chapter investigates how the concept of well-being and human security are interconnected in the circumstances of elderly Sámi in Finnish and Swedish Lapland. Our observations pinpoint the benefits of promoting the well-being of the region's elderly in response to the challenges we identify. We describe the threats that face elderly Sámi – either directly or indirectly – and that pose potential obstacles to their overall well-being. One of our main aims in this chapter is also to heighten awareness of the issue in view of the need to promote the well-being of elderly Sámi in response to the significant transformation which the region is undergoing.

Our findings draw on previous research, a literature review and field studies. The literature includes scientific research on the Sámi population, relevant health and policy reports on the well-being of the Arctic and northern populations and other relevant resources. The field studies comprise data collected using interviews conducted between 2012 and 2014 in Finnish and Swedish Lapland. Our research questions relate to informants' experiences of the ongoing transformation of the region, livelihoods, the importance of traditional activities, changes in livelihood practices and the impact of those changes on their social lives. All discussions were recorded using a tape recorder and some were also summarised in notes. In most of the cases we had received permission from informants by e-mail and telephone before conducting the interviews. In a few instances, we also sent a sample of the research questions by e-mail and ultimately obtained permission before starting the interviews. The participants' consent to participate in the research was completely voluntary and all were competent to give consent.

We interviewed nine elderly Sámi, three active members of the communities, one healthcare professional and three researchers working on indigenous issues. The elderly people ranged in age from 65 to 85. Six were from Ivalo and Inari (Finland), two were from Jokkmokk (Sweden), and one from Tärnaby (Sweden). The community members, researchers and health professional were between 40 and 70 years of age and involved with Sámi people's well-being

16 Einarsson, Niels, Joan Larsen N. and Fondahl Gail, ed. *Arctic Human Development Report* (Copenhagen: Nordisk, 2014).

in the Finland and Sweden. In order to gain insights into the human security challenges facing elderly Sámi, we needed to know, among other things, about their culture and its importance to them.

2 Brief Overview of the Sámi in Finland and Sweden

The Sámi in Finland and Sweden

The northern parts of Finland and Sweden are more sparsely populated[17] than the corresponding areas in other Nordic countries. It is in this region that the indigenous Sámi people live.[18] It is difficult to estimate the total Sámi population.[19] The number of Sámi people is estimated to be some 70,000, but the statistics differ from source to source. In addition to Finland and Sweden, there are Sámi communities in the Kola Peninsula in Russia and in Norway, the largest population being in Finnmark County. Based on the characteristics of the locations in which they live, Sámi are referred to as Sea Sámi, Forest Sámi and Reindeer-herding Sámi. Both in Finland and in Sweden the Sámi are classified as belonging to one of the inland groups of Sámi even though sometimes their livelihoods are connected to river fishing and lake fishing.[20]

In Finnish, a Sámi is called *'saamelainen'*, and in Swedish *'Same'*. The Sámi have been recognized as an indigenous people in the Finnish Constitution since 1995; they received corresponding recognition in Sweden 1989.[21] The Sámi are the only the indigenous people of Europe and their rights are protected under the international conventions on indigenous peoples.[22]

Sámi Culture and Livelihood in Finland and Sweden

Despite some variations from area to area, the Sámi share similar cultural practices. In both Finnish and Swedish Lapland they strive to maintain their

17 Hassler 2008, *supra* note 5, 106.

18 Bogoyavlenskiy and Siggner 2004, *supra* note 5, 27–41.

19 Hassler, Sven, Siv Kvernmo, and Andrew Kozlov. "Sámi," in *Health Transitions in Arctic Populations*, ed. Young, T. Kue and Peter Bjerregaard, (Toronto: University of Toronto Press, 2008), 148.

20 *The Sámi* – an indigenous people in Sweden (The Sámi, Ministry of Agriculture, Food and Consumer Affairs). Accessed 1 March, 2015 http://www.samer.se/2137.

21 *The Sámi of Northern Europe – one people, four countries.* Accessed 1 March, 2015. http://www.unric.org/en/indigenous-people/27307-the-Sámi-of-northern-europe--one-people-four-countries.

22 Johnson, Daniel, "Indigenous Land Threatened By Mine," 21 August, 2013. Accessed 4 May, 2015. http://www.mediacoop.ca/story/indigenous-land-threatened-mine/18648.

traditional culture, which encompasses certain activities, such as fishing, herding, farming, making of handicrafts, gathering, trapping and, in some locations, berry picking. These nature-based activities show the Sámi's special relation to their surrounding natural environment. Indeed, their cultural identity has traditionally been built around these activities. Today, in addition to the Sámi languages, *duodji* (Sámi handicraft), *gakti* (the traditional clothing) and reindeer husbandry are the emblematic elements of Sámi culture to the outside world.

The iconic livelihood in the Sámi region is reindeer herding, even though only about 10 per cent of Sámi are involved in it and it is gradually becoming more commercialized. There are differences in the right to practice reindeer herding in Finland and Sweden. In Finland the Reindeer Husbandry Act of 1990[23] provides that, regardless of whether they are Sámi or not, citizens of the European Economic Area who reside permanently in the reindeer husbandry, as well as reindeer-herding cooperatives, may own and herd reindeer. In Sweden, in contrast to, reindeer herding is restricted to the Sámi only by virtue of the 1971 Reindeer Husbandry Act, which was amended in 1993. In Sweden this law regulates only the rights of reindeer-breeding Sámi; the Sámi who are permitted to practise reindeer herding also enjoy special land and water rights. The amended Act does not cover the land and water rights of Sámi fishers in the country.[24] In any case, the importance of reindeer herding and other such activities keep the crucial element of the culture – the language – alive, which provides the group's identity. According to Martin Scheinin, cited in Linus:[25]

> The Sámi language lives and dies with the Sámi way of life because the social activities around reindeer herding and in the nature-based forms of livelihood really keep up the living language. If it is isolated to a museum piece I think there will be no future for the Sámi language.

As regards protection of the Sámi culture and identity, the Sámi often refer to the ratification of ILO Convention No. 169, which deals specifically with the rights of *indigenous* and *tribal peoples and* which is a legally binding

23 *Ministry of Agriculture and Forestry*. Accessed 16 April, 2015. http://www.mmm.fi/en/index/frontpage/Fishing,_game_reindeer/Reindeer_farming.html.

24 *The Sámi People in Sweden*. Accessed 25 May, 2015. http://www.samenland.nl/lap_Sámi_si.html.

25 Linus, Atarah, "Rights: Finland&#39s Sámi Fear Assimilation," April 7, 2008, IPS, Helsinki, accessed 16 April, 2015. http://www.ipsnews.net/2008/04/rights-finland39s-Sámi-fear-assimilation/.

international instrument.[26] Several Sámi informants from both Finnish and Swedish Lapland mentioned that this convention would indeed be important for promoting Sámi people's socio-economic, cultural and political rights. Neither Finland nor Sweden has ratified the Convention despite its importance for the Sámi. In a recent lecture, the UN Special Rapporteur on the Rights of Indigenous Peoples, Victoria Tauli-Corpuz, re-iterated the importance of the ILO Convention for the protection of the Sámi people's rights.[27] Whereas both Finland and Sweden are parties to the International Covenant on Civil and Political Rights (ICCPR) and to the International Covenant of Economic, Social and Cultural Rights (ICESCR), neither of these covenants is applicable to indigenous peoples – despite the fact that indigenous groups as a minorities sometimes invoke Article 27 of the ICCPR, which concerns the protection of cultural rights broadly connected to identity. However, the article only protects the rights of individuals not of a group as a whole. Both Finland and Sweden have also endorsed the United Nations Declaration on the Rights of Indigenous Peoples (UNDRIP), which is a comprehensive document designed to protect the culture and identity of indigenous peoples. While the adoption of the Declaration is a huge achievement for the protection of all aspects of indigenous rights, it is nevertheless not a legally binding document.

Sámi Parliaments have been established in Norway, Sweden and Finland to promote Sámi culture. In 2010 (12th December), Kuelnegk Soamet Sobbar (The Kola Saami Assembly) was established in Murmansk but the Russian government did not recognize it as the Russian Sámi Parliament.[28] The Parliaments are composed of members elected by the Sámi themselves. In Finland only Sámi inhabitants of the Sámi homeland are eligible to vote in elections for the Sámi Parliament, whereas in Sweden all registered Sámi residents are entitled to vote. The existence of such institutions is naturally important to let the Sámi voice be heard as a channel for promoting Sáminess and thereby preserving the Sámi identity. However, in our interviews (the respondents were Sámi activists and professionals) we found concerns in both countries that the competence of the Sámi Parliaments is limited because of structural weaknesses and poor allocation of funding.

---

26 *Convention No. 169*. Accessed 4 May, 2015. http://www.ilo.org/indigenous/Conventions/no169/lang--en/index.htm.

27 UN Special Rapporteur on the Rights of Indigenous Peoples Victoria Tauli-Corpuz gave a lecture at the University of Lapland, 25 February, 2015.

28 *Fighting for Sámi parliament in Russia*. Accessed 30 May, 2015. http://www.barentsobserver.com/fighting-for-Sámi-parliament-in-russia.4530696-16149.html.

In the following section, drawing on literature reviews and field interviews, we go on to point out regional developments and circumstances that affect the well-being of elderly Sámi.

3 Impacts of Ongoing Changes in Lapland

Climate Change

Climate change has both positive and negative impacts, ones that pose distinct challenges in social as well as economic perspective in Arctic communities.[29] The literature review and interviews both indicate that the global warming caused by climate change is one of the greatest environmental threats to the Arctic region.[30] Lapland, being part of the region, is also affected. Indigenous and rural populations are more vulnerable to negative impacts of climatic and environmental changes.[31] It has been documented in both scientific research and discussions with elderly informants that health effects[32] are among the most obvious consequences of climate change in the Arctic.[33] According to the ACIA (2005) report, climate change results in various challenges to the region: for example thawing permafrost causes damage to roads and water supplies[34] and toxic contaminants released from snowmelt pollute water and the food chain, which is a particularly serious threat to human health.[35] The

29 Rasmussen, 2009, *supra* note 13, 525.

30 *Arctic Threats: The Arctic region is under threat from Climate Change, increased exploitation, and a lot more.* Accessed 19 April, 2015. http://www.greenpeace.org/international/en/campaigns/climate-change/arctic-impacts/arctic-under-threat/.

31 Furberg, Maria et al. "Facing the limit of resilience: perceptions of climate change among reindeer herding Sámi in Sweden," in *Glob Health Action*, 4 (8417) (2011). Accessed 1 May, 2015. http://www.ncbi.nlm.nih.gov/pmc/articles/PMC3204920/.

32 Parkinson, Alan J., "Arctic Human Health Initiative," in *Circumpolar Health Supplements* 6 (2010): 9, accessed 12 November, 2012. http://www.circumpolarhealthjournal.net/public/journals/32/chs/CHS_2010_6.pdf.

33 Scheraga, Joel, "Overview of the health implications of climate change in the Arctic" (paper presented at the Workshop held in Anchorage, Alaska, 13–15 February, 2008). Accessed 19 October, 2012, http://www.circumpolarhealthjournal.net/index.php/ijch/article/viewFile/18295/20987.

34 McCarthy et el., "Climate Change in the Context of Multiple Stressors and Resilience," in *Arctic Climate Impact Assessment* (ACIA), ed. Symon, Carolyn, Lelani Arris and Bill Heal (Cambridge: Cambridge University Press, 2005), 945–988

35 Berner, Jim et el., "Human health," in *Arctic Climate Impact Assessment* (ACIA), ed. Symon, Carolyn, Lelani Arris and Bill Heal (Cambridge: Cambridge University Press, 2005), 863–906.

Intergovernmental Panel on Climate Change (IPCC) clearly recognizes that climate change mainly affects particular parts of the population, for example, the elderly, the powerless, indigenous peoples and recent immigrants. The effects of climate change are considerable for marginalized people all across the region,[36] including the Sámi. Within these groups, the elderly have been identified as the most exposed segment.[37] Climate change has impacts on food safety and security and heightens the risk of environmental contamination and the spread of viral diseases,[38] all of which affect the health of the region's inhabitants.[39] Risks such as these impact the elderly most significantly. Heat stroke has caused deaths and exacerbated cardiovascular diseases amongst elderly and socially isolated people in Europe,[40] and Lapland is no exception. Moreover, as elderly persons lose physical and mental stamina with age and their economic situation generally deteriorates as well, their coping capacity declines significantly. In addition to health-related challenges, the elderly, especially the Sámi elderly, are threatened by a psychological fear that the group's distinct identity cannot be sustained, a central consideration here being that climate change will bring about sweeping societal changes.[41] In her research Lena Karlsson found that trends in health and demography among indigenous people have followed a different course compared to those for non-indigenous groups living in the same area. The main finding of her research suggests that Sámi have higher mortality rates and a shorter life expectancy at birth than

---

36 Schumann, Barbara, "*Climate change in Lapland and its role in the health of the elderly and rural populations,*" in *Ageing, Wellbeing and Climate Change in the Arctic: An interdisciplinary analysis*, ed. Naskali, Päivi, Marjaana Seppänen and Shahnaj Begum. (Routledge – Earthscan, Forthcoming, 2015).

37 Rakkolainen, Maria and Monica Tennberg, "Adaptation in Russian Climate Governance," in *Governing the Uncertain*, ed. Tennberg, Monica (London: Springer, 2012), 42.

38 Haines, Andy et al., "Climate change and human health: Impacts, vulnerability and public health," in *Public Health* 120 (2006): 585–96. Accessed 19 April, 2015. http://www.bu.edu/sph/files/2012/08/Haines_2006_Climate_Change_and_Human_Health_-_Impacts_Vulnerability_and_Public_Health.pdf.

39 Arbour, Laura, Alan Parkinson and Judith Kulig, "Human health at the ends of the earth," in *Rural Remote Health* 10 (2010): 153.

40 Luber, George and Natasha Prudent, "Climate Change and Human Health," in *Trans Am Clin Climatol Asoc* 120 (2009):113–117. Accessed 19 April, 2015. http://www.ncbi.nlm.nih.gov/pmc/articles/PMC2744549/; Haines et al. 2006, *supra* note 38, 585–96.

41 Parkinson, Alan J., "Climate Change and Infectious Disease: Impact on Human populations in the Arctic," *Centers for Disease Control and Prevention* 156 (2) (2008): 104–178.

the population at large.[42] This is probably a result of their having a different lifestyle or of psychosocial and/or genetic factors.[43]

Human Activities Threatening Traditional Activities

The Sámi informants, especially the elderly ones, reported dramatic changes in what for them had been a stable environment. The changes noted have mainly been caused by numerous human activities, such as mining, tourism and other commercially oriented developments. Traditional activities are gradually being replaced by more modern ones. There is a mixed opinion about this development amongst the Sámi. An 83-year-old woman who was born in Sodankyla and now lives in Ivalo in an elderly service institution made the following comments on mining:

> Mining will just destroy our nature and environment. Our water, fishes and berries which we collect from the forest will be contaminated. When I was young, everything was fresh!

One young female informant who has a handicraft business in Jokkmokk and whose husband is a reindeer herder talked about the impact of mining in their community. In talking about the test mining at the Kallak Deposit, she presented a number of views about mining:

> Herding and *duodji* are both closely related to our cultural identity and now mining has already affected these activities. Most of the people are concerned about the future impact of mining activities on our traditional activities and environment. I am also worried about our young generation. People can easily earn good money by working in the mining industry and because of that many young people are not motivated to pursue higher studies. In the future, there will be a huge job crisis when the mining company leaves the area. There will not be good options to compensate for the effects of the crisis.

42 Karlsson, Lena, "Indigenous life expectancy in Sweden 1850–1899: Towards a long and healthy life?" in *Demographic Research* 28 (2013): 433–456.

43 Hasler, Sven et al. "Causes of death in the Sámi population of Sweden, 1961–2000," in *International Journal of Epidemiology* 34(3) (2005): 623–629. Accessed 1 May, 2015. http://diva-portal.org/smash/record.jsf?dswid=_e_03rO&faces-redirect=true&language=en&searchType=SIMPLE&query=&af=%5B%5D&aq=%5B%5B%5D%5D&aq2=%5B%5B%5D%5D&aqe=%5B%5D&pid=diva2%3A154024&noOfRows=50&sortOrder=author_sort_asc&onlyFullText=false&sf=all&jfwid=_e_03rO.

While some say these activities bring revenue to the region and hence boost the region's economy and bring new jobs for young adults, others intend to resist such developments, which impact the environment. We interviewed a 69-year-old woman from the Kallak area who is not a Sámi. She is retired but active in social life; her daughters work in the southern part of Sweden. She has supported the mining in Kallak, her logic being the following:

> Without job opportunities the young generation is leaving the village. They are only seven elderly persons living in this area. The family members are coming in the summer time and during holidays to visit their elderly. If there were jobs available, then people could stay here. Otherwise, in the future the village will not exist anymore. I know about the negative impacts of mining on our water resources and environment, but I am more concerned about our ageing population being isolated from the younger one.

As regards mining developments in Sámi areas, even though the research suggests that "[t]he legal protection that the Sámi people now enjoy against mining and its adverse impacts is relatively strong",[44] the reaction of the locals – Sámi as well as non-Sámi – is mixed. In both Finnish and Swedish Lapland, mining activities cause serious tension especially amongst the Sámi. In response to the initial development of the Kallak mine project, a series of protests were organized which even became violent at some point. The Sámi activists were at the forefront of these protests, joined by other local Sámi. In Finland, however, protests were mostly aired using popular media such as in newspapers by Sámi politicians, activists and journalists. It could be mentioned that currently there are no mines within the Finnish Sámi homeland. In 2014, the Irish mining company Karelian Diamond Resources received provisional approval from Tukes (The Finnish Safety and Chemicals Agency) for exploration in Utsjoki but had to pull out because of resistance from the local people.[45] In the case of elderly Sámi, we found that in Jokkmokk many of them took part in the protest. Some of the respondents stated with great frustration that if they could not continue

44 *Koivurova, Timo et al.*, "Legal Protection of Sámi Traditional Livelihoods from the Adverse Impacts of Mining: A Comparison of the Level of Protection Enjoyed by Sámi in Their Four Home States," in *Arctic Review on Law and Politics* 6(1), (2015). Accessed 19 April, 2015. http://arcticreview.no/index.php/arctic/article/view/76.

45 *YLE news, May 11, 2015. Barents Observer, "Local opposition buries plans for diamond mine in Arctic Finland,"* accessed 11 June, 2015, http://barentsobserver.com/en/nature/2015/05/local-opposition-buries-plans-diamond-mine-arctic-finland-11-05.

reindeer herding, which will be affected by mining developments, they – the whole community – will die mentally. "We would like to keep on our herding practices as long as our legs are working", said an elderly Sámi in Inari.

Changes in Health and Well-Being

Health is one of the most important concerns for elderly Sámi as they suffer from the loss of physical strength to resist diseases in old age. As discussed, a number of viral diseases may enter the region as a consequence of climate change, and such diseases are expected to increase, particularly among the very young and the elderly.[46] In addition, environmental pollution, caused for example by extractive industrial developments in the region, puts people's health at risk. Amongst the Sámi, acculturation has already been shown to cause numerous health problems,[47] especially among the elderly, who feel threatened and psychologically depressed as a result.

We have observed that in remote villages in Lapland elderly Sámi are generally happy about their health. They consider health and well-being connected to individuals' physical, socio-economic, cultural and environmental surroundings. Their nature-based culture and environment have a huge influence on their physical and mental health. Our informants reported that they live close to nature, which gives them space to breathe and comfort to enjoy life. Even though regular services, such as access to healthcare centres, post offices and shopping malls are not readily available, they feel that they are well adapted to this reality. They eat fresh and traditional food, which allows them to meet their dietary needs. This sort of understanding of well-being is very important for elderly Sámi in determining whether they are healthy.[48] However, as stated before, the pureness of nature is now increasingly being contaminated, for example, by gradual expansion of mining throughout Lapland. A 54-year-old activist from Sevettijärvi, highlighting the importance of water resources for the maintenance of good health, expressed her concerns:

> Mining activities starting in Kittilä are located just around 100 km from Inari at Kevitsa, which will pollute the water of Lake Inari. People in Inari

46 Parkinson, Alan J. and James Berner, "Climate change and impacts on human health in the Arctic: An international workshop on emerging threats and the response of Arctic communities to climate change," in *Circumpolar Health Journal* (2008). Accessed 5 April, 2015 http://www.circumpolarhealthjournal.net/index.php/ijch/article/viewFile/18295/20987.

47 Hassler, Sven, Siv Kvernmo and Andrew Kozlow, "Sámi," in *Health Transitions in Arctic Populations*, ed. Young, T. Kue and Peter Bjerregaard (Toronto: University of Toronto Press, 2008), 155.

48 Hassler 2008, *supra* note 47, 148–170.

> and in Utsjoki rely on the water from the lake. Decision makers think that mining is important and water treatment would eventually solve the problem, whereas the people in the community are concerned about environmental pollution. We are dependent on clean water for our health.

Generally speaking, in the Nordic countries, especially Finland, Norway and Sweden, the health of the populations, including the elderly, is much better than elsewhere in the world,[49] and they live independently. In Finland, for example, the government has worked to promote well-being in 40 municipalities by raising the nutritional level of people's diets. In the year 2012, the National Nutrition Council, in collaboration with local and regional governments,[50] conducted a study showing the importance of nutrition to the well-being of municipal residents. The study stated: "A healthy diet is an essential part of not only physical and psychological health, but also social well-being, community spirit, cultural and behavioural education, sustainable development, quality of life, and life management skills". It also mentioned that healthy food is important for elderly people's well-being. However, this project did not include Lapland; the city of Oulu was the northernmost site studied. Consequently the dynamics prevailing in Finnish Lapland in general have been neglected, not to mention the concerns of elderly Sámi in particular. In Sweden, a national public health policy was adopted in the year 2003 and updated in 2008.[51] According to this policy, which is based on 11 public health objectives, the government should create social conditions that will contribute to equally good health for the whole population.[52] However, as indicated, the lives of elderly Sámi are structured differently from those of the population at large. The characteristics

49 Tuomilehto, Jakko, "Health status in Finland and other Nordic countries with special reference to chronic non-communicable diseases," in.*Ann Nutr Metab* 35(1) (1991):41–52. Accessed 28 April, 2015. http://www.ncbi.nlm.nih.gov/pubmed/1888127.

50 *Well-being through nutrition: A guide for municipal decision-makers* (2012), *National Nutrition Council in Finland In collaboration with Local and Regional Government Finland With the support of Ministry of Agriculture and Forestry and Ministry of Social Affairs and Health*. Accessed 1 May, 2015. http://www.stm.fi/c/document_library/get_file?folderId=501339&name=DLFE-23602.pdf.

51 Anell, Anders, Anna H Glenngård and Sherry Merkur, "Sweden: health System Review," in *Health Systems in Transition*, 14(5), (2012). Accessed 16 April, 2015. http://www.euro.who.int/__data/assets/pdf_file/0008/164096/e96455.pdf.

52 Suorsa, Katri, "Regionality, innovation policy and peripheral regions in Finland, Sweden and Norway," in *Fennia* 185 (1), (2007):15–29. Accessed 1 May, 2015. http://www.researchgate.net/publication/228460641_Regionality_innovation_policy_and_peripheral_regions_in_Finland_Sweden_and_Norway.

of the region in which they live and their indigenous culture warrant a special focus on their physical and mental health.

Changes in the Food Supply-Chain

The Sámi believe that traditional food provides the diet needed to keep them healthy. Any impact on the traditional food supply chain may bring problems related to health. Studies have found that diseases such as diabetes, asthma, cancer and high blood pressure are common among elderly Sámi in the Finnish and Swedish north. Climate change in the region has reduced the availability of traditional food, and the resulting reliance on imported food has significantly changed the local diet, with major health-related implications.[53] Traditional food is also important in social and cultural terms.[54] Research has shown that imported food has increased the risk of cancer, obesity, diabetes, and cardiovascular diseases among elderly Sámi.[55]

An elderly woman from Inari, aged 87, expressed her view on traditional food in the following way:

> I was 14 years old during the war time. We had a cold room where we stored fish. We used to get fish from our lakes and to sell them to German soldiers. But now fish stocks are not what they used to be. A variety of foodstuffs from outside sources come to the shops and these give us more options to choose from, but we still miss some of our local fish and traditional sources of foods for our dietary needs.

Another woman, aged approximately 90, living in an elderly institution in Ivalo stated: "In addition to our language, the food we used to eat before is very important for our culture, but this food is now less available in the service institutions".

The interviews indicate that it is good that elderly Sámi have access to a wider choice of food. At the same time, the informants expressed their concerns about the poor availability of traditional food. An additional concern is that

53 Parkinson, Alan J., "Arctic Human Health Initiative," in *Circumpolar Health Supplements* 6 (2010): 9. Accessed 12 November, 2012. http://www.circumpolarhealthjournal.net/public/journals/32/chs/CHS_2010_6.pdf.

54 Begum, Shahnaj, "Impact of Climate Change on the Elderly People in the Arctic with special focus on the European High North: A Human Rights Perspective," in *The Yearbook of Polar Law* 5 (Publisher: Brill Academic Publishers, the Netherlands, 2013): 571–602.

55 Jorgenson, Marit and Kue Young. "Cardiovascular Diseases, Diabetes, and Obesity," in *Health Transitions in Arctic Populations*, ed. Young, T. Kue and Peter Bjerregaard (University of Toronto Press, 2008), 291.

the traditional food supply chain has been contaminated by the numerous commercial activities in the region, making consumption risky. One example noted by local Sámi informants is the expansion of mining in Swedish Lapland. This will have devastating effects on the Luleå River, the water of which is important for the Sámi community and many other local residents who rely on fishing from the river. Most of the Sámi respondents viewed the contamination of the river as a threat to their very survival.

Increased Out-Migration

Out-migration is one of the acknowledged challenges in the north. Research suggests that the trend is common amongst young adults and women.[56] Finnish and Swedish Lapland are both experiencing out-migration, from the Inari-Ivalo and Jokkmokk regions, respectively. Out-migration creates a threat to elderly care and other relevant issues. It is mostly the younger population who move to the south for better education and for better jobs. This trend is also common amongst the Sámi of the region,[57] creating an imbalance in the social structure. The number of elderly amongst the Sámi population is increasing, which brings new challenges. Especially in the region's more remote locations, the elderly Sámi live with little public support, fewer communication services and insufficient access to community health and acute care.[58] These issues have a great impact on their overall well-being as both the lack of essential services and isolation cause considerable suffering. In old age, when they are not physically able to live independent lives, elderly Sámi who have no relatives nearby are required to move to the nearest elderly care institution. Our interviews indicate that had their children or neighbours continued to live in the village, elderly Sámi would have had a network to help them and could stay at home rather than moving to elderly care institutions.

Unavailability of Essential Services

Given that health care services in remote communities are not as efficient as they are in cities, elderly Sámi sometimes find access to healthcare problematic.

56 Rasmussen 2009, *supra* note 13, 525.

57 Gergils, Håkan, "Dynamic innovation systems in the Nordic Countries? Denmark, Finland, Iceland, Norway and Sweden," in (*Sueco*) *Tapa dura* 2 (2006): 423. Accessed 25 May, 2015. http://pdfqr.com/dynamic-innovation-systems-in-the-nordic-countries-denmark-finland-iceland-norway-and--9185355356.html; Jauhiainen, Jussi,S., "Regional and innovation policies in Finland – Towards convergence and/or mismatch?" in *Regional Studies* 41, (2007); Suorsa 2007, *supra* note 52.

58 Kozlo and Lisitsyn 2008, *supra note* 8: 96.

For example, our field studies conducted in the village of Angeli in Inari reveal that some of the elderly Sámi living in the village need to come to the Ivalo health centre, which is around 80 kilometres from their home. Sometimes their physical mobility is poor and driving to Ivalo by themselves in an emergency is difficult. They frequently rely on help from family members or other relatives. Immediate health service is extremely difficult. Those who live in the care institutions also face numerous problems. In both Inari and Jokkmokk individuals mentioned that services require public funding, but the extra expense involved in providing them for the elderly living in remote villages is not looked upon favourably. Moreover, home services for elderly are less available because of the remoteness of the region. Even the sporadic home services that are available are not as effective as they should be. In regard to moving to elderly service institutions, we observed that elderly Sámi prefer to speak Sámi with caregivers, or at least they would like the caregivers to know the Sámi culture and norms. This is important especially when the elderly suffer from dementia. For clearer and better communication specially trained care professionals with knowledge of the Sámi language and culture could make elderly clients feel better.

4 Discussion

The threats to the well-being of elderly communities in the north in general, and Sámi elderly in particular, are not given special attention despite the fact that the Nordic countries are regarded as advanced in promoting the quality of life for all their citizens. The basic universal welfare system guaranteed by the constitutions of both Finland and Sweden offer all the residents equal rights and opportunities irrespective of their sex, age and the region where they live. The focal region for this study is Finnish and Swedish Lapland, which have distinctive environmental and cultural characteristics compared to the southern regions of the respective countries. The discussions above have indicated that the elderly Sámi population studied here is affected in a number of ways by the ongoing transformation in the region, and they can be identified as objects of human security threats. While the impacts vary depending on the characteristics of each of the smaller districts of the region, there are threats that are common to elderly Sámi in both Finnish and Swedish Lapland.

We have identified how culture and cultural identity, as essential components of human security, have a clear link to the well-being of elderly Sámi. Traditionally, elderly Sámi have been regarded as the holders of customary norms and values, which are now at risk of disappearing because of the adoption of new life styles. Their authority to transmit the customary values to the younger generations has diminished, as development has been rather rapid and traditional practices representing the Sámi culture and cultural identity are gradually being altered. This transformation poses obstacles to the elderly Sámi in transmitting culture-based practices to the younger generation, making them feel threatened with losing their identity.

We have also observed that in many areas human activities such as mining have caused mixed feelings amongst the elderly. Our interviews show that there have been valid reasons for these mixed feelings, as economic sustenance and socio-cultural survival run counter to one other. While all the respondents acknowledged the negative effect of mining, the elderly Sámi respondents in Jokkmokk, for example, seemed to object to it more forcefully than the non-Sámi elderly in the area. The former are more concerned about cultural sustenance whereas the latter are more worried about the threat from out-migration of the young generation to big cities. For the latter group, mining at least brings economic incentives that create more jobs for young people, allowing them to live closer to their elderly relatives.

The elderly are concerned about inclusion in matters that affect them. The elderly Sámi in both countries find that their voices go unheard in the decision-making process. For example, even though it has been claimed in the literature that there are enough legal tools to protect Sámi culture and practices amid the mining activities in Finnish and Swedish Lapland, we found that the views of the people in the communities studied – indicators of the socio-cultural and psychological impact of mining – were not given due regard.

In both Finland and Sweden, elderly Sámi are in many cases engaged in reindeer herding, making and handicrafts, for example, and are thus also directly affected by the loss of jobs as new modern means take over these traditional practices. It should be mentioned here that reindeer herding activities are regarded as emblematic of Sámi culture, even though in Finland, unlike in Sweden, non-Sámi can also engage in herding. The risks affecting elderly Sámi thus are not only confined to a fear of losing community identity, but include other threats that will affect their economic sustenance, living conditions and personal safety.

Overall, the situations in the northern parts of both countries are essentially the same. Access to healthcare facilities, availability of traditional food, secure livelihood practices, preservation of cultural identity and environmentally sound development are the principal concerns of elderly Sámi, either directly or indirectly. The lack of a policy focus attuned to the situation of elderly Sámi results in a gap in the understanding of human security. For purposes of future research on this issue we propose that the concerns of elderly Sámi that we have highlighted in this chapter should be specifically addressed. We also see the need for inclusion of the relevant stakeholders in determining the policies for the promotion of the human security of elderly Sámi.

5 Conclusion

In this chapter, we have brought to light the challenges facing the elderly population, in particular the elderly Sámi of the Finnish and Swedish north. While the ongoing transformation in the Arctic generally affects the socio-cultural lives and livelihoods of all the residents, the elderly – and more specifically elderly Sámi – face distinct challenges. We have identified a number of considerations, such as health, food, culture and livelihoods, shortcomings in which pose risks to the well-being of the region's elderly. As far as the concept of well-being is connected to human security, we submit that these risks threaten the security of elderly Sámi in the northern parts of Finland and Sweden. We also contend that while the elderly in these countries in general are well treated, and supported by the states' social security networks, policy documents fail to adequately address specific regional characteristics affecting the elderly Sámi in particular. As part of bringing this issue to the fore in this paper, we propose that in-depth research should be initiated to identify the special risks facing elderly Sámi so that they may live healthy and full lives. We recommend that states should not only promote policies in this regard, but also undertake efforts to implement those policies with adequate monitoring mechanisms.

CHAPTER 13

Human Security for Mongolian Herders: Evolving Risks and Opportunities

*Vigya Sharma**

Abstract

The Arctic region shares a number of socio-cultural and ecological parallels with Mongolia. Reliance on traditional livelihoods, fast paced changes to the natural climate, conflict with existing industries such as tourism, a rapid mining boom, and remote and sparse population centers are only some of the similarities underlining the Arctic and Mongolian contexts.

This chapter applies the lens of human security to unpack tensions underlying Mongolia's development. It provides a robust understanding of how these tensions interact with one another to infiltrate socio-economic and environmental insecurity amongst Mongolia's traditionally pastoralist communities.

The chapter argues that Mongolia's ongoing experience in navigating human security risks and opportunities may provide useful pointers to northern Indigenous peoples, including those from the Arctic. To that extent, the chapter highlights a number of important take-home messages that may: (a) not only help pro-actively counter some of the challenges that the Indigenous people of the North may increasingly experience in relation to societal security, but also (b) help build their capacity over the long-term to preserve their cultural and ecological identities.

1 Introduction

As a sovereign state, Mongolia is not 'indigenous' in conventional interpretation. Yet, it is often referred to as the 'last frontier' and one of only a handful of places in the world with true unspoilt wilderness.[1] The country is currently undergoing a change so rapid that its identity is suddenly under threat from

* Vigya Sharma is a Research fellow with the Energy & Poverty Research Group at the University of queensland (UQ) Australia. This chapter is based on her recent postdoctoral research at the Centre for Social Responsibility in Mining, also at UQ.

1 Togtokh, C. "Mongolian Gobi," (2011). Retrieved 2 June, 2015, from https://www.youtube.com/watch?v=bU8Q8Vz3LNk&feature=share.

 | DOI 10.1163/9789004314399_015

insecurity across political, environmental, economic and socio-cultural functions. While some of these threats are externally driven, others remain internal to Mongolia's choice of development pathways.

This chapter applies the lens of human security to unpack tensions underlying Mongolia's development and better understand how these tensions interact with one another to infiltrate socio-economic and environmental insecurity amongst Mongolia's traditionally pastoralist communities. In particular, the chapter has a twofold purpose: firstly, there is a serious paucity of literature that goes beyond political and territorial dimensions to interrogate human security implications for Mongolia.[2] The chapter therefore, aims to advance knowledge in this space with a view to inform national policy debates on Mongolia's future sustainability. Secondly, and importantly in relation to the theme that this book explores, Mongolia's development trajectory boasts a number of characteristics that resonate strongly with the nature of challenges that the Indigenous peoples of the northern hemisphere, including the Arctic are either experiencing already or will do so over the coming decades. To that extent, Mongolia's experience in successfully navigating – or succumbing to – human security risks and opportunities may provide useful pointers to northern Indigenous peoples and build capacity to preserve their own cultural and ecological identities.

The chapter is organized as follows: the next section proposes a theoretical underpinning of human security as a concept, including its manifestations. Section 3 provides an overview of Mongolia's current development pathways, and grounds them in its rich cultural, socio-economic and political past. Section 4 outlines contemporary human security implications for Mongolia, and likely future challenges. Section 5 concludes with key findings and lessons from the Mongolian experience for the Indigenous peoples of the northern hemisphere, including the Arctic.

2 Human Security and Sustainability: Theoretical Observations

Over the last two decades, the concept of human security has evolved from being an idea that allows 'grappling with the complexities that face humanity'

2 Enkhsaikhan, J., "Human security factor in Mongolia's National Security Concept,"in *The Mongolian Journal of International Affairs* (November, 2000); Jargalsaikhan, M., *Unkept Human Security Promises In Developing Countries. The Case of Mongolia* (Washington DC, Elliott School of International Affairs. The George Washington University. Number 4, November 2012).

to one that argued for vulnerable communities to address 'freedom from fear and freedom from want'.[3] It is now recognized as a universal approach founded on the complementary roles of 'protection and empowerment' to address threats to human security at multiple levels.[4] It offers a framework that helps safeguard the survival, livelihood and dignity of citizens, irrespective of race, gender, religion, culture, income and power. To that extent, it pushes conventional boundaries to invoke a sense of safety that goes beyond physical and territorial; it seeks to operationalize a holistic view of wellbeing.[5] A number of principles thus remain central to the concept of human security, including: people's freedom and dignity of life; inter-linkages between peace, development and human, socio-cultural, political and civil rights; national ownership; and government responsibility to seek solutions that foster security in light of local realities.

These principles necessitate that governments and international and regional agencies employ approaches that are grounded in the local context while remaining people-centered, pro-active and comprehensive. It is important that the role of local context is given particular consideration in understanding, planning and managing human security. Local conditions provide a unique interpretation to both immediate demands and long-term needs-driven priorities and can therefore, widely vary among regions within a country or across nations. In other words, local context relies on individual knowledge construction and de-construction to influence how it manifests itself across communities worldwide.

Furthermore, human security provides an all-encompassing platform for policy making that allows contemplating potential future challenges in light of current and past local realities. In doing so, it encourages both policy makers and the regulating institutions to work towards a coherent program of work

---

3 UN, "Human Security 'More than an Abstract Concept' — for Hungry Family, It's Food on the Table, for Refugee, It's Shelter from Conflict, General Assembly Told," (2012, 4 June 2012). Retrieved 23 May, 2015, from http://www.un.org/press/en/2012/ga11246.doc.htm; UN, Strategic Plan 2014–2017 (New York, Human Security Unit, United Nations: 22, 2014).

4 Gomez, O.A. and D. Gasper, *Human Security: a thematic guidance note for regional and national human development report teams*, United Nations Development Programme, Human Development Report Office, 2013; GDRC. (n.d.). "Definitions of Human Security". Retrieved 30 May, 2015, from http://www.gdrc.org/sustdev/husec/Definitions.pdf.

5 Human Security Initiative, "Definition of Human Security" (2011). Retrieved 25 May, 2015, from http://www.humansecurityinitiative.org/definition-human-security; UN, Strategic Plan 2014–2017 (New York, Human Security Unit, United Nations: 22, 2014).

that not only calls for improved national social, economic and environmental planning processes on an enduring basis but also interrogates emerging risks and challenges, such as those related to increasing economic inequality, declining stocks and quality of land and water and climate change. The latter – although ubiquitous in nature and gradual in effect – may have long-term irreversible, but differentiated consequences which will require early thinking and pro-active strategies.

Finally, in light of the overarching objective of this chapter, Table 13.1 below encapsulates current discourse on human security in a framework of key security threats and their manifestations across the world. Drawn from a systematic critique of literature on the evolution and implementation of the human security approach, the framework is not exhaustive *per se*, but provides helpful pointers towards the changing meanings, and interpretations of human security over time. It acknowledges that various sources of threat result in varied outcomes depending upon local contexts and a range of associated values. This framework will provide a useful lens to analyze contemporary human security issues in Mongolia, explored later in the chapter.

Climate change and related disaster events negatively influence both the accessibility and quality of natural resources (e.g. loss of land and increasing salinity in a coastal area), thereby impacting resource dependent livelihoods and poverty levels in an irrevocable fashion.[6] In particular, climate change-induced droughts and decline in food production may lead to regional social and economic crises, greater distributional inequality, in turn, enhancing the chances of potential conflict.

In the discussion of the relationship between climate change and conflict, the capacity of states to cope with both long- and short-term changes to natural and socio-economic conditions is particularly important.[7] For existing states that have relatively weaker governance structures, climate change impacts on livelihoods may further constrain the state's capacity – through

6 Connell, J., "Climatic change: a new security challenge for the atoll states of the South Pacific,"in *Commonwealth & Comparative Politics* 31(2) (1993): 173–192.

7 Barnett, J., "Security and climate change," in *Global Environmental Change* 13 (2003): 7–17; Raleigh, C. and H. Urdal, "Climate change, environmental degradation and armed conflict," in *Political Geography* 26 (2007): 674–694; Gartzke, E., "Climate change and interstate conflict" (paper presented at the 250th Anniversary Conference organized for The Royal Norwegien Society of Sciences and Letters, 'Climate Change and Security', Trondheim, Norway, 2010); Parsons, R., "Climate change: the hottest issue in security studies?" in *Risks, Hazards & Crisis in Public Policy* 1(1) (2010): 87–116.

TABLE 13.1 *A framework to identify sources of, and outcomes from human security threats*[8]

Primary Sources of Threat	Manifested in/Key Impacts
Climate and weather-related	• Loss of livelihoods • Physical relocation – temporary or permanent • Loss of social capital • Resource scarcity-based violent conflict
Political/institutional	• Human rights abuse • Place-based violence and armed conflict • Corruption
Environmental – degrading quality and quantity of land, water and biodiversity	• Impacts on agriculture and food security with widespread national and local economic repercussions • Loss of natural resources-based livelihoods like farming, pastoralism • Resource scarcity-based conflict
Social	• Gender-based violence • Loss of cultural heritage
Economic	• Growing income inequality • Globalization-influenced loss of traditional lifestyle and associated cultural value

significant losses in broader social and natural capitals – to maintain high levels of governance and institutional prudence.[9]

The literature argues that the most direct connection between climate change and conflict is via population displacement.[10] Although, there have

8 Human Security Initiative, 2011; UN, 2012 (4 June 2012); Gomez and Gasper, 2013; UN, 2014.

9 Salehyah, I. "From climate change to conflict? No consensus yet," in *Journal of Peace Research* 45(3) (2008): 315–326; Adger, W., "Climate change, human well-being and insecurity," in *New Political Economy* 15(2) (2010): 275–292.

10 Nordas, R. and N. Gleditsch, "Climate conflict: common sense or nonsense?" (paper presented at the International Workshop on 'Human Security and Climate Change'. Oslo, International Peace Research Institute, Buhaug, 2005); Gleditsch, H., N. and O. Theisen, "Implications of climate change for armed conflict" (paper presented at the World Bank Workshop on 'Social Dimensions of Climate Change'. Washington D.C., World Bank, 2008).

been certain situations in the past where environmental degradation has led to migration which, in turn, has resulted in conflicts (e.g. Bangladeshi migration-related conflicts in India's eastern states, the Darfur conflict),[11] these cases remained limited to particular regions and were based on a range of context-dependent factors. To that extent, these cases are not representative of any direct links between changing environmental conditions, resulting migration and conflicts.[12]

Nevertheless, it is accepted that migration of large populations may lead to greater competition for access to scarce and or limited resources but also to gain a dominant share of existing resources that may not necessarily be scarce, causing unbridled socio-economic inequality.[13] In the absence of efficient institutions, growing inequality may lead to local and regional conflicts. As Parsons argues, "density increases the likelihood of violent collision". Internationally, the absence of an appropriate law concerning environmentally-displaced communities may further provoke inequality and raise arguments seeking distributional justice for both migrant and host communities.[14]

However, the nexus between climate change, migration and conflict (See Figure 13.1 below) has thus far ignored the critical role of industrial development in abetting or inciting further threats to human and societal security in regions and markets that are relatively late entrants to globalization. Newly industrialized nations may host activities that may, in particular, aggravate existing socio-economic dysfunction on the one hand, but bring along immense promise for improved lifestyles and greater resilience to climate disasters in the future.

3 Mongolia – Past and Present

Before we identify what human security risks there might exist for Mongolia, it is important to develop an appropriate understanding of Mongolia as it stands today – politically, socio-economically, and environmentally. Hopefully, this will highlight what internal and external forces existed that may have not only played a role in shaping Mongolia's development trajectory more broadly but may have also influenced the nature of human security challenges that Mongolia's peoples and governments might face, moving forward.

11 Reuveny, R., "Climate change-induced migration and violent conflict,"in *Political Geography* 26 (2007): 656–673.

12 Nordas and Gleditsch, 2005.

13 Barnett, 2003; Salehyah, 2008.

14 WBGU, World in transition: Climate change as a security risk – summary for policymakers. Berlin, German Advisory Council on Global Change, 2007; Parsons, 2010.

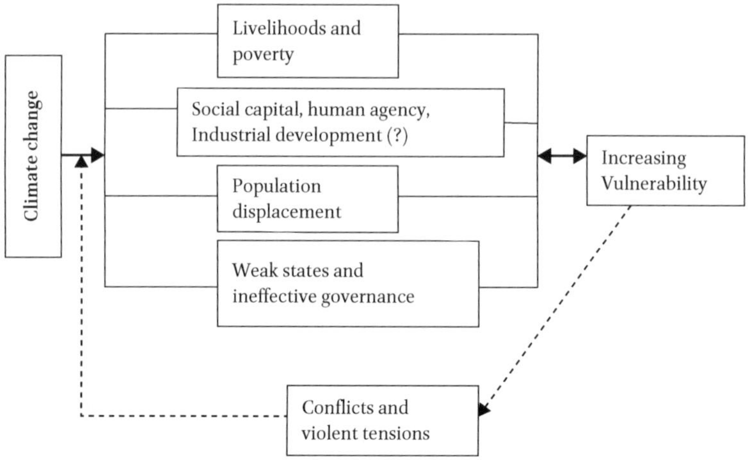

FIGURE 13.1 *Climate change impacts on human security and potential conflict*

Mongolia provides a unique landscape of diverse socio-cultural, economic, institutional and environmental forces that challenge its current course of development across both time and space.[15] These forces include, high climate variability; geographical remoteness, with extremely low rates of population density; high dependence on the natural environment for livelihoods; increasing urbanization; and a series of economic and institutional changes since 1991 including, democratization after decades of Soviet rule, and subsequent opening of its economy to global market forces.[16]

15 Nixson, F. and B. Walters, "Privatization, income distribution, and poverty: the Mongolian experience," in *World Development* 34 (9) (2006): 1557–1579., Lioubimtseva, E. and G.M. Henebry, "Climate and environmental change in arid Central Asia: impacts, vulnerability, and adaptations," in *Journal of Arid Environments* 73 (2009): 963–977.

16 It has been reported that a majority of 'these' unregulated rural–urban migrants live in the outskirts of the capital city of Ulaanbaatar in impoverished settlements with poor services and infrastructure. Refer to Section 4 below, for more detail; Nixson and Walters, 2006; Ochirsukh, Y., "Mongolia 2010 population census: main findings," (2011). Retrieved 20 October, 2013, from http://www.slideshare.net/Ochiro/mongolia-2010-population-census-main-findings; Reeves, J., "Mongolia's environmental security," in *Asian Survey* 51 (3) (2011): 453–471, Sietz, D., M.K.B. Ludeke and C. Walther, "Categorisation of typical vulnerability patterns in global drylands," in *Global Environmental Change* 21 (2011): 431–440.

Approximately 40% of all Mongolians are currently involved in herding for their primary livelihood.[17] History has played an important role in shaping pastoralism as an economic enterprise in Mongolia; a strong pastoralist past provides Mongolians with a strong cultural identity rooted in the philosophy of co-existence with land. For the better part of the 20th century, Mongolia was a socialist Soviet satellite state. As part of the Soviet Bloc, Mongolia groomed an educated population that, in the absence of a solid industry, took over the role of the Bloc's meat producer and exporter. At the same time, Mongolia's nomadic pastoralist sector transformed into a collective enterprise that flourished with state's support for herding and related services and infrastructure.[18]

As the Soviet Union eventually collapsed in 1991, Mongolia transitioned to a capitalist democratic model and almost instantly, faced grave institutional and socio-economic challenges. State-led services were removed while food and other imports stopped, causing extremely high rates of inflation and a steep decline in the quality of life.[19] Herding-related dependency on centralized service provision, now withdrawn, resulted in the pastoralist economy to crash and with meat export markets closed, the economy remained in turmoil until the turn of the century.[20] The new government followed a 'free market' policy to rein in economic decline. This manifested in two important changes, both of which would play an instrumental role in shaping Mongolia's future: (a) privatization of the herding sector, and (b) the passing of the Mining Law in the late 1990s.

On the one hand, privatization of herding coincided with a failing economy and growing demands – mostly, Chinese – for cashmere. In the absence of other sustainable ways of raising revenues, Mongolia's newly free and democratic government encouraged herders to raise the share of goats in their total livestock. Goats outnumbered other animals including camels, sheep and horses such that by 2010, up to 50 per cent of Mongolia's

17 UN Stats, "2013 World Statistics Pocketbook Country Profile: Mongolia," (2013). Retrieved from http://unstats.un.org/unsd/pocketbook/PDF/2013/Mongolia.pdf

18 Dierkes, J., *Introduction: research on contemporary Mongolia. Change in Democratic Mongolia: social relations, health, mobile pastoralism, and mining*, J. Dierkes and B. Dalaibuyan, (Leiden, Brill, 2012).

19 Ibid.

20 Ibid.

total national livestock comprised of goats.[21] Not only did this lead to a significant digression from Mongolia's traditional nomadic herding lifestyle that relied upon a balanced stock of all types of animals, but the move allowed only short-term economic gains at the cost of severe irreversible environmental – and thereby, socio-economic – repercussions that would inhibit the country's post-Soviet rebuild in the years to come. In its decision to encourage herders to increase the number of goats to raise cashmere-led economic revenue, the government ignored critical facts that not only were goats known to be naturally less resilient to harsh climatic conditions that Mongolia was often subjected to (see more below) but also that their grazing patterns were highly unsustainable in that they grazed by the roots on a continuous basis, leaving little time for the land to rehabilitate organically.[22] An alarming number of goats as a percentage of the total livestock would therefore, exacerbate land degradation across Mongolia over the coming years.

On the other hand, the new Mining Law allowed lifting all controls to seek foreign investment in the mining sector and was widely recognized as a necessary pathway for Mongolia's future development. The country's rapid resource boom has played a crucial role in uplifting its status as a nation state at the forefront of international geopolitics.[23] Vast undeveloped resources of copper, coal, gold, fluorspar, and uranium have caught the imagination of some of the world's largest mining corporations. Table 13.2 below provides key statistics to summarize the role that the extractives sector has played in shaping Mongolia's current and future development.

21 Endicott, E., *A History of Land Use in Mongolia: The Thirteenth Century to the Present* (London, Palgrave Macmillan, 2012); Heshmati, G.A. and V. Squires, *Combating Desertification in Asia, Africa and the Middle East: Proven practices* (London, Springer, 2013).

22 Osman-Elasha, B., *Building Resilience to Drought and Climate Change in Sudan* (2009 State of the World: Into a Warming World, WorldWatch Institute, 2009); Bittner, P. and K. Niemeyer, *Strengthening the Resiliency of Herders Facing Climate Change: The Case for Drought-Resistant Fodder* (The UB Post. Ulaanbaatar, 2015).

23 The World Bank, "Mongolia's Natural Resources: A Blessing or a Curse?" (2006). Retrieved 23 May, 2015, from http://www.worldbank.org/en/news/feature/2006/02/28/mongolias-natural-resources-blessing-or-curse; Combellick-Bidney, S. *Mongolia's mining controversies and the politics of place. Change in Democratic Mongolia: social relations, health, mobile pastoralism, and mining* (J. Dierkes. Leiden, Brill, 2012), 271–296.

TABLE 13.2 *The role of mining in Mongolia's economic development*[24]

Contribution of the mining sector as a % share of GDP	8.9% (2001) 21% (2005) 27.4 (2007) 19.8% (2009) 17.8% (2012) 15.9% (2013) 17.6% (2014)
% Share of export revenues (2007)	43–78
% Share of total revenue (2007)	32
% Share of industrial output (2007)	70
% Share of total land exposed to exploration work (2008)	24.8
% share of total land under mining license (2013)	11.4
% share of total employment	5

Mongolia's emerging minerals boom is further demonstrated by its double-digit GDP rise of 17.3% in 2011.[25] The minerals sector already employs in excess of 14,000 people and contributes to more than 70% of Mongolia's total export earnings.[26] Recent census data reveals that the two major mining centers of Khanbogd and Tsogttsetsii in the South Gobi region have witnessed an exponential growth in their population between 2000 and 2010 (approximately 201% and 229% respectively).[27] In 2012, mining accounted for approximately

24 EconomyWatch, *Mongolia industry sectors*, Economy Watch, 2010; Snyder, J., M. Wagler, O. Lkhagvasuren, L. Laing, C. Davison and C. Janes, "An equity tool for health impact assessments: Reflections from Mongolia," in *Environmental Impact Assessment Review* 34 (2012): 83–91; NSO, *Statistical Database by Sector: Industry* (Ulaanbaatar, Mongolian Statistical Information Service, National Statistical Office, 2015).

25 UN Stats., 2013.

26 Austrade, *Mongolian mining projects* (Canberra, Australian Trade Commission, Commonwealth of Australia, 2011).

27 Ochirsukh, 2011.

9% of all new employment opportunities in Mongolia.[28] Ongoing growth in Mongolia's mineral exports is expected to lead to doubling of the national GDP every two years for the next ten years.[29] Oyu Tolgoi (OT), besides being one of the world's largest copper mine, is projected to contribute to approximately 34% of Mongolia's total GDP once fully operational by 2020.[30]

Besides numerous political and socio-economic changes, Mongolia has also witnessed a steady – and permanent – decline in its ecological health and biodiversity. Currently, Mongolia is recognized as one of the world's most arid regions with desertification affecting '44% to 90% of the country's territory'[31] and up to 70% of its total land degraded through overgrazing and deforestation.[32] Climate has played an important role in this decline, particularly given the intricate dependence between the Mongolian herders and natural climatic conditions. Currently, approximately 80% of the total national territory is considered extremely vulnerable to climate-influenced disaster events.[33] Historically, Mongolia has experienced high natural climate variability with significant inter-and intra-annual and daily variation in temperature and extremely low rates of precipitation.[34] Throughout Mongolia's past, there have been recurring instances of natural disasters, commonly known as *dzuds* that typically result when intense summer droughts are followed by harsh, extremely cold winters.[35]

The frequency and intensity of dzuds have increased significantly in the last two decades, causing 'mass debilitation, starvation, and death of

---

28 Dalaibuyan, B., *Scoping the potential for enterprise facilitation in Mongolia* (Brisbane, International Mining for Development Centre, 2013).

29 Snyder, et al., 2012; NSO, 2015.

30 Dalaibuyan, 2013.

31 Reeves, 2011.

32 IFAD, "Mongolia: Rural Poverty-reduction Programme," Project Performance Assessment. Rome, International Fund for Agricultural Development, 2013; ADB, "Preserving Mongolia's Pastures to Counter Climate Change" (2014). Retrieved 1 June, 2015, from http://www.adb.org/features/preserving-mongolia-s-pastures-counter-climate-change.

33 ADB, 2014.

34 Tachiiri, K., M. Shinoda, B. Klinkenberg and Y. Morinaga, "Assessing Mongolian snow disaster risk using livestock and satellite data," in *Journal of Arid Environments* 72 (2008): pp. 2251–2263; Bittner, P. and K. Niemeyer, *Strengthening the Resiliency of Herders Facing Climate Change: The Case for Drought-Resistant Fodder* (The UB Post. Ulaanbaatar, 2015).

35 Lioubimtseva and Henebry, 2009; Wang, J., D.G. Brown and A. Agrawal, "Climate adaptation, local institutions, and rural livelihoods: a comparative study of herder communities in Mongolia and Inner Mongolia, China," in *Global Environmental Change* (In press, 2013).

livestock … [thereby damaging] the livelihoods of the herder households who depend upon them'.[36] It was, however, the intense and tragic events of 2009–10 that highlighted the complex climate-livelihoods nexus in Mongolia and the serious consequences for its herding communities that continue to remain vulnerable to a life consumed by an uncertain natural environment. The dzud of 2009–10 resulted in an enormous loss of livestock populations across the country, whereby 40% of total national livestock perished during and after the event.[37] The loss of livestock, in turn, spiralled into a series of socio-economic and ecological crises across Mongolia, particularly in rural remote areas.[38]

Mongolia thus provides a particularly timely – although dichotomous – case of the marriage between the traditional and the modern, whereby the interaction between a harsh climate, growing institutional focus on minerals development and a deepening crisis in the traditional livelihoods sector creates a range of human security concerns, as discussed below.

4 Human Security in Mongolia – Emerging Risks and Opportunities

The national security concept of Mongolia encompasses a broad suite of conditions that include, but are not limited to, the existence of the Mongolian people and its civilization, independence, sovereignty, territorial integrity, economic independence and sustainable ecological development.[39] Mongolia is grappling with a number of challenges that threaten its long-term social and human security. Geo-political pressures from neighboring Russia and China; market-led forces of globalization and ongoing volatility in mineral commodity prices; an increasing occurrence of more intense natural disaster events; and limited capacity within the herding communities to maintain resilience to both internal and external drivers of change are issues at the heart of Mongolia's security conundrum. Albeit in different ways and at different times over the past two decades, each of these factors has influenced Mongolia's

36 Tachiiri et al., 2008.

37 Ibid.; UNOCHA, "Mongolia Dzud Appeal 2010" (2010). Retrieved 30 May, 2015, from http://www.unocha.org/cap/appeals/mongolia-dzud-appeal-2010.

38 Wang, Brown and Agrawal, 2013.

39 NSC, "National Security Concept of Mongolia" (2012). Retrieved 3 June, 2015, from http://nsc.gov.mn/sites/default/files/National%20Security%20Concept%20of%20Mongolia%20EN.pdf.

traditional lifestyles, and continues to play an important role in the way Mongolia's institutions address human security in the future.

In light of the discussion so far and the complexity that underlines climate-mining-livelihoods nexus in Mongolia, there are four key human security implications that warrant further attention: social change, resource curse, disaster-induced loss and damage, and innovation. While the first three are what would be conventionally considered human security risks, the fourth is an opportunity, not only to address identified risks, but to enhance resilience and build internal capacity to withstand any unforeseen risks that might appear in the future. Each is discussed in further detail below.

4.1 *Migration-Induced Social Change*

Post-Soviet era has seen Mongolia open up its national borders to both in-and out- international migrants. While most Mongolians have sought international destinations, most notably, South Korea and Russia for better employment and or education purposes, the total number of in-migrants arriving in the country has seen a particularly sharp rise since the country's booming mineral economy caught worldwide attention.[40]

Statistically however, migration within its borders – primarily rural to urban – has been more pronounced and an important contributor to social change. The Soviet era witnessed a controlled rural to urban migratory wave as urban centers were established, and industries flourished under state control. Post-soviet times experienced a reversal of sorts whereby the shutting down of services and industries prompted the unemployed urban population to seek livelihood opportunities in the herding sectors and thus increased migration to rural areas caught pace immediately following the transition.[41]

Soon however, the reality of living in remote locations became clear as did the low productivity and high climate vulnerability of the livestock sector. Not only has the appeal of traditional herding gradually faded over the last two decades, loss and damage resulting from extreme natural disasters has forced herders and dependent households to explore newer opportunities for livelihood.[42] Additionally, successive democratic governments have achieved little

40 Algaa, S., *Growth of Internal and International Migration in Mongolia* (8th International Conference of Asia Pacific Migration Research Network Funian Normal University, Fujian, China, 2007).

41 Ibid.

42 Algaa, 2007; Wang, Brown and Agrawal, 2013; UNICEF, "Migration profiles: Mongolia" (2015). Retrieved 31 May, 2015, from http://esa.un.org/MigGMGProfiles/indicators/files/Mongolia.pdf.

in terms of building infrastructure and providing services in remote and rural communities following the decline of Soviet style centralized system of support services. Together, these factors have resulted in contemporary Mongolia facing an extremely high rate of rural to urban migration (see Table 13.3 below). According to some, most migrants to the capital city of Ulaanbaatar are witnessing a wave of 'cultural transition from rural to urban life [that] is painful and irreversible'.[43] Ulaanbaatar has been reported to have one of the highest levels of air pollution in the world.[44] Unrestrained rates of rural to urban migration has on the one hand, led to extensive urban poverty and pressure on already underprovided urban services. On the other hand, migration to urban centers has caused a steep loss in the availability and quality of human and social capital in rural areas.[45]

It is feared that mining may further encourage this trend by providing improved – often only perception-based – opportunities for employment and skills development in mining-focused larger urban centers. Greater minerals

TABLE 13.3 *Migration flows*[46]

	1990	2013
Total population (millions)	2.18	2.83
% urban population	57	70
% rural population	43	30
Remittance inflow (international, as a % share of GDP)	1.1 (2000)	2.8 (2012)

43 Horwood, C., *Tomorrow's crises today: the humanitarian impact of urbanisation* (Nairobi, United Nations Office for the Coordination of Humanitarian Affairs (OCHA) and Integrated Regional Information Networks (IRIN), 2007).

44 Sayed, A. "Ulaanbaatar's air pollution crisis: Summertime complacency won't solve the wintertime problem" (2010). Retrieved 24 May 2015, from http://blogs.worldbank.org/eastasiapacific/ulaanbaatar-s-air-pollution-crisis-summertime-complacency-won-t-solve-the-wintertime-problem.

45 Algaa, 2007; Horwood, 2007; Reeves, 2011; Allen, R.W., E. Gombojav, B. Barkhasragchaa, T. Byambaa, O. Lkhasuren, O. Amram, T.K. Takaro and C.R. Janes, "An assessment of air pollution and its attributable mortality in Ulaanbaatar, Mongolia," in *Air Quality, Atmosphere and Health* 6 (2013): 137–150.

46 Algaa, 2007; UNICEF, 2015.

revenue and investment may cause urban centers to expand that will result in an increased rate of unidirectional migration of young, healthy Mongolians to urban areas seeking employment in non-herding jobs; currently, 53.4% of Mongolia's total migrants are youth aged between 15 and 29 years.[47] This trend of young emigration from rural areas may not only have acute repercussions for human capital-intensive traditional pastoralism but also increase socio-economic dependency upon mining, thereby contradicting Mongolia's core value system that thrives on peoples' deep connection with their lands.[48] Anecdotal evidence suggests that there has been limited success thus far for herders seeking jobs in the mining industry largely due to lack of relevant skills and qualifications. On the other hand, ongoing institutional neglect towards rural and remote areas may further aggravate in light of the constitution of the remaining herding population represented largely by women, children, and the elderly, who have traditionally experienced disadvantage in asserting their 'distant voice'.[49]

Together, these varying forms of migration are creating a series of security challenges that threaten the quality of social and human capitals that have sustained Mongolia for generations. Instances of Chinese migrants working across Mongolian mine sites and resulting violence and lack of respect for cultural differences, the spread of migrant-induced social evils such as prostitution, alcoholism, and sexually transmitted diseases, and wider economic inequality between the host and migrant groups, although anecdotal at this stage, provide vital pointers towards challenges threatening Mongolia's social security into the future.

4.2 *Resource Curse*

As highlighted in Section 3 above, there is little doubt about the critical role that the mining industry has played in Mongolia's socio-economic development thus far. Combellick-Bidney captures the spirit of resource development and its importance for Mongolia and its people by arguing that 'mining became a symbolic and material manifestation of a wide range of development issues ... [that] range from democratic governance (transparency, consultation

47 Ochirsukh, 2011.

48 Upton, C., *Mining, resistance and pastoral livelihoods in contemporary Mongolia. Change in Democratic Mongolia: social relations, health, mobile pastoralism, and mining* (J. Dierkes. Leiden, Brill, 2012), 223–248.

49 Sietz, Ludeke and Walther 2011.

and information access) to equality (share of profit, civil society involvement in profit allocation), from environmental preservation (local and ecological efforts) to economic viability (economic stimulus, domestic and foreign investment, domestic development of technological capacity).'[50]

As an economic activity, mining has far-reaching social, cultural, ecological and institutional consequences.[51] Lessons from other world regions that have hosted mining operations provide useful insights into what conditions may exist in mining contexts that may contribute to them succumbing to – or successfully withstanding – the 'resource curse' syndrome. The latter argues that institutional focus on any particular industry, most notably those based on extractives, is actually counter-productive to long-term social and economic development. Resource curse claims therefore, that regions with 'large primary export sectors (oil, rubber, diamonds, minerals) often, though not always, grow more slowly than their peers'.[52] On the contrary, regions experiencing resource curse allow minerals wealth to make the rich richer, often via institutional corruption and continuing neglect of fundamental human rights for a large majority of affected peoples.[53] Over-dependence on natural resources for social and economic development, often leading to dysfunctional governments and communities; eroding of human capital; and institutional neglect towards other economic sectors are examples of key by-products of resource curse as experienced in typical mining regions across Asia and Africa.[54]

As noted above, the nature and quality of institutions and governance structures that are in place are particularly important instruments to regulate, steer

50 Combellick-Bidney, 2012.

51 Ali, S.H. and A.S. Grewal, "The ecology and economy of indigenous resistance: divergent perspectives on mining in New Caledonia," in *The Contemporary Pacific* 18 (2) (2006): 361–392.

52 The World Bank, 2006.

53 Leite, C. and J. Weidmann, *Does mother nature corrupt? Natural resources, corruption, and economic growth* (Washington DC, IMF working paper, International Monetary Fund, 1999); Hilson, G. and R. Maconachie, *The Extractive Industries Transparency Initiative; panacea or while elephant for sub-saharan Africa? Mining, society and a sustainable world* (J.P. Richards. London, Springer, 2009), 469–491.

54 Ross, M., "The political economy of the resource curse," in *World Politics* 51 (2) (1999): 297–322; Sachs, J. and A. Warner, "The curse of natural resources," in *European Economic Review* 45 (2001): 827–838; Robinson, J.A., R. Torvik and T. Verdier, "Political foundations of the resource curse," in *Journal of Development Economics* 79 (2006): 447–468.

and monitor returns from resource development – whether these remain with a select elite group, mostly comprising bureaucrats and business leaders, or are shared more equitably with the larger populace.[55] Mongolia's institutions are relatively new and inexperienced, thereby making them more vulnerable to conditions that favor inequitable returns from mining. While it remains too early to suggest any conclusive signs of Mongolia experiencing a resource curse, there indeed remains an urgent need to foster a strong policy environment and credible institutions to address any risk from a potential 'resource curse' on Mongolia's future human security.

4.3 *Disasters, Loss and Damage*

Over the past two decades, climatic changes – both slow onset and extreme events – have severely impacted the livestock sector in Mongolia, resulting in devastating losses and damages to herder livelihoods across the country. In the most recent 2009–2010 dzud, 19 out of the country's 21 provinces were impacted with about 8 million livestock – perished.[56] In living memory, the scale of livestock loss – affecting nearly 30% of the country`s population – was unheard of and immediately highlighted Mongolia's unique context underlined by the close relationship between the land and its peoples and livestock. Impacts of such dzud events negatively affect the economic, social and psychological wellbeing of a large proportion of Mongolians every year.[57]

Culturally, the health of the environment, including natural climate embodies a strong sense of emotional and spiritual connection with the Mongolian way of life. Loss and damage – both tangible and intangible – occurring due to disruption in natural environmental conditions may therefore have several enduring implications for human security. The latter is manifested across Mongolia's rural and urban communities in a range of biological, cultural,

55 Mehlum, H., K. Moene and R. Torvik, "Institutions and the resource curse," in *The Economic Journal* 116 (January, 2006): 1–20; Wagner, M. and F.-W. Wellmer, *A hierarchy of natural resources with respect to sustainable development – a basis for a natural resources efficiency indicator* (Mining, society and a sustainable world. J.P. Richards. London, Springer, 2009), 91–121.

56 Tachiiri et al., 2008; Sayed, A., "Dzud: a slow natural disaster kills livestock -and livelihoods- in Mongolia" (2010). Retrieved 24 May, 2015 from http://blogs.worldbank.org/eastasiapacific/dzud-a-slow-natural-disaster-kills-livestock-and-livelihoods-in-mongolia; UNOCHA, 2010.

57 Sayed, 2010; Wang, Brown and Agrawal, 2013.

economic and spiritual capitals.[58] The accumulation, maintenance, and recovery of these capitals prior to, during and after a disaster event is vital to addressing human security challenges that may surface as a result of extreme events.

While Mongolia has had many extreme events in the past, the intensity and frequency of some of these events has increased over the last two decades.[59] Combined with institutional changes and policy shifts around service provision, local and national vulnerability to natural disasters has increased dramatically. Considering the deep dependencies that Mongolia holds on the natural environment, socially, culturally and economically, any increases in the scale and or frequency of natural disasters are expected to lead to crises with far-reaching consequences for its human and societal security.

For particular parts of the country, most notably the Gobi desert, local experts are advocating for developing a comprehensive understanding of what comprises natural and social capitals within these regions.[60] Improved knowledge of critical issues is expected to strengthen the effectiveness of appropriate government interventions and planning instruments to identify means of building resilience, both in the present and future, to address climate disaster-induced loss and damage to herder livelihoods and wider socio-economic quality of life.[61]

4.4 *Opportunity for Innovation*

Besides the risks for Mongolia's human security identified above, there is a vital potential opportunity that this chapter identifies. There is little doubt that Mongolia is currently experiencing a concurrent flux from a number of contemporary challenges including, but not limited to, mining, climatic disasters, urbanisation and threats to traditional livelihoods. This experience in and of itself provides a timely trigger for Mongolia's institutions and policymakers to undertake 'reflective' learning, one that is future-orientated but drawn together from its own as well as other world regions' past experiences of dealing with lasting drivers of change.[62]

58 Togtokh, 2011

59 Tachiiri et al., 2008; Sayed, 2010.

60 Togtokh, 2011.

61 Taylor, M., *The Political Ecology of Climate Change Adaptation: Livelihoods, Agrarian Change and the Conflicts of Development* (London, Routledge, 2014).

62 Sharma, V. and D. Franks, "In situ adaptation to climatic change: mineral industry responses to extreme flooding events in Queensland, Australia," in *Society and Natural Resources* 26 (11) (2013): 1252–1267.

A key element that may mobilize in-house resources and capabilities to allow such learning and move towards sustainable pathways in the future is the recognition of local indigenous knowledge and its potential to drive positive change. Local knowledge may provide lessons for addressing a number of contemporary challenges that confront Mongolia including, but not limited to, addressing natural disasters, integrating culturally diverse communities, managing external changes brought about by globalization and mining, and steering the changing role of civil society in Mongolia. There is much scope and opportunity for further integration of traditional knowledge, particularly in the way national and local institutions support pastoralist communities and acknowledge the full range of contributions the latter can make towards Mongolia's future sustainability. There are currently calls from various domestic quarters to create a repository of indigenous knowledge that will allow oral histories to play an important role in capturing and disseminating this knowledge over time.[63]

Another opportunity is to better identify knowledge gaps and current needs in relation to managing climate risks, developing robust adaptation strategies, and managing resultant loss and damage. Currently, climate adaptation efforts across Mongolia are undertaken in silo with little attempts to develop synergies with other industries and coordinate resources and knowledge to address common concerns.[64] Considering the presence of strong mining and herding industries as key backbones of Mongolia's future development, the potential of public-private partnerships in Mongolia is enormous, yet immensely underdeveloped.[65] Recent disastrous dzud events and associated risks for human and societal security may have well pushed people's resilience thresholds and in doing so, may provide a timely and much needed prompt to question current *modus operandi*, innovate and experiment.

Ecological and cultural tourism, scaling up of organic farming, maintaining an effective level of commercial cashmere production for export, up-skilling labor force for improved employability, transitioning into a renewable energy regional hub, investing in infrastructure and fostering an economic climate conducive to small and medium enterprise development are examples of opportunities that will allow a development model based on economic

63 Sharma, V. and B. Dalaibuyan, *Can mining and traditional livelihoods co-exist in a changing climate? Exploring the role of public-private partnerships to reduce risk and address Loss and Damage* (Brisbane, University of Queensland, 2015).

64 Ibid.

65 Ibid.

diversification.[66] Importantly, such a pathway will strengthen local and national resilience to climate disaster events such as dzuds, as well as help the country avoid falling prey to a vicious resource curse.

7 Conclusion and Lessons for Indigenous Peoples of the Northern Hemisphere, Including the Arctic

This chapter has argued that Mongolia's human security challenges are complex and interwoven with several direct and indirect drivers of change, some of which are externally driven and therefore, remain beyond national capacity to manage. The emergence of a strong mining sector at the same time when Mongolia is grappling with a growing climate uncertainty creates a number of environmental and socio-economic challenges for its people.

Traditional livelihoods are at the core of any discussion on Mongolia's human and social security. It is thus important and within national interest to recognize that herding-based lifestyles provide much more than just livelihoods. They are 'inherently situated within and shaped by a wider set of socio-ecological dynamics and institutional transformations'.[67] While pastoralism in Mongolia is far from declining, there are genuine concerns within the country in relation to its future contribution to Mongolia's socio-economic development. These concerns are gaining increasing momentum as mining and climate disasters take center stage in Mongolia's policymaking milieu.[68]

7.1 *Relevance for the Indigenous Peoples of the North, in Particular in the Arctic*

The Arctic region shares a number of socio-cultural and ecological parallels with Mongolia. Reliance on traditional livelihoods, a fast paced change in the natural climate, conflict with existing industries such as tourism, a rapid mining

66 Togtokh, 2011; GGGI, Interview with Sanjaasuren Oyun, Mongolian Minister for Environment and Green Development, Global Green Growth Institute. Reuters, 2013 Mongolia eyes renewable energy as climate warms. The Sydney Morning Herald; ADB, 2014; Making It, "Mongolia: looking to diversify" (MakingItMagazine.net, 2014). Retrieved 10 June, 2015, from http://www.makingitmagazine.net/?p=8446; Bold, R; "Sandwiched Mongolia looks beyond its two gigantic neighbours" (The Australian, 2015). Retrieved 12 June, 2015, from http://invest-mongolia.apip.com/blog/sandwiched-mongolia-looks-beyond-its-two-gigantic-neighbours.

67 Taylor, 2014.

68 Upton, 2012; Taylor, 2014.

boom and, remote and already sparse population centers are only some of the similarities underlining the Arctic and Mongolian contexts. Although it may be too early to draw any conclusive lessons from Mongolia's experience, these contextual similarities allow us to consider how human security challenges currently experienced in Mongolia can be useful tools and pointers towards Arctic's experiential learning.

The minerals boom in the Arctic is expected to grow further in both scale and scope as the region experiences a more permanent nature of changes to natural climatic conditions. This is expected to, on the one hand, allow the extractives sector to flourish and create along the way a promise for long-term economic development by way of mineral revenues and the emergence of new support businesses. On the other hand, as experienced across different parts of the world that have hosted mining operations, the industry accompanies a large footprint and has the potential to alter – in some cases, permanently – both local and regional socio-cultural, ecological and institutional landscapes.

The discussion above has highlighted a number of clear take-home messages for the Indigenous peoples of the North that can help pro-actively counter some of the challenges they experience in relation to societal security: disintegration of social capital with both in- and out-migration catching pace (as a large proportion of foreign workers and investors turn to Arctic to partake in the mining boom); impacts on the natural landscape that may have spiralling effects on tourism and reindeer industries; opportunity to restore traditional indigenous knowledge for future generations; and diversifying economic opportunities to avoid a potential resource curse, among others.

Although for Arctic, which spans across several nation states, developing a regional understanding of key concerns and local priorities would be far more challenging than Mongolia. Yet, much like the latter, the international community continues to reiterate the importance of good governance and long-term institutional reforms to facilitate transparent mechanisms of revenue management, encourage public private partnerships, and undertake multistakeholder consultations to manage conflicting demands.[69] A steady investment in building institutional capacity can play a critical role in capitalizing the socio-economic promise offered by an extraordinary mining boom in the Arctic, while simultaneously addressing socio-cultural and environmental threats to human security in the region.[70]

69 Taylor, 2014.

70 Isakova, A., A. Plekhanov and J. Zettelmeyer, *Managing Mongolia's resource boom* (London, Working paper no. 138, European Bank for Reconstruction and Development, 2012).

Index

Printed in the United States
By Bookmasters